7/20

# *The* LAST SECRET

## by Michael H. Brown

## CHARIS

SERVANT BOOKS
CINCINNATI, OHIO

© 1998  Michael H. Brown

Charis Books is an imprint of Servant Books.

Published by St. Anthony Messenger Press
28 W. Liberty St.
Cincinnati, OH 45202
www.servantbooks.com

Cover illustration courtesy of the Merciful Mother Association.

03  04  05   10  9  8

Printed in the United States of America
ISBN 1-56955-023-9


LIBRARY OF CONGRESS CATALOGING-IN-PUBLICATION DATA

Brown, Michael Harold, 1952-
The last secret / by Michael H. Brown.
    p.   cm.
Includes bibliographical references.
ISBN 1-56955-023-9 (alk. paper)
1. Mary, Blessed Virgin, Saint—Apparitions and miracles.   2. End of the world.   I. Title.
BT650.B75   1998
232.91'7—dc21                                              97-42592
                                                           CIP

◆

For my grandmother,
who taught me much about the Holy Spirit
and the Virgin Mary

◆

Then Mary said, "My soul proclaims the greatness of the Lord, my spirit finds joy in God my Savior, for He has looked upon His servant in her lowliness; all ages to come shall call me blessed."

LUKE 1:46-48

With jewels set in gold, and dressed in brocades, the King's daughter is led in to the King.

PSALM 45:13-14

You will know the truth, and the truth will set you free.

Jesus in JOHN 8:32

# CONTENTS

# ACKNOWLEDGMENTS

First and foremost my wife Lisa put up with tremendously early and long hours of work. For her patience and dedication to Mary, and for her love, I am eternally grateful. My parents always have been there for me, and their spiritual support has been crucial. While there are too many names to list here, I would like to specially thank the staff at the Marian Library at the University of Dayton for its fine assistance and also the staffs at the Sanford Library in Colonie, New York; the New York State Library in Albany; the library at the State University of New York at Albany, and especially the library at Siena College. I am also grateful for those many hundreds of people I have met during the past six years who are devoted to Mary. Your support and input have been invaluable. I can only urge you to maintain prayer and vigilance. I am grateful to Don Cooper, Bert Ghezzi, Heidi Hess, and the fine staff at Servant Publications for their able publishing. Grytha Drerup did yeoman's work in translating documents for me from German, and Elizabeth Buck helped me with French. I am grateful for the assistance in distribution by the Riehle Foundation and for our long and fruitful relationship. I am also grateful to Marian Messengers in Framingham, Massachusetts, for spiritual support, and to them and dozens of others who aided me at various stages of this project, especially the prayers of the Intercessors of the Lamb, Robert Duff, Sondra Abrahams, and all my friends in the Medjugorje network, I am very grateful and I love you all and will pray for you too in these times and those ahead.

# 1

---

# A Huge Mystery

She is a mystery, a huge mystery, and every century, every decade—now, every *year*—her mystery has grown. She is the most loved, revered, and renowned woman in history, but her role goes far beyond that of any human. She is a spirit. She is supernatural. She is a deliverer and a healer. She is an advocate of grace, empowered by Christ, and we are beginning to see her role both in heaven and on the world stage in ways unavailable just a few short years ago. She's a mother—the great mother—and all generations have indeed called her "blessed" (Luke 1:48), but she is also a great warrior against evil, the woman who crushes the head of the serpent, the one Christ sends as a messenger, and her message, her weapon, is love.

In great droves now, in Catholic but also in other Christian denominations, the Blessed Virgin Mary is seen in a new light as history plays out and God's plan, His secrets, begin to unfold. She is the woman of Genesis and Revelation, she is prophesied in Isaiah, but beyond that she is a maternal spirit who tends to God's children as her own.

She is the Queen of Angels. She is the Spouse of the Holy Spirit. She is everyone's mother, and whether or not you know or believe it, she is closer to you than anyone in the world.

She is not a deity. She is not an idol. The mediator between God and men is Jesus (1 Timothy 2:5). Mary is the great assistant or "co-mediator." For her great sufferings, for her great loyalty, and for her great holiness she has been given a special role by Christ and her time is now. No one in human history knew Jesus as Mary knew Jesus, and while the role of women kept her from a greater presence in Scripture, it was Mary who had to have provided much of what was later to enter the New Testament, she alone, with Joseph, who was at Christ's birth, she alone who tended to the Child and whose own sufferings, whose sufferings as a mother, were united with and only slightly less than His own. As the Second Vatican Council declared, "In an utterly singular way she cooperated by her obedience, faith, hope, and burning charity in the Savior's work of restoring supernatural life to souls."

It was the Virgin Mother who helped usher in the very beginning of the Church (Acts 1:14) and who alone was privy to Christ's greatest secrets. No one could have been as close. No one was more loved by Christ. It would have been extraordinary had Mary *not* been given a special role, and far from taking anything from Christ, her veneration has time and again proven to be the best guarantee for purity of belief in the incarnate Word. As the great John Paul II once said, what we now desire is to be the same Church that was born of the Holy Spirit when the apostles devoted themselves to prayer with Mary in the Upper Room. She is the new Eve. She came to correct the wrongs of the Garden. She turned history around by obeying where Eve had disobeyed and by restoring what Eve had lost and as the Mother of Christ she is Mother of the Church itself.

Although her detractors don't want you to know it, Mary's special role was spelled out as far back as the second century in the *Protevangelium of James*, as well as by men like Ignatius of Antioch, who lived around A.D. 110. Since her Assumption she has been able to manifest and show herself. By the fourth century—more than one thousand years before the Protestant Reformation tried to diminish her—Mary was considered a coredemptrix in Syrian devotion, and major popes such as Leo XIII and Pius X have since acknowledged that Mary, the humble peasant teenager, the demure woman of the New Testament, the suffering mother at Golgotha, has played a critical and redeeming role in assisting her Son.

As another ancient theologian named Irenaeus put it, Mary is the pure womb who regenerates men unto God. In the fourth century Mary and Jesus were seen as an inseparable team, and it was the great theologian Origen who first called Mary "Theotokos" or "Mother of God."

Her special status has been confirmed by her countless apparitions. She has been appearing for two thousand years and today her appearances only intensify. This book traces the entire history of her miracles and places them in an historical context. What follows is an account of the Virgin Mary's apparitions since the first century and, unlike the current media, I give miracles the benefit of the doubt. I believe the supernatural is not only a force in our lives but the *major* force. And I believe that Christ has chosen His mother to demonstrate that force. She is real and operates by the Holy Spirit. That's my belief. She is miraculous. She is metaphysical. I have seen her phenomena myself. I've seen her inexplicable cures. I have sat in on her apparitions in the company of bishops.

According to the International Marian Research Institute at the University of Dayton, there have been at least eight thousand significant apparitions of the Virgin since the early centuries. But scholars stress that no one can give a real estimate. If one considers visions to ordinary, private people who have never formally reported them, the figure would be astronomical. She appeared to martyrs. She appeared during the early persecutions. She appeared to the major saints. She appeared as the Church was forming—during the famous Council of Nicaea—and she appeared each time mankind passed through a hard moment. Plague, famine, war. She especially appeared to those who, like herself, were poor, simple peasants, but she has also appeared to kings and popes. From earliest times she has come to eliminate paganism. She has come to replace occult deities. She has come to supplant temples with chapels and to replace goddesses with Christian maternity. She was with Constantine. She was with Charlemagne. She rode with Columbus on the *Santa Maria* (the first Christian prayer ever recited in the Western Hemisphere was the *Salve Regina*) and her holy days were listed in the oldest English prayer book published in America. The greatest river in the United States, now known as the Mississippi, was once called the "River of the Immaculate Conception" and the second largest city, Los Angeles, was known more fully as "Saint Mary Queen of the Angels of the Portiuncola." In accordance with the will of Jesus, Who wants His mother esteemed, her images and churches span the breadth of Christendom. No one has established more places of worship. No one but Christ has had more of a role in shaping Christianity. While there are always those who seek to denounce Mary as usurping Christ's power or who slander her as an idol, she is in fact just the opposite, a humble handmaiden whose mission has been to fight the most diabolic of heresies—from gnosticism to Communism—and to magnify God (Luke 1:46). Secular historians have tried to hide her overwhelming influence but as the veil lifts, as we have revelations for the new millennium, her historical appearances take on an entirely new and fascinating perspective. They show that for two thousand years we have been embroiled in an apocalyptical battle between good and evil, a battle that is reaching a culmination in our own time, and that Christ has posted her on the front lines. She helps fulfill His promise to send the Holy Spirit (Acts 1:8). She is empowered only by the Spirit and has appeared in countless places from Europe to Australia.

Hers is a story of biblical magnitude and her presence has skyrocketed as a counter to the great darkness. She comes to crush the serpent, who has all but assumed control of our popular culture. She comes to a world whose financial, legal, and educational systems are corrupt. She comes to warn of murder, suicide, and abortion, which are the devil's attempt to invert the word "live" into the word "evil" and to kill at every opportunity. We see perversions at new heights and a blurring of the genders and the return of paganism and *selfness* as the most corrupt members of our society—the most immoral and, yes, the most vulgar—have been given money and power.

As you will see, this spiritual mayhem brings to a head two millennia of spiritual warfare. Since Christ there has been a pitched battle between those who support God and those who have been blinded or seduced by the forces of the world, those whose prince is Satan (John 12:31). Our evil is not new because, as it says in Ecclesiastes 1:9, there is nothing new under the sun. But in a world of nearly 6 billion humans (there were only 100 million at the time of Jesus), the evil is of monumental proportion. And as a result we face monumental consequences. I'm not speaking "gloom and doom." I'm not talking about far-out prophecies or the end of the world. I'm talking about reality. I'm talking about how the violence of our own time resembles the violence of gladiators and how the obscenity resembles the obscenity of Caligula.

We are Sodom. We are Babylon. That's why Mary is among us. That's why her statues weep. That's why she comes to pray for our salvation. Her very presence is the great warning and her prayers are those of the great advocate. She is the definition of mercy. She pleads our case before her Son. She did this in the time of the Romans and in the Middle Ages and she does so in the age of modernism.

She is the bride in the Canticle of Canticles, the first daughter in the Book of Wisdom, the sanctuary in Psalms. She is the woman of Zion, a light to enlighten the pagans, the glory of Israel. She is venerated but not worshiped, loved but not idolized. She is God's answer to the pagan goddesses and most of all she is our dear and blessed mother. Since Ephraem in the fourth century she has been known as the "lyre of the Holy Spirit," a woman whose stature has grown since her earthly death because Christ *wants* it to grow. She is His stand-in before the Second Coming, and she enrages Satan because she was a mere human and because he is powerless against her love, simplicity, and humbleness. The prince of pride is defeated by humility, and those he seduces are warned by this incredible mother to hurry from his darkness. She reminds us of heaven. She gives us warnings. She reminds us of Jesus. She personifies the glory of heaven, informing us of its beautiful promise while dissuading us from the netherworld. In every decade of every century she has been there to help in the struggle called life and today she comes as we fall into turmoil. She comes as we encounter disarray not only in society but also in nature. God has always spoken in storms and quakes and He continues to do so. According to the Federal Emergency Management Agency, there were 75 major disasters during 1996 in the United States alone. Floods. Tornadoes. Since then other indications have continued. We hear God's whisper in the wind, His echo in thunder. The more we sin—the more we stray from God—the more we'll see regional disasters. They will spread and grow, one after the other, and if we keep up the sin, if we let it continue into the new millennium, we will tempt God to awaken us in a more powerful and singular fashion.

That's what Mary has always warned about; that's what she is warning about in our own challenging era. These are special times. There will be special trials. Their nature is hidden in history but the veil is lifting and Mary accompanies God's warnings. She's His prophet. She's His messenger. Most importantly, she is our mother. We can go to her. We can flee to her. We are held in her arms just as she held the Christ Child. We don't know God's timetable and we must be careful not to emphasize man-made dates, but as we enter a new millennium we sense great danger.

And so we go to the Madonna. We go to Mary, Mother of God. We go to the mystery known as the Virgin. She is there for us. She has always been there for us. She was there for the Christians in the first century and she was there during the Black Death and she comes amid the current evil just as she came to dispel evil at the time of the Moors and Turks and Huns.

She has manifested in the remote corners of every habitable land.

She has manifested so many times, she has guided so many, that we can easily reckon her as the mother of entire continents.

As you will now see, she formed our world in a way that historians have not allowed us to realize, and she continues to form it, to protect it, and to guide it as we head for rough water and as we see from the past what soon may come.

# 2

## Strong and Demure

It started on the plains of north Spain, along the Ebro River, wide but not so swift, cutting into the red soil that James the Apostle, on mission from Jerusalem, walked in search of souls.

It was A.D. 40, seven years since the death of Christ, and James had ventured from Jerusalem to the Iberian Peninsula as Peter and John evangelized Samaria. He was near a place called Caesar-Augustus or "Saragossa," which recently had been conquered by Rome, and the territory was mysterious, the domain of fierce tribesmen whose origin was a puzzle. There was a strangeness in the air, a feeling of occultism. Since the time of the Neanderthals, skulls had been ritually gathered and that custom had evolved into the more recent form of the occult known as paganism, with all its gods, goddesses, and spirits that hovered over the ramparts.

This was the kind of territory that James, son of Zebedee, had been told to evangelize by Jesus. It was dangerous, lonely work, and often his only consolation was in prayer. In fact James was praying when he encountered the first known manifestation of Mary. According to tradition the apostle, accompanied by eight of his own disciples, was in deep prayer and may have dozed off when, as in Revelation 11:19, a flash of light jarred him awake and he heard the distinct, unforgettable sound of heavenly music.

We don't have many details about Saragossa (also spelled Zaragoza) but we do know that after the flash James saw the heavens "open" to reveal an apparitional woman. Immediately he recognized her as the mother of Christ, Mary of Nazareth. She had been in the care of his own brother John, and since Christ's death she had frequently prayed with the apostles in Jerusalem or Ephesus. If early images are correct, she had a small straight mouth, a thin chiseled nose, and a drawn look that was sometimes sorrowful. She was of medium height and had brown hair with dark bangs and eyebrows, her face neither long nor round but oval, her hands and fingers tapered, delicate, and long. She was a regular peasant in a small, regular hillside house, and her life had been one of prayer and toil: drawing water, cooking, and repairing clothes. She had subsisted on fruit, fish, and bread; in manner always serene and demure. Her complexion was the color of wheat, her clothing wool in winter and linen in summer, a veil over her head if she had gone into the streets, feet bare or with sandals of wood and leather, wearing two garments: a chaste chemise and a robe or a gown.

Often James had seen her that way, the sweet and gentle matron who kneaded bread and prayed for the apostles. But now she was different. Now she was in splendor. Now her face was the same and her sweetness was the same but James was seeing her in apparition or bilocation—seated on a throne of light or a marble pillar and accompanied by angels. Some angels knelt on transparent clouds while others sent forth the music.

James was certainly not new to unusual occurrences. He had been on the mount when Jesus transfigured (Matthew 17:2). He had witnessed the apparitions of Elijah and Moses. He had also been present at the raising of Jairus' daughter from the dead (Mark 5:39). He had seen many of Christ's wonders. But now he was witnessing something else. Now he was seeing a new miracle. Gazing in ecstasy, perhaps in the same way that Stephen had gazed upon a vision of Christ (Acts 7:56), James watched as the angels suspended Mary's pillar or throne and, according to some legends, gave him a statue.

Then the apparition spoke.

*James, servant of the Most High, blessed be thou by God, and may He fill thee with His divine grace. My son James, the Most High and Mighty God of heaven has chosen this place that you may consecrate and dedicate here a church and house of prayer where, under the invocation of my name, He wishes to be adored and served, and all the faithful who seek my intercession will receive the graces they ask if they have true faith and devotion, and in the name of my Son I promise them great favors and blessings, for this will be my chapel and my house, my own inheritance and possession, and in testimony of my promise, this pillar will remain here, and on it my own image, which, in this place where you will build my church, will last and endure with the holy faith. Note well this pillar on which I am seated, which my Son and your Master sent down to me from on high by the heads of angels and around which you shall set up the altar of my chapel. On this spot the Most High will work miracles through my intercession for those who implore my protection in their need. And this pillar will remain in this place until the end of the world....*

The Virgin told James to build the chapel at once and then to return to Jerusalem, where it was correctly prophesied that he would be martyred. According to legend, the apostle constructed a tiny chapel. Sxteen feet long and just eight feet wide, it marked the first church dedicated to Mary and placed her in direct opposition to the prevailing pagan goddesses.

There along the Ebro was a chapel that would one day grow into a huge domed basilica the precise size of the most famous goddess temple in Ephesus.

There was also the small statue of Mary holding Jesus, the first of many times she would be shown with Him.

# 3

---

# *Days of Darkness*

She had made her mark. It was her first mark and a little mark but it was a permanent mark. She was showing Jesus as she had shown Him on earth. She was watching over His mystical body just as she had watched over His physical one. If Jesus could not as openly show Himself, lest it be confused as the Second Coming, He *could* present His mother as a visible sign and He could use her to establish shrines, chapels, and churches that replaced the rampant pagan idols, the shrines to gods and goddesses that in cities like Pompeii stood on every corner.

Those were the deceptions; those were the forces of destruction. They were of the serpent, and Mary as the new Eve was sent to counter them. In A.D. 47, just a few years after Saragossa, she appeared in the pagan stronghold of Le Puy, France, to an ill woman named Villa, who while praying for a cure suddenly had a vision and was told by Mary to climb a hill known then as Anicium (today Mount Corneille). There she rested on a large stone, fell asleep, and found herself free of fever and cured when she awoke.

Word of the miracle reached George of Velay, who had been sent to evangelize Gaul by the apostle Peter. He visited the site, which was notorious for its occult Druids.

When he got there George was astonished to see the hill covered with a sparkling veil of snow even though it was July 11 and the height of summer.

As the missionary and his companions surveyed the phenomenon, a stag leapt from the woodland and circled the spot, leaving track marks that were then used to indicate the area for a future altar.

Two appearances, two churches. The intervention had started. The replacement of paganism had started. Where goddesses were arrogant, Mary was humble. Where goddesses were flamboyant, Mary was a wallflower. Where goddesses were seductive, Mary was a virgin. Most importantly, where goddesses were rebellious—which was the very seed of occultism (see 1 Samuel 15:23)—Mary was obedient.

She was sent to correct the mistake of Eve. She was sent to help cast away the snake and his idols. She replaced the Druid May Queen. She replaced the earth mother. She replaced occult feast days with holy ones, for she was the great sign. She was the "woman clothed with the sun" (Revelation 12:1).

She was also a warning. On earth, she had been a wallflower, avoiding notice and taking a back seat. Now, in heaven, in glorified form, she was still exquisitely humble but her flower was in bloom. As it said in Revelation 12, she had a mission against the dragon. Near Toulouse, France, a shrine was instituted in her honor (allegedly by the publican Zaccheus) while near Madrid a small chapel was built around a statue said to have been given by the apostle James to a man named Calocerus. There was also an oratory dedicated to her in Soulac, France, and a church on the island of Malta. At Ein Karim in Palestine was a miraculous well rumored to have been used by Mary when she visited Elizabeth. And far to the north was an island called Yniswitrin (now Glastonbury, England) where in A.D. 64 they built a church for the Virgin.

Pagans polluted men with their graven and devilish images—with the idolatrous picturing of creeping things—and heaven countered with Jesus and Mary, images that brought the Gospels alive and had the warmth of family photos. It was widely claimed that the apostle Luke painted or carved images of Mary (he may have presented one to Eterius, the first bishop of Barcelona), and though it wasn't easy to separate fact from legend, such images carried an anointing. Such images could neutralize evil. Such images countered pagan symbols like the sun sign or "swastika" and stood against the promiscuity that was illustrated with lewd graffiti in the public places of Pompeii and Rome.

It was the time of Caligula. It was the time of Nero. And it was a time of warnings. On February 5 in A.D. 62 an earthquake had rocked the city of Pompeii, and two years later another disaster struck when Rome was swept by an historic fire that sent residents shrieking on the streets and destroyed the pagan temples.

While Rome was burning, Nero sang to the accompaniment of his lyre.

Then he decided to persecute the city's small colony of Christians. Catholics were thrown to the animals, impaled on sharp stakes, or smeared with combustible materials and ignited like torches. They were blamed for starting the fire because Nero needed a scapegoat. The persecution claimed the life of Peter, the first pope, who was taken to the emperor's gardens and crucified upside down (a torture that was soon symbolized by the "witch's foot" or Cross of Nero, an inverted cross inside a circle).

Such transgressions cried for heavenly justice, as did Rome's tolerance of fornication, infanticide, and abortion. Jesus had warned that sin would be met by war, fire, and darkness (see Luke 21 and Matthew 24), and as if to serve as an omen, Halley's Comet hung over Palestine in A.D. 66 like a sword.

It was the year Jerusalem revolted against Rome, and that rebellion provoked a horrifying war. Tens of thousands were massacred and others starved when Roman soldiers moved into Israel. As prophesied by Christ, Jerusalem was surrounded and its temple ruined. At the same time, Rome itself was hit by unprecedented disaster. In the words of the historian Tacitus, that corrupt city was turned into "a theatre of horrors." Flood and famine struck the very vicinity of Peter's execution. The entire empire was thrown into an uproar. Christ had said there would come a time when "the sun will be darkened, the moon will not shed her light" (see Matthew 24:29), and his words were fulfilled on August 24 of A.D. 79 with the eruption of Mount Vesuvius. For three terrifying days Pompeii and its pagans suffered through quakes, soot, and total darkness. Sheets of fire leapt on the mountain, while violent tremors shook buildings from their foundations. Some attempted to escape by sea, but as Christ predicted (see Luke 21:25), the waves were too high and the sea was roaring.

There was lava. There was sulfur. Pompeii was about to disappear and, as the historian Pliny observed, there loomed "a horrible black cloud ripped by sudden bursts of fire, writhing snakelike and revealing sudden flashes larger than lightning."

It was the beginning of the first great chastisement of the Christian era. Hell was causing rents in the earth and sending fire into the wind, fire and brimstone, as at Gomorrah. According to a chronicler named Pliny the Younger, residents of Pompeii at one point

debated whether to stay indoors or take their chance in the open, for the buildings were now shaking with violent shocks, and seemed to be swaying to and fro as if they were torn from their foundations. Outside, on the other hand, there was the danger of falling pumice stones, even though these were light and porous…. As a protection against falling objects they put pillows on their heads tied down with cloths. Elsewhere there was daylight by this time, but they were still in darkness, blacker and denser than any ordinary night, which they relieved by lighting torches and various kinds of lamps…. Then the flames and smell of sulfur which heralded the approaching fire drove the others to take flight…. For several days we had experienced earth shocks, which hardly alarmed us as they are frequent in Campania. But that night they became so violent that it seemed the world was not only being shaken, but turned upside down.

# 4

## "Mother of the Lord"

It was the bloodiest and spookiest episode in all of Rome's history. Soon at the burial site of Nero there would be rumors of spirits plaguing the area, and apparitions in the neighboring district were said to take the form of crows.

Such ghastliness was dispelled only by the mercy of Christ, Who sent His mother and His own miracles.

Some twenty-five miles northeast of Rome, on a mountain called Guadagnolo, a Roman officer named Placidas, who served under the emperor Trajan (A.D. 98 to 117), was hunting one day when he and his companions spotted an unusual and noble deer. History doesn't reveal what exactly made the animal unique, but it was so grand that Placidas decided to capture it. He drove it to a spot on the mountain where there seemed no way out, but just as he came within grasp, the stag gave a sudden leap and planted itself on a rock beyond his reach, looking at him boldly.

To his amazement, Placidas saw the body of Christ on a luminous cross that appeared between the stag's magnificent antlers.

There was also a voice and what seemed like the light of divinity piercing Placidas' soul. He felt compelled to worship the God of the Christians. When the officer returned to Rome he and his family were formally committed by baptism and his name changed to Eustachius.

A convert, he was also a martyr. News of his conversion reached Roman authorities and when Eustachius refused to renounce his new faith, he and his family were thrown into a boiling cauldron.

Countless others met the same fate as Satan sought to immediately stamp out the great threat of Catholicism. Christians were stoned, trampled upon, skinned alive, beheaded, and even dismembered or eviscerated while still conscious. They were starved. They were flayed. They were crucified. These were the people who established Catholicism and, far from extinguishing Christianity, such deaths were the seeds for its growth.

Like a young tree buffeted by wind, the more the Church was persecuted, the stronger its roots grew. Devotion to Mary began to supersede the worship of heathen goddesses. Where Mary was, where she manifested, there was faith, love, and perseverance even to martyrdom.

It was faith that extinguished the fiery darts of Satan, and as Paul stated in a letter to the Ephesians (6:12), the battle was not against human forces "but against the principalities and powers, the rulers of this world of darkness, the evil spirits in regions above." Satan stood as prince of the world, but Christ was sending His mother to take it back. That notion was expressed in an image of Mary and Child that may date back to the year A.D. 170 in the catacomb of Saint Priscilla. Her intercession was also expressed by apparitions to important founders of the Church like Bishop Gregory of Caesarea. Gregory was seeking divine guidance on the Trinity one night just before his episcopal consecration in A.D. 240 when the apparition of an older man materialized before him.

It was John the Evangelist, saintly and noble, in holy garments. Startled and rising from his bed, Gregory asked John why he was there. In a gentle and tranquil voice the apparition said, *"Calm yourself, my son. I have come to help you."* John then extended his hand and pointed to one side.

When Gregory looked in that direction, he was amazed to see the form of a woman, more than human, with a brightness that was compared to a torch. She was beautiful and graceful and majestic beyond measure, addressed by John as "Mother of the Lord." She told the Evangelist to make the mystery of piety known to Gregory.

John did that in powerful and unforgettable words. *"The Father has never been without the Son, nor the Son without the Spirit,"* said the apparition, *"and this same Trinity is immutable and forever unalterable."*

Such was the foundation of Trinitarian doctrine. Such was a formula for the Church.

Such was also the beginning of incredible events.

Both friends and enemies looked upon Gregory as another Moses, for the apparitions of Mary and John seemed to have empowered him. They seemed to have given him the grace of healing and conversion. Encyclopedias repeat legends of his ability to foresee the future. He also caused physical effects. On one occasion he stuck his staff in a river or stream and caused it to divert course, and he had special powers against evil spirits. Upon entering one pagan temple, he began its purification with the sign of the Cross. The temple guardian became enraged when he could no longer summon the spirits, but even he converted once he saw that Gregory had command over demons.

As a test, Gregory was asked to command a great stone to move, and indeed against reason and logic the stone moved to a different location.

Crowds gathered. People were healed. Others were exorcised. And soon the city of Neocaesarea, home to only seventeen Christians, was converted. Mary's strength was clearly seen in establishing entire dioceses and also in defending Catholicism against endless heretics like the Gnostics and Montanists, who thought themselves the true Christians and arrogated themselves above Church tradition.

Clearly the Holy Spirit, Who had been sent down in a special way since the Resurrection, was now working many wonders to build up the Church. Miracles had not stopped with Christ's Resurrection. If anything there was now a profusion. The Holy Spirit was on earth and if official public revelation had ended with Sacred Scripture, the Church still allowed and was indeed nurtured and brought to key traditions by private ones. The

Church was Christ's mystical body, not a mere institution. The mysticism often came through Mary and its cement was mixed with the blood of martyrs. Near Naples a priest named Felix was scourged, loaded with chains, and cast into a torture cell, but soon was visited by an apparition that filled the cell with bright light and caused the locked doors to open.

There was also supernatural help against invading pagan tribes from the Germanic regions. When Christians were trapped by German "barbarians" in what is now Austria, the sky suddenly darkened and lightning struck with such ferocity that the barbarians fled and granted the Christians victory.

# 5

## *Above the Sun*

But barbarians kept pounding at the Roman Empire, and so did famine and plague. The chastisement continued. In a single day five thousand died in Rome, and violence was such in Alexandria that dwellers didn't venture out of their neighborhoods.

The empire was under judgment, had suffered woe after woe for more than two centuries, had seen twenty emperors die violently between A.D. 211 and 284 alone, yet it continued its paganism. It continued its persecutions. It continued the attempt to annihilate Catholicism, whose heroes soon included a seer named Nicholas of Myra (who was later integrated into the myth of Santa Claus) and Catherine of Alexandria, a young pagan girl who had been converted by a vision of Mary.

There were also two Egyptian martyrs named Julian and Basilissa who, on the day of their execution in A.D. 312, saw Jesus and Mary surrounded by angels. *"Victory to thee, Julian,"* they said. *"Victory to thee, Basilissa!"*

It was a time in which altars blazed with deference to idols like Dionysius, while those who refused to worship the pagan gods, the gods of earth and sun and of love and war, were stretched on the rack or had their skin peeled while they were still alive or their limbs hacked off and spread around their writhing torsos. These martyrs suffered in the most excruciating manner because they knew a secret, they knew that the goddesses who were now immortalized in Rome were the same goddesses who had been worshiped by the pharaohs and Babylonians, by the ancient Greeks and Spanish tribesmen, by the pagans of Ephesus—and that all were actually devils in disguise (1 Corinthians 10:20), all were in contravention of Jesus, and all would be conquered one day by the Mother of God.

In the typical case a Catholic was brought before an emperor like Diocletian or one of his henchmen and commanded to renounce the "Nazarene," then imprisoned and usually condemned to the ugliest of deaths if he failed to worship an idol or if he even slightly insulted the emperors, who were known on occasion to dress as Jupiter.

According to legend, one martyr was a young woman named Philomena from Macedonia who was imprisoned about A.D. 312 when she stood up to the emperor. Her vermin-ridden cell was illumined one night with a light from which stepped the Blessed Virgin.

> *Do not be afraid. I am she who is never called in vain. I am Mary your mother and I have come to give you glad tidings. In three more days, your captivity will be over. But you must suffer a great trial beforehand. Have courage, for in the midst of your troubles my Son will help you mightily. And I have commanded the great angel Gabriel to watch over you and always be at your side. His power will do great things for you, my beloved daughter. My Son has prepared for you everlasting happiness, so be joyful. The angels are already awaiting your coming.*

Then Mary placed the Christ Child in Philomena's arms.

True to the reputed prophecy, Philomena supposedly escaped several attempts at execution but was finally beheaded on the third day.

While the story of Philomena remained a myth, there was no doubt that major miracles were occurring in a way that was changing history. Around this same period, something extraordinary happened to Constantine the Great while he was on the way to do battle with the superior forces of a rival emperor named Maxentius. Half-convinced that Christians were correct in their concept of one God, Constantine was praying for victory and asking the Lord to show Himself when, late one afternoon, he and his men saw the radiant form of a crosslike emblem above the setting sun. Once used by pagan sun worshipers, it was sort of an X with a perpendicular line drawn through it and turned at the top. It had recently been taken over by Christians who used it as the cipher of Christ. It was surrounded by the words, *In This, Conquer.*

There it was, in daylight above the sun, seen by a force of at least twenty-five thousand soldiers, most of whom were pagans: The cipher of Christ. These men also claimed to see angels coming to their aid as they prepared to fight a force that was probably twice or several times their number.

Even scholars of our own day agree that *something* happened to Constantine, something hard to explain, something way out of the ordinary, described by earlier and more believing historians as an event *divino monitus instinctua*—advised by the divine instinct.

Constantine swore to the vision and said it had been followed by a dream in which Christ told him to use the emblem for protection.

Obeying that advice, Constantine immediately ordered the monogram placed on his soldiers' shields and marched to a miraculous defeat of Maxentius at the Battle of Milvian Bridge, which made him the sole emperor. He then set about legalizing Catholicism, donating land to the Church, and building a basilica over Peter's tomb.

That was how swiftly God could work. That was the fruit of a legitimate apparition. At every turn Christ and Mary were watching their flock. They were looking down on the struggling Church and while the Virgin wasn't saying much these first few centuries, while she would be a subtle presence for most of the first millennium and into the next, while her main mission would be quiet prayer, she made every visit count, she continued to replace pagan shrines, and she appeared not only to men like Nicholas of Myra—who saw her during the Council at Nicaea—but also to prayerful women like St. Monica of Thurgaste.

Monica's husband had recently died and she was disturbed not only by her widowhood but because her son, a brilliant scholar, was wallowing in immorality and involved with another heresy called Manichaeism.

According to legend, while Monica was deep in prayer she saw Mary with a cord or cincture around her waist. The cord was glowing. *"Daughter of mine, in the future you are to dress yourself as I am dressed,"* said the Virgin. *"Let this cincture be a pledge of my love for you, this very cincture that encircles the womb wherein the Word was made flesh. Let it be yours from now onward, and may you wear it constantly. Never remove it. Spread devotion to it as far and wide as you are able. All who wear a cincture like this one I shall look upon as my special children. This cincture will become a wonder of the universe in a future time."*

Monica did as she was told and soon witnessed the conversion of her son.

This was of no small consequence, for her son would soon become a great bishop and doctor of the Church whose many followers would wear the cincture through the ages and whose own name was Augustine.

# 6

## *Gog and Magog?*

S uch miracles said one thing: no matter how much dissidents and heretics would try to destroy it, no matter how much they would attack its traditions, Catholicism was here to stay and its sacraments were the will of Jesus.

By now the Eucharist had been celebrated for nearly three centuries, and such observances became more clearly defined as the sacramental meal was turned into an independent rite with reading and preaching on Sunday mornings, which Constantine had declared a special day. Resurrecting the rituals of ancient Jews, Catholics employed altars, incense, and priestly garments much like those described in Exodus, and they also used certain rituals such as genuflection and candles that were taken from pagans and reconsecrated.

While paganism would continue to rear its head and while Rome would continue to endure purification, Catholicism and its mother, Mary, became a significant and even vast presence.

The Virgin appeared to a bishop in Tours, France, and sent a message to a king named Julianus during a battle with the Persians. In Italy the shrine discovered by Placidas was officially dedicated to Mary, and in the same nation a bishop named Eusebius established a sanctuary that became famous for a miraculous statue. By A.D. 347 there was a shrine dedicated to the Virgin in Belgium and on August 5, A.D. 352, a dramatic manifestation occurred in Rome when the Virgin appeared in a dream to a nobleman and his wife, as well as Pope Liberius, telling all three to construct a church at a site she would designate with snow, as she did at Le Puy. (Though it was August, snow or frost was indeed reported the next day by those who flocked in amazement around Mount Esquiline, which became the site for the Basilica of Mary Major, the greatest church in her honor.)

Mary brought grace everywhere. Images said to have been painted by Luke and obtained by venturers like Constantine's mother, Helena, during missions to the Holy Land, found their way to Constantinople, Lebanon, and Athens. They were cypress-board paintings and precious little statues that ended up in magnificent places like Montserrat—a towering mountain overlooking northern Spain—and Mount Sumela in Turkey, where a famous portrait was deposited by a Christian called Basilius Soterichus who was instructed to do so by a vision. Though not dogma, already Mary was being described as a "co-redemptrix," and already her divine maternity and her perpetual virginity had been established as doctrine. When Mary was honored and invoked, her power grew, and few things so irritated Satan. He especially despised her images, which were potent tools of conversion. They were images for veneration, not worship, and they brought to mind holy images of the past, such as the gold images of cherubic angels on the Ark of the Covenant (Exodus 25:18). They were used to deepen prayer. They created a holy atmosphere. They sparked faith and were an invitation to heaven, reminders that wherever Mary was, so was Christ, listening quietly and blessing those who came to pay His mother homage.

His Presence was seen in a great sign that appeared during the first year of St. Cyril's episcopate in Jerusalem. This was the era of the Arian heresy, in which the relationship of Christ to God the Father had been placed into question. In a letter to the Emperor Constantius, Cyril wrote:

On the nones of May, about the third hour, *a great luminous cross appeared in the heavens,* just over Golgotha, reaching as far as the holy mount of Olivet, seen, not by one or two persons, but clearly and evidently by the whole city. This was not, as might be thought, a fancy-bred and transient appearance: but it continued several hours together, visible to our eyes and brighter than the sun. The whole city, penetrated alike with awe and with joy at this portent, ran immediately to the church, all with one voice giving praise to our Lord Jesus Christ, the only Son of God.

Such graces were crucial as Christians struggled with heretics and the Roman Empire continued to endure barbarians who burned villages, sacked cities, and hung captives from trees as sacrifices to a pagan war god called Woden. They were fierce shaggy-haired men from the Germanic north, once called Scythians (Colossians 3:11), known now, perhaps, as Gog. Were they in Scripture? During the first centuries the prophecies of Jesus in Matthew 24 and Luke 21 had been largely borne out. His prophecy of fire and darkness had been met in both Rome and Pompeii, His prediction of roaring seas had been witnessed with the accompanying quakes. His remarkable prophecy of the temple's destruction had come true. Now His predictions about war were further realized during a great chastisement (wars and rumors of wars) that showed no signs of letup.

Gog! They were Gothic men armed with clubs, bows, battle axes, and swords. They would later become a rootstock for Western Europe but for now were brutal warriors set on overthrowing the equally cruel though more refined Romans.

It was a terrifying and apocalyptical time, so evil that learned churchmen foresaw the Antichrist and expected him to arrive by the year 500. In Milan a bishop named Ambrose believed the world was coming to an end and if that was a recurrent prophecy, something predicted since the Montanists in the second century, it *did* seem like a day of judgment as Goths were joined by clans known as Vandals, who spilled over the borders or arrived in slashing raids.

"He will do the things which Christ did, except only for raising a corpse," an ancient writing known as the *Apocalypse of Elijah* had warned. "By this you will know he is the Lawless One: He has no power to give life!"

He had only the power to take it. He had only the power of death. He was like a horde of locusts. And Rome had invited it. She had laid out a red carpet. Through idolatry her citizens had invoked demons for centuries, and now here were barbarians. It was the end of the Classical Period and the beginning of the Dark Ages and, on the afternoon of August 9, 378, two-thirds of the Roman army were annihilated in the Battle of Adrianople. For several more centuries the empire would have to suffer Northern tribes that sacked France and Athens and in 410 Rome itself (with war, famine, and pestilence everywhere, again fulfilling Scripture).

The Goths may have been the legendary Gog and they'd been forced from their homeland and into Roman territory by a second and yet more barbarous horde known as Hunnica or "Huns," an Asian tribe identified ominously with Scythian werewolves. The Huns probably originated beyond the Volga River in the land of Magog and were widely seen as the apocalyptical horsemen (Revelation 6:4), eating, sleeping, and fighting on their horses. Short and broad-shouldered with bowed legs and "horrible" faces, they were derived of Mongolian nomads and beyond ferocious. They were accused of drinking blood, cannibalizing the young, and destroying so many towns no one could number the dead or the pillaged churches.

The Huns were said to come with flames and the smell of sulfur, to be infested with vermin and disease. They attacked not only in great numbers but also with speed, their howls deafening, their arrival in Constantinople presaged in 447 by a great earthquake. They also broke into Italy, France, and the Balkan provinces, right out of Ezekiel 2:2-10: "Before them peoples are in torment, every face blanches. Like warriors they run, like soldiers they scale the wall.... They assault the city, they run upon the wall, they climb into houses.... Before them the earth trembles...."

While the Huns went down to defeat, other barbarians took over much of the empire and as they did, as the face of Europe changed, Mary came as the Mother of Transition. She came first as a warning and if unfortunate events and tumult still ensued, then as the comforter. Her maternal power was officially recognized in 431 when she was given the title "Mother of God" at the great Council of Ephesus and her power was seen at a chapel in Santa Margherita that by this time had been dedicated to the "Madonna of the Rose" (and in Oropa at the shrine founded by Eusebius, where "stupendous" miracles were reported).

Mary could even be seen by the blind, as in 450 when she appeared in a dream to a sightless man named Simeon and told him to find his way to Constantinople where he would witness the crowning of a new emperor.

Simeon did as he was instructed, but it was a long, dusty road and somehow he lost his dog, either by dropping its leash or because it collapsed from the heat (there are various versions). Trying to make it on his own, the blind man soon became thirsty. Realizing there were dangerous cliffs nearby, he let himself collapse into a hopeless heap, dehydrated and crying, "Holy Virgin! I have always had confidence in your protection. Do not let me perish here!"

Soon Simeon heard footsteps and the clank of metal. It was a Greek soldier named Leo. He was carrying messages from his field commander to headquarters. He comforted the old fellow and asked him what he was doing. It was then that Simeon told him about the dream, the vision of going to Constantinople and watching a new emperor take his throne. The vision made little sense. How could a blind man see a coronation? And anyway, thought Leo, no new emperor was expected; the current one was in good health.

Leo helped Simeon to his feet and they may have trudged a while, but it was obvious the old man couldn't go farther without water. Certainly he couldn't make it to Constantinople. Finding him shade and setting him down, the soldier wondered where he could find a spring. There was nothing in sight. It was hopeless.

Then he heard a voice.

*"Leo, why are you troubled, while just before you is a pond full of water?"* said a soft, womanly tone.

Looking to a small mountain, Leo realized that its top was covered with trees, which meant there was a source of water. Climbing the hill, he found only caked holes. Ready again to give up, he prayed to Mary and heard her voice a second time telling him to continue through a thicket, where Leo indeed came upon a small pond of cool clear water. She instructed him not only to bring water for the blind man, but also to bring a handful of mud to rub on Simeon's eyes (see Mark 8:23). Then she allegedly said, *"Because your soul is compassionate and your heart open to the appeal of the unfortunate, and because you have confidence in my intercession, and have honored me with a persevering devotion, I have obtained for you the highest earthly dignity man can seek. You will be proclaimed emperor, and you shall sit on the throne where Constantine my servant sat"* (see Mark 9:41).

To Leo's astonishment the pond seemed to turn from a muddy yellow to a rich golden hue. Quickly Leo did as instructed, filling his helmet. He brought it back to Simeon, who drank voraciously. Then he applied the mud, which took away Simeon's blindness. The old man could see! He could see the soldier and the sky and the dry road. He could see the hill!

As the story goes, several years later there was political upheaval in Constantinople and before it was over this military man named Leo, this man who had stopped to help a blind man on a dusty road, this man who obviously had had a certain stature, rose miraculously through the ranks and in a dramatic series of events was named emperor of the Byzantine Empire in 457!

That was the legend of Leo I, also known as Leo the Great.

It would sound like pure myth if there weren't so many similar accounts and if Leo had not built a church for Mary, Our Lady of the Golden Fountain, on that hill.

These were important events because with every miracle and every church Mary was taking turf back from the devil.

That was the plan. That was her first secret. She would crush the serpent's idols, and the devil would not be ready because in his arrogance he'd never suspected that his great foe would be a humble woman. He could never understand that it was precisely her humility, her self-effacement, which connected Mary with the power of God. It was precisely her humility that set in play the most mysterious plan which revolved around Christ but constituted her as the woman in Genesis. She had to pray and she had to beseech God but what a place she was in and what a warrior! Her power was her love, and her beauty was her love, and her message was her very loveliness, the way she opened secretly, softly, like a dew-laden flower, sparkling and fragrant. Madonna of the Rose! Christ wanted her glorified—every son wants praise for his mother—and He had to have been happy after the Ephesus council when a large throng carried 260 bishops in a candle-lit ceremony rejoicing over their proclamation and shouting, "Hail Mary! Treasure of the world! Hail Mary, Mother of God! It is through you that the prophets raise their voices, and that the pastors of the Church celebrate the praises of the Almighty, singing with angels, 'Glory be to God on high, and on earth peace to men of good will!'"

# 7

## Through the Streets of the City

She was a sublime woman, certainly more than your standard saint, elevated upon death to a standing that would have *shocked* those who'd hardly taken note of her on earth, those who thought of her only as a peasant mother, the woman in the manger, when in fact she was the most blessed of all women and queen of the angels and at the highest place below Christ. In Genazzano, Italy, she'd eclipsed Venus as Our Mother of Good Counsel while in Armenia she was called co-redemptrix in a liturgical prayer that showed how instantly she could move across boundaries.

She came where she was called, where she was welcome. She came to the humble and lowly, to those who, like her, were peasants in stony hill country or who, like Patrick, were laboring for her Son and trying to take back Druid territory. Ireland became "Mary's Island" as pagan wells were reconsecrated into Christian springs and monuments like Stonehenge in nearby England were turned into pagan ruins. While no one knows how often she appeared during the Dark Ages, in Greece she manifested to a hymn writer named Romanus and in Constantinople to an abused Jewish boy. During the same sixth century she appeared in Italy to a general named Narses and informed him of the best time to engage in battle with a powerful barbarian named Totila, who was indeed turned back at the Battle of Taginae.

Her appearances came as society changed and as signs of the times included disaster. On May 20, 526, Antioch was struck by a quake that killed 250,000. Subsequent tremors were accompanied by outbreaks of plague that killed at least a fifth of the Europeans south of the Alps and 40 percent of Constantinople. The plague recurred at regular intervals and when it struck Italy between 588 and 591, it even claimed the life of Pope Pelagius II. The rampant fever and swellings called "buboes" only added to the woe caused by Lombard invaders and a flooding of the Tiber as chastisements that had commenced with a similar flood after the time of Nero now came full circle. "Everywhere death, everywhere mourning, everywhere desolation!" lamented Pope Gregory the Great, who was astonished at the devastation. "Cities are destroyed, armed camps overturned, districts emptied of peoples, the earth reduced to solitude. Not a native remains in the countryside, nor scarcely an inhabitant in the cities; nevertheless, these small remains of humankind are still being slaughtered daily and without cease. The scourges of heavenly justice have no end because even in their midst there is no correction of the faults of our actions."

The scourges caused Gregory to wonder if mankind was approaching the Final Judgment. In a letter to King Ethelbert of Kent, he speculated that "the unending kingdom of the saints is approaching." He predicted there would be many "unusual" signs, including "climatic changes, terrors from heaven, unseasonable tempests, wars, famines, pestilences, earthquakes. All these things are not to come in our own days, but they will all follow upon our times."

In January of 590, the pope led a three-day procession through the streets of Rome in a desperate effort to call down heavenly intervention. The processionists carried a statue from Mary Major Basilica. The image in unstained wood was of Mary and the Christ Child and was believed to have special power. It moved with solemnity past the flooded homes, the shops and consular offices closed because of the plague, past the old pagan strongholds and the destructions caused by barbarians, past the baths of Diocletian. It passed people falling and dying, exorcising a city where

Christians had been killed for refusing to eat meat which had been offered to a goat's head, where debauchery had reigned for centuries, but now where God's justice was breaking down the evil as Pope Gregory and the processionists prayed and shouted, "Lord have mercy! *Kyrie eleison!*"

That's when it happened. That's when the chastisement ended. As the procession crossed an old stone-arched bridge over the Tiber and arrived at the mouth of Via Conciliazione near St. Peter's, the processionists caught sight of a mirage above an old round funerary: the incredible sight of an angel identified as Michael putting away his sword and marking the end of God's justice.

It was an apparition atop what is today called Castel Sant'Angelo, and almost immediately the plague stopped, and soon so did the general chastisement. The long-running trial had been a spiritual punishment but it had not come from God so much as from men who had *refused* God, who had ignored His protection, who had pushed away the shield of grace and who were thus left to their own devices and to infiltration by demons loosed through sin from the netherworld.

Demons could come as seductive women or fearsome animals but were more like insects. They crawled in and infested whenever there was a hole in the spiritual armor, and proliferated as long as they were unnoticed (flourishing like cockroaches in the dark). They affected the mind with oppression, confusion, pride, and anxiety. Pride was one of the best signals of their influence. Left alone, they could cause not only mental and societal ills, not only personality disorders like arrogance, but also ailments of the body, as Jesus had shown when He cured so many by first casting out their demons.

They were like insects, but they could also appear as a crow, a centaur, or a sea monster (Isaiah 27:1). They were bats. They were werewolves. Not a soul lived who had not encountered them, yet few paid attention to Christ's admonishment that in His name such spirits should be bound, isolated, and cast off or exterminated (Matthew 10:8).

Fewer still paid heed to the Apocalypse where it explained that Mary's appearance signaled the great conflict with evil and the arrival of Michael (Revelation 12:7) just as he was now seen at Castel Sant'Angelo after her statue was invoked and just as he was honored with her at a new shrine in Glastonbury. When Mary was invoked, there was Jesus. When Mary was invoked, the archangels came and demons made a quick exit. The whole cohort of heaven was with her, and she was a special scourge because as prince of pride Satan could not possibly bear her humility. She could defeat him at every turn by simply submitting to God. This was her second secret. It was like water on fire. It was alkaline on Satan's acid. His fiery darts couldn't affect her because she was separated from self and full of the Spirit. More and more recognized this. More saw the woman in Revelation 12 not just as a symbol of the Church but as a symbol for the great Virgin to whom even angels sang. In 590 at Castel Sant'Angelo, it was even said a celestial choir was heard. She was a queen and mom and she shielded men from the devil just as she had shielded Jesus from Herod. She was even invoked in barbarian lands like the Black Forest where her image was enshrined by a missionary named Gallus.

There was something about her eyes, something about her demeanor, something about her softness that rose above human delicateness and brought the touch of heaven and a sense of well-being to those in the spiritual war. If there were always those who would seek to detract from her, who would do Satan's bidding in denigrating her role, there were that many more who defended her, who invoked her on May 13, which was a feast of martyrs, or on August 15, which by A.D. 600 commemorated her Assumption. There were men like Archbishop Ildephonsus of Toledo who wrote a long treatise defending her virginity and who as a result was favored with an apparition of Mary seated on a throne. This occurred on August 15, 657, when Ildephonsus and two deacons noticed a church illuminated by a brilliant light. They entered and saw Mary surrounded by a choir of virgins (Psalm 45:14). She beckoned the bishop and fixing her eyes on him said tenderly, *"You are my chaplain and notary of faith. Receive from me this chasuble which my Son sends you from His treasury."*

It's said the chasuble, an outer priestly garment, is still preserved at Oviedo, and while we can't verify most relics, not all are the euphoria of anoxic hallucination. The most respected men of Ildephonsus' day believed in Mary. Legend says she helped end the siege of Constantinople and appeared to Bishop Bonitus in Clermont. Another bishop, Egwin of Worcester, witnessed an apparition in 708 after being summoned by an excited herdsman to a thicket in the southern part of England now known as Evesham. The bishop saw Our Blessed Mother accompanied by two other virgins who were chanting the most exquisite psalms. She was engulfed in an ineffable fragrance and was as white as lilies. The Blessed Mother was even brighter than the virgins. She was like the noon sun—and in her right hand she held a golden cross with which she blessed the bishop.

Her role became yet more crucial as Christians faced a new threat from Muslims. While their founder Mohammed had accepted the one true God and while his followers were often courageous against evil, their insistence that Christ was just a prophet and not the Son of God placed these two religions—both with roots in Abraham—in mortal combat.

Mohammed had tolerated images of Mary and Jesus, but after he died his followers set about to destroy Catholicism, attacking entire Christian nations.

As if foreseeing this holocaust, Pope Gregory sent the statue from Mary Major to Seville, Spain, but Seville was attacked by Arabs a century later and the statue was covertly carried out of the city and hidden in a cave in A.D. 711.

Records indicate the unstained-wood statue was placed under a church bell or sealed in an iron case with an explanation of what it was. Then it was buried.

The hiding place was near the mountains of Estremadura, a hundred miles southwest of Madrid, near a river or "hidden channel" which translated as "Guadalupe."

# 8

## *From Highest Mountains*

I n France, a hot spot second only to Italy, there were other supernatural events which, like Guadalupe, would figure into Europe's
future. Since the time of Le Puy the French had been warm to *la
Vierge Marie* and that love, that respect, and especially the recognition of
her purity had led to yet more wonders.

During the reign of King Dagobert I a sort of ghost boat, a vessel without sails, oars, or crew, reportedly wandered into the mouth of the Liane
River on the northern coast just across from England. When the curious
townsfolk boarded, they found a forty-inch statue of the Virgin that
seemed to have a strange radiance about it.

Records don't afford much detail, but it's a matter of the historical regis-
ter that people flocked to the riverbank, lifted the statue in procession, and
carried it to the upper part of Boulogne, where it was housed in a chapel
that became the site of miracles.

Across the English Channel in Ireland, which by this time had accepted
the spiritual authority of Rome, an angel representing Mary was said to
have transmitted a message to a group of lawmakers requesting passage of a
law known as *Cain Adamnain*, which sought to alleviate burdens on
women and exempt them from duties that belonged to men.

While the day would come when spirituality and politics would be
strictly separated, religion in seventh-century Europe was not only a part of

governance but often its most fruitful component. I've mentioned the apparition to Bonitus of Clermont but didn't say he was the former governor of Marseilles and chancellor to King Sigebert III. That apparition had occurred in the church while the influential Bonitus was praying on Christmas of 694.

As Mary received recognition, as still more Christians discussed her purity and the concept that she had been free from original sin, as they spoke of her Assumption into heaven and accepted the powers of her intercession, so was she empowered to unleash more signs, so could she help more directly.

In 714 she appeared in Constantinople to the mother of Saint Stephen the Younger, predicting the birth of that holy martyr, and showed herself to the abbess of a monastery in Montreuil, France, half a century later. Most awesome was her place high up Montserrat, the extraordinary mountain north of Barcelona with soaring pillars and ramparts that reached a height of 4,055 feet. There was a hermitage and during the Arab invasions it was a major place of refuge as Muslims swept across the Iberian Peninsula—across the old territory of James—and sought to destroy anything Christian, causing the frenzied Catholics to hide many of their most precious relics, including the statue that had been given to Bishop Eterius (which on April 22, 718, was taken to Montserrat and like the image of Guadalupe and many others, hidden in a hole or cave).

Up there with eagles, the image transformed Montserrat into a huge altar that seemed to look upon the entire continent. Below, across Europe, the spiritual landscape was greatly influenced by the Blessed Mother, who continued to work spreading her purity in areas that had long been contaminated by Druids. It was a most serious form of idolatry and the human sacrifices by long-robed occultists in wooded areas had alarmed even the Romans. There was something unusually spooky about the Druids (perhaps it was because they operated in darkness or because of the legends that they could conjure remarkable magic, creating an actual fog). Like other pagans, the Druids worshiped the moon and sun or nature spirits such as those thought to inhabit the mighty oak and other trees of the forest.

Such occultism had been targeted by Christians from the very start and was dangerous because it revered creation instead of the Creator. It spread the false notion that utopia—heaven—could be achieved on earth. As Paul had indicated, the worship of nature spirits was devil-worship. And just as Mary had quietly and secretly ushered in Jesus to a world of pagans seven centuries before, so was she now quietly but powerfully moving into Druid Western Europe; so was she now overcoming occultists not with warfare, not with an inquisition, but by the simple sweet grace which the Holy Spirit had formed in her.

She had an intimate relation with the Church from its very beginning and now, while never equating her with Jesus (see 1 Timothy 2:5), the Church in both the West and East, Rome and Byzantium, knew her as a most extraordinary intercessor, an ambassador, an exorcist. Her prayers were heard in a special way because of her purity and obedience. When humans asked for her prayer, when they sought her in the name of Christ, she answered. In some way she always answered.

She drew grace from Christ. She had a reservoir of it. And she shared. She shared with those who implored her and placed them under the cloak of her protection. While the Antichrist had not arrived in 500 as many had foreseen, there was still plenty of evil. Mary was sent because no one doing evil, no one infested with a demon, could stay near her. They had to convert or take leave. She was stronger than the dark angel. She had to struggle when on his territory but it was already written that she would win, that Christ would triumph, even if the devil in his pride refused to accept the inevitable. Clearly the victory at Calvary had brought Satan into a near panic and he was determined now to do anything to erase that victory and claim the earth by the end of time.

It's what I call the "endgame." How could he be prince of the world if people turned to Jesus? He *desperately* wanted to stop the lowly, humble Christians who were dismantling his idols. What was now unleashed was the horrendous attack on Catholics by Muslims who were ravaging southern France and who controlled territories from Asia to Spain. In 718 they swept with special force toward the mountains near the Bay of Biscay where a band of Christian patriots was encamped. It was near a little cavern known as Covadonga in Mount Auseva and hidden there was another statue, one of hundreds that had been concealed from the invaders. As sixty thousand Muslims moved in for the kill, a man named Don Pelayo sought emergency help at the blessed cavern. He was the band's leader and shortly before, while pursuing a criminal at the cave, he had run across a hermit who had pleaded on behalf of the outlaw. "If you will pardon this culprit, and give him time to repent of his sins, you too will someday find haven in this holy cave," said the hermit. "And through you there will here be born a new and powerful empire, which shall make thy name a glory to thy people."

Pelayo granted the old man's request and instead of apprehending the criminal got on his knees and paid homage to the Mother of God at the hidden shrine. He prayed for deliverance from the Muslims and not long after, when the Moors arrived, Pelayo took his men to the cave and watched as the Muslim leader, Alcamah, maneuvered in the area of Covadonga and sent an emissary demanding that the patriots surrender or face certain disaster.

When Pelayo refused, preparations were made for attack. The Moors were going to destroy them. They were swarming all over. Although inhibited by forbidding ravines, the Moors moved into the valley and were soon close enough to let loose a terrifying array of darts, stones, and arrows.

But they never did conquer Pelayo. Few of the missiles found their targets and as the Arabs tried to reach the plain at the foot of Mount Auseva, a huge storm arose with sheets of rain that caused the Deva River, which originated in the holy cave, to sweep over its banks and flood the spooked Moors. There was also a landslide so large it seemed like the mountain had been torn from its base, sending Alcamah's men fleeing and granting Pelayo, like Constantine, an unlikely victory that changed history.

For Pelayo was then crowned king of Asturias, and created an alliance that would one day form a nation called Spain.

# 9

## Little Secrets

But it took centuries for Spain to completely wriggle free of the oppressing Muslims. While the Arabs still swarmed over the countryside, Mary's images were also under assault up north by Vikings who slew monks, destroyed shrines, and raised the banner of Woden, the evil war god.

Like Druids the Vikings chanted spells, associated oak trees with power, and had another god symbolized by the swastika. They bore an abhorrence of Catholicism, wrecking its sacred spots in England and Wales. They killed priests and presided over their own occult altars.

The Vikings' anti-Catholicism, and especially their iconoclasm—their hatred of relics—was paralleled in other parts of the world by a Byzantine emperor named Leo III who at this same time had his soldiers perched on ladders in Constantinople removing figures of Christ and destroying them just as Vikings and Arabs destroyed statues.

While there were occasionally those who were overly preoccupied with statues, worse were those with an obsessional dislike of them, those who set about *destroying* the images and who in so doing betrayed error and even demonism. As usual Satan could spot one extreme and set it off against another, causing division and further separating the Eastern Rite, the Byzantine Catholics based in Constantinople, from the Western or "Roman" Rite. The bottom line was that there was nothing wrong with holy images. Christ Himself had lent God a visible form. In Him "the full-ness of deity" had resided (Colossians 2:9) and as Byzantium's own patri-arch Germanus had noted in a letter to Leo, "Pictures are history in figure and tend to the sole glory of the heavenly Father. When we show reverence to representations of Jesus Christ we do not worship the colors laid upon the wood: we are venerating the invisible God Who is in the bosom of the Father."

Grace and spiritual presence came with statues. And many people who supported their cause became martyrs. In Egypt, John Damascene was accused of treason for defending sacred icons, and his right hand was cut off. Kneeling beside a statue of the Blessed Lady on the night of his dis-memberment, John cried, "O stainless Mother of God, in defense of holy images I have lost my hand. Help me, heal me, that I may still write of thy praises, and those of thy divine Son!"

When sleep arrived, so did a voice. *"Thy hand is whole,"* said a mysterious female. *"Be it as thou hast said, as the pen of one who writeth swiftly."*

When John awoke, his hand was supposedly restored. Only a thin line showed where it had been severed.

While such accounts sounded like fables and while there was often a medley of fact and allegory in ancient parables, the most outlandish cases were frequently based on real events. There was fantasy and embellishment but miracles were happening just as miracles were recorded throughout the New Testament. When they did occur, when they occurred at Constantinople or Covadonga, when they affected great men and great nations, or when they touched a holy man like John Damascene, history often shifted as a result.

When they affected men like Charlemagne—the greatest leader during the Dark Ages—they reshaped the entire Holy Roman Empire and thus the entire future of Europe.

While many know Charlemagne as the famous Frankish king who fought Vikings and barbarians and conquered part of northern Spain to keep it from the Muslims, few know that Charlemagne was devoted to the Virgin Mary and that, in fact, an apparition was associated with him. In 772, during a war that had erupted between Franks and Saxons, soldiers reported fleeting visions of a "majestic" woman on the outskirts of Charlemagne's camp at Ostro, Germany. No one has said that Charlemagne himself witnessed the Virgin, but there can be no doubt about the emperor's unusual devotion. In another German town called Aachen, Charlemagne constructed a cathedral with chapels containing relics gathered from the Holy Land and Rome, including a cloak which once had belonged to the Virgin. On his way to fight the Spanish Muslims, he visited Our Lady of Rocamadour, the old Marian shrine near Toulouse which was said to have been established by Zaccheus. And Charlemagne climbed the 216 steps from town to the basilica on his knees!

He also secured an old portrait of the Madonna thought to have been painted by Luke and presented it to a prince in Ruthenia. This image, showing Mary with a long and serious look, would one day be honored at the Polish shrine of Czestochowa.

Behind many great men, behind many of history's movers and shakers, was the Blessed Mother. It was a divine plan, a secret design. She glided into a region and quietly turned paganism into Christianity—with no fanfare, no lances. Largely due to her evangelization the occult use of sacred eggs was turned into an ornament of Easter, and pagan evergreens were converted into the decorations for Christmas. In Rome the great pagan temple known as the Pantheon was reconsecrated as St. Mary Rotundo.

Jesus knew His people needed a mother and as the world reshaped itself after the great Roman chastisement she was there behind the scenes, forming Christendom, making the world safe for Catholicism, but doing it so quietly she would rarely be mentioned by historians. And even when her work *was* known, it would be ignored, downplayed, or ridiculed by academicians who, to quote Paul, were "always learning but never able to reach a knowledge of the truth" (2 Timothy 3:7).

The simple, humble, and unconfused people, the peasants who didn't own a book, had a clearer perception. They knew Mary. They *felt* her importance. They knew that when she was present, so was the Holy Spirit. Their knowledge was visceral. No book learning was necessary. That's why there were so many statues. That's why there were so many images. It didn't matter how much Mary was excluded from universities and libraries. People sensed her importance and stationed her images throughout Europe, where there were more and more miracles. Near the town of Itri south of Rome a devout shepherd accustomed to pasturing his herd on Mount Civita noticed that one of the oxen was roaming and disappearing for hours at a time. After this happened for several consecutive days the shepherd finally went to see where on the mountain his ox was hiding, and near the summit he found the animal in front of an oak tree, its knees bent in an attitude that resembled veneration. Approaching, the shepherd looked up at the tree and among the branches at its center, in what was described as a "bright burst of light," he saw a picture of Mary with the Infant. How it had gotten there was a mystery but the purpose seemed clear. An oak! An oak like the oaks that pagans had worshiped. Instinctively the shepherd fell to his knees and then hurried off to get a little lamp, creating a shrine in the formerly pagan woods.

During the 800s a similar shrine was constructed by a hermit named Meinrad in the dark woods southeast of Zurich. The center of his chapel was a lovely three-foot statue of Mary with Jesus. So holy was the place that word spread and many visited the chapel despite its remoteness. On approaching the hermitage one visiting monk saw a brilliant light issuing from the chapel. Looking in, he saw Meinrad kneeling on the step of the altar reciting the night office while a beautiful "child" dressed in white and surrounded by brilliant rays held the book.

In Toulouse, Mary appeared to a prelate named Archbishop Gondisalve beseeching him to defend the concept of her immaculate or sinless birth, while in Germany, Kaiser Ludwig I sent workmen to the former spot of a spring goddess named Frigga in the foothills of Hildesheim and erected a round chapel in honor of the Blessed Mother. The Hildesheim shrine was consecrated under the title of "Mystical Rose" (it is now known as Our Lady of the Oak) and was based on an image that inexplicably found its way into a tree and could not be pried out.

In Europe the Virgin was known as the "Star of the Sea" and also the "Mother of Mercy" for deeds like those in the legend of Theophilus, who had made a pact with the devil but was freed by the Blessed Mother. "Through a woman I have been wretched until now, through a woman I am now blessed," wrote a Byzantine bishop at Argos.

In the Black Forest, where the missionary Gallus had once enshrined an image of Mary, people reported the mysterious sounds of music. There were other miracles, other little secrets as well. In Coimbra, Portugal, the Virgin was credited with a great victory over invading Moors.

In 915 at Utrecht in the Netherlands she appeared to a bishop on his deathbed and on Athos in the Aegean Sea a shrine was established that, like Montserrat, would claim numerous miracles.

In Herford, Germany, Mary informed nuns through a beggar whose name has been lost to time that she wanted a cross erected at their monastery. When they did, the cross often seemed to change into a dove.

At Sion Les Saintois in Switzerland, Mary was seen by another bishop.

During 980 she likewise appeared in Canterbury, England, to a bishop named Dunstan in the east part of a monastery, preceded by a light that filled the chapel.

In Einsiedeln near Zurich, where Meinrad once had his little chapel, a magnificent church was completed in 948 and on September 13, Bishop Conrad of Constance arrived to consecrate it. At midnight, while the bishop was praying in preparation for the event, he and other clergy heard strange harmonious voices and a heavenly melody. Looking up, Conrad saw to his astonishment that the structure was now illuminated with what chroniclers called a "marvelous splendor." The altar was completely lit, and the bishop reportedly saw a procession from heaven: angels and saints swinging golden censers and chanting celestial psalms. *"Sanctus Deus in aula gloriosoe Virginis, miserere nobis,"* they sang. "Holy God, have mercy on us in the court of the glorious Virgin! Blessed be the Son of Mary who has come to this place and Who is to reign world without end!"

Bishop Conrad later testified that among the apparitional figures were Matthew, Mark, Luke, Gregory, Augustine, Ambrose, and Peter, along with the Archangel Michael and the Blessed Virgin. Then the bishop saw Christ arrayed in pontifical vestments and wearing a violet chasuble. As Conrad watched, the heavenly visitors prepared for Christ to celebrate Mass and consecrate the holy shrine to the Immaculate Mother.

Before Mass began, Mary took her place above the altar, radiant with "dazzling glory" and attended by a train of angels.

Conrad experienced the extraordinary vision for more than an hour. When Jesus and the angels suddenly left, the light was magically extinguished.

We know such details because a full investigation was later initiated by the highest civil and ecclesiastical authorities, and formal confirmation of the event came in a bull issued by Pope Leo VIII in 964. Further documentation was found in Conrad's book *De Secretis Secretorium,* where we're told that Conrad remained kneeling in ecstatic meditation for hours after the apparition, hesitant now to go through with ecclesiastical consecration because the chapel had already been consecrated by God.

# 10

## The Stroke of Twelve

The apparitions came as the millennium, the first thousand years since Christ, was approaching its close. It was still a period of transformation. It was still a time of danger. There were still the Vikings and still the Arabs, who conquered Crete and sacked Rome. The darkest moment came in 998 when a great Arab named Al-Mansur invaded the shrine at Santiago de Compostela where the apostle James was buried.

Borders shifted. Kings and popes rose and fell. In the six hundred years since the end of the Roman chastisement men had become much more moral and Christianity had made great leaps, but there were also periods of faltering. In the 900s, evil rose again with the Church encountering every form of distress as monasteries were burned, a pope was physically assaulted, and secular powers took over the appointment of pontiffs, often choosing immoral men to assume the throne of Peter, men who were selected for political and not spiritual reasons. Italy was dominated by powerful nobles who appointed and dismissed the popes at whim and filled the papal quarters with friends and relatives. Some popes flirted with female visitors or lived with mistresses; in the case of John XI (931–36), the mistress' son later became pontiff and so did her nephew and grandson.

The papacy reached a nadir in 955 with Pope John XII, who gained the throne at age eighteen, turning the papal palace into a stage of lurid scandal as he consorted with prostitutes and was accused of both incest and raping nuns. He also sold Church offices to the highest bidder, castrated a priest who criticized him, and reportedly drank wine in honor of the devil, toasting with raised cup and invoking Venus and Jupiter.

Pope John was finally forced out by Saxon King Otto I, but power struggles still left corpses at the Vatican. John even regained the papacy for a short while until he was killed by the husband of a lover.

Persecution joined the deplorable scandals. There was renewed iconoclasm and tension between the Eastern and Western churches to the point where the Roman and Orthodox leaders excommunicated each other.

With such turbulence it was no surprise that common folk began wondering whether the year 1000 would bring the Antichrist. If historians are correct, the millennium didn't really occur in A.D. 1000. That was a miscalculation. Herod the Great had died around 4 B.C., it is now said, and thus Jesus, Who had been born under Herod, actually arrived before 4 B.C. But still the year 1000 seemed mystical, and with all the evil there was bound to be trepidation.

In England a meteor caused great fear and so did the rumbling of Mount Vesuvius in Italy. Nuns in France saw fiery armies fighting in the sky while others reported visions of the sky splitting open or the specter of a dragon. An image of Christ shed crimson tears and perhaps His sorrow was over the Church turmoil and the intermittent famines that had led to robbery and even cannibalism. One man was executed for selling human flesh and upon arrest another cannibal was found with forty-nine skulls.

While society still had a way to go before it accumulated the evil of Roman times, and while most of the Middle Ages saw tremendously strict moral codes, that morality began to deteriorate and did so quickly. "A mixture of frivolity and infamy corrupts our way of life," fretted a monk named Raoul Glaber. "Therefore our minds have lost their taste for what is serious and dwell upon what is shameful. Honor and justice cannot be had now at any price. Women walk about in shortened dresses, moving wantonly.

Among men, degeneracy gives way to effeminacy. Fraud, violence, and every imaginable vice vie with each other for dominance."

In Rheims, Archbishop Hervee added that "like the first people of earth, men live without law and fear of punishment, abandoning themselves to their passions. Everyone does as he pleases, defying the laws divine and human, as well as the orders of their bishops. The strong oppress the weak. Everywhere there is violence against the poor who are helpless to resist— and equally helpless the churches and cloisters who cannot defend what is theirs."

Hervee warned that, as a result, the world approached "the day, majestic and terrible, when we, together with our flock, shall stand before the Great Shepherd of all."

And so the end appeared to be in sight, and many expected the Last Judgment to take place soon at Jerusalem. Throughout 999—which, of course, was "666," the sign of the devil, upside down—pilgrims converged on the Holy Land. Many had sold all they owned to make the journey, and they came from all over the known world. This great wandering was itself seen as a sign of the Antichrist, whose appearance would signal the end of the world. "And so the pilgrims thronged the miserable roads," writes author Richard Erdoes. "On foot, in carts, riding horseback, and singing psalms, they fearfully scanned the sky, which they full expected to be rent asunder at any moment. Every phenomenon of nature filled them with alarm."

Although there was no major panic, enough folks were worried to fill the old basilica of St. Peter's on the last day of 999. Many of those sought God's forgiveness with weeks of fasting and other acts of penance. As Pope Sylvester II was celebrating the midnight Mass, they were lying with their faces to the floor, arms outspread, waiting.

Finally the fearsome moment of twelve approached. Many were afraid to look. Others were in ecstasy. A few actually died of fright, and only the voice of Pope Sylvester was heard intoning the words *"ite missa est"* when the midnight bell rang out.

Midnight came and went and after an hour passed the people embraced each other with joy.

Weeping. Laughing. The bells of the basilica as well as those of the Lateran and Aventine—every church in Rome—began to sound as if to thank the Lord.

It wasn't the end of the world after all but rather a period of birth pangs. While there were still purifications in various regions, there was not yet the need for general chastisement. It was a period of reshaping. The Dark Ages were melding with the Middle Ages and while evil abounded, other trends were good ones. During the past few centuries, since the end of the Classical Age, a wholly new spiritual empire known as Christendom had begun to form across the European continent. This empire was linked with temporal powers, but had no real boundaries. It was a commonwealth of Christian peoples organized in various states yet united in a common faith. Countries like Russia, Sweden, and Denmark were converted. In Spain the Arabs were being forced out and though still troublesome, Islamic power had reached its peak and was now in decline. When Viking descendants called Normans besieged Chartres, France, the bishop took a relic from what was believed to have been the Virgin's veil and advanced into the midst of the invaders, causing them to flee in panic.

A huge and august cathedral, one of the most impressive in all the world, would rise at this site, forever obscuring the previous occupation by Druids. There was also a great devotion to the Blessed Mother in London. When that city was attacked by Denmark and Norway on the Feast of Our Lady's Nativity, the prayerful Londoners hurried to the walls and succeeded in repelling the invaders in a fashion so successful and unanticipated that, like Covadonga, it was ascribed to the Virgin's assistance.

A major shrine called Willesden was established in England, while in Italy shrines were built after strange flames were seen in forests. During 1001 an apparition was reported by an Italian duke at Incoronata and the next year in Cologne, France, by Archbishop Herbert. In 1008 Mary protected Valencia from an outbreak of plague and in 1050 she appeared to Muslim Prince Hali, who was not only converted but painted her picture. In 1066 she was seen by Saint Albert in Espain, France (a year marked by another appearance of Halley's Comet), and in Arras, France, the entire town saw a vision of Mary in the clouds. They called her "Queen of the Universe." The Blessed Mother also appeared to a royal helmsman in Denmark during a bad storm on the North Sea, guiding him to Normandy, and to the founder of an abbey in Belgium whose request to die on Ascension Day was granted.

From the British Isles to the Mediterranean, and from east to west, Mary had planted many seeds, kernels that would at first sprout into little chapels but eventually grow into towering monuments. From such sanctuaries would come missionaries who would be sent beyond the borders of Europe to those many other parts of the world where the gospel of Christ was still unknown and where the native people were still in bondage to nature spirits. Although given different names, the same spirits that deceived the Druids and Vikings also deceived the sun and animal worshipers from Africa and China to South America. These spirits were revered on totem poles or at gravesites or in pyramids eerily similar to those of ancient Egypt even though these people had no known contact with each other.

Against those idols came the Virgin, who was about to appear as never before. The eruption was accompanied by the dramatic development of a prayer traced to Irish monks who had long recited the 150 Psalms of David.

When laymen who couldn't read or memorize the long Psalms wanted to do the same, the monks devised a new system whereby the people carried a pouch with 150 pebbles. Instead of a psalm the people recited an *Our Father* with each pebble.

The commoners next developed a rope with 150 knots, then strings with fifty wood pieces.

Soon the technique spread to other parts of Europe, where the faithful began to recite the Angelic Salutation with each piece of wood and where it became famous as the Rosary.

# 11

## Lights, Sounds, Graves

"*Hail Mary, full of grace.*" The words rang with power. "*The Lord is with thee.*" That was how the Rosary began. "*Blessed art thou among women.*" They were quoting the angel, an archangel, in the salutation (Luke 1:28) and every time it was repeated, it requested intercession. It asked Mary to come. It was recited in the same way that a hymn or song was repeated, not a vain repetition but an invocation, and although it wasn't the whole *Hail Mary*, each recitation magnified her. It brought power because it was an invitation. The Lord was with those who invoked Mary. She was the one to go to when a person wanted His ear and the best way of doing it was by simply quoting the salutation because any quotation of Scripture shooed away the devil and brought the Holy Spirit.

Each salutation parted the veil just as Gabriel had parted the veil, and the more it was recited in conjunction with a meditation on the mysteries of Christ, the more of a heavenly atmosphere enveloped the person and the greater was the call for Mary to come to earth.

It prepared her way.

No vain repetition! It brought Mary. It brought the angels. It drowned out the pagan incantations. And the result was an explosion. The more folks acknowledged her, the more Mary was allowed to intercede, and so the first century of the new millennium rang forth with apparitions that were not only significant enough to enter the records but would increase vastly every century thereafter.

In Turin, Italy, an old neglected church was replaced by a chapel after Mary appeared to a nobleman called Marquis Arduino of Ivrea and promised him his health if he would build the chapel in honor of Our Lady of Consolation, which he indeed started on November 23, 1014. (He was cured of his affliction.) In Rome at St. Mary Major Basilica, Emperor Henry of Italy, who had recently driven an anti-pope from Rome, was praying when he saw "the Sovereign and Eternal Priest Christ Jesus" enter to celebrate Mass, along with saints, angels, and the Blessed Virgin, who sent an angel to touch Henry on his thigh and say, "*Accept this sign of God's love for your chastity and justice.*" (From that time the emperor was lame, an affliction he recognized as the gift of suffering.)

Like the miraculous Mass at Einsiedeln and many other places, the reality of seeing something not of earth, the experience of touching up against eternity, however briefly, changed the emperor's entire perspective. Shortly afterward he used his treasury—state money—to build cathedrals. That was another of Mary's motifs: establishing great structures that stood as flagships of Jesus instead of glorifying emperors, instead of standing as tribute to men and their riches, instead of glorifying the world. Westminster Abbey was built in England, while at Chartres, France, where Mary had replaced the Druid stronghold, men were seen "humbly dragging carts and other conveyances" to help in the construction of an august cathedral that would rank among the world's top ten. The humility of the workers was rewarded with miracles and healings.

Wonders were also reported at the heights of Montserrat, where the hidden statue from Barcelona, which was given to Eterius and reputedly dated to the first century, was discovered by two shepherds from Olesa who heard singing and saw lights as they were tending their flocks on the banks of the Llobregat River.

It was a Saturday evening. There was the sweet mellow music and a peculiar light shining in the eastern part of the mountain. It was as if a thousand candles were descending. Nearby was a cave. "The astonished boys explained their vision to the priest of Monistrol, who did not believe them and wished to see the sight with his own eyes," wrote José María De Sagarra.

It appeared again the next Saturday. When the whole town had seen the marvel and the priest of Monistrol had told the bishop of Manresa, a long procession went to the luminous cave behind the bishop. The canticles, the lights, and the fragrant aroma that arose from this mysterious place affected the people so much that the bishop, filled with the deepest devotion, ordered that the cave be entered, and there they found the image which since then has been a fount of miracles and an object of universal veneration. The bishop wanted to take such a wonderful treasure to his cathedral at Manresa, but when those who were carrying the Virgin reached the place where today the monastery rises, they found that they could not move a single step backward or forward, and this new miracle was interpreted as a sign that the Virgin desired her sanctuary to be erected on that very spot, as was done.

The phenomenon was witnessed on four consecutive Saturdays as crowds sang hymns and prayed near the river. The wonders rose shortly after sunset one of the evenings when a bright light suddenly split the gloom. It illuminated the sharply cut rocks, rising and falling over the one spot, according to a later narrative, and then a most exquisite music filled the air and the crowd became silent, speechless with both fear and astonishment. The phenomenon lasted for about ten minutes, after which the light sank among the crags and the music faded away.

"The following day an expedition was organized to visit the place where these strange things had occurred, and it was with the greatest difficulty that those chosen for the task succeeded in their undertaking," wrote another chronicler, Isabel Allardyce. "They had to cling to one another to avoid falling over the narrow ledges, making large detours when the obstacles were insurmountable, and often being obliged to hew a foothold in a perpendicular rock that barred their passage. Near the summit of the mountain they came across a cave whose entrance was partly covered by stones, and after removing these they found inside a beautiful image of the Virgin and Child, carved in wood with great skill."

Soon the image was placed in a small church erected on the towering rock, which was destined to turn into a huge complex of chapels and churches and eventually the splendid monastery, and become one of the world's great pilgrimage spots. I have visited this spot and have felt the power of Montserrat in a remarkable and nearly tangible fashion.

Time and again, from Iberia to Austria and all around the Mediterranean, various miracles would repeat themselves. There would be luminosities that indicated the location of an ancient and lost relic or Mary would appear at the spot of burial, resurrecting what had been hidden from the Muslims. Or a farm animal, a mule or an ox, at times sheep, would hover at a location and refuse to budge, leading to the discovery of another lost icon. Many such images were found in trees as Mary now took over the Druid places of worship. In some cases an image would be found and moved to a better location but the next day would be back at the original place, repeating this mysterious relocation until the local people realized that Mary wanted a chapel built at the original spot for reasons that were mysterious. In still other cases workmen building a chapel would awaken the next morning to find their materials in a different place or would see birds lifting chips of wood to indicate the actual spot where the Virgin wanted a place of prayer as she set about constructing many sites of worship throughout Christendom.

These were the fortresses. This was the rock. They stood in the time of knights and feudal lords and they would continue to stand as months turned into years and years into decades. They would witness the Crusades and the rise of Turks as well as the fierce Mongolians who would challenge Europe. They would stand despite the split between Rome and Constantinople in 1054 and they would stand in the dark days of dukes with names like Robert the Devil.

They would stand—they would bear their august countenance—even in the face of Emperor Henry IV, who stormed Rome after he was excommunicated and for all practical purposes kept the pope hostage.

But no longer were noblemen in charge with their puppet pontiffs. The pope had gained vast secular power. There were periods of attack and weakness, but through the Middle Ages Catholicism became the most powerful institution in history, the papacy now its own unique monarchy. It had control over the forty to seventy million who belonged to the Western Church, and besides presiding over the crowning of kings and emperors, it controlled huge stretches of land. From its farms came revenue which was inching the Church toward a dangerous level of worldliness but which was used for its untiring evangelistic purpose. "The imposing papal monarchs of the twelfth century carried on in the Gregorian spirit, devoting themselves with exceptional energy to the task of supervising the well-being of Christendom," writes Church historian Thomas Bokenkotter. "When they clashed with secular princes they usually managed to come out on top."

It was the Catholic Church that preserved sacred writings and formed them into the Bible, and without its traditions Christianity would not have survived beyond the first centuries. It also sent military missions to stem the Muslim onslaught. While there were abuses during its Crusades, these missions had been initiated for the entirely noble cause of wresting control of Jerusalem and other cities from Muslims who had gone so far as to damage the Church of the Holy Sepulchre. If the Church could seem austere, excluding sinners from reception of Communion for years at a time and publicly whipping adulterers, it *had* to be strict if mankind was not to spin out of moral control, and it bravely fought the evils of violence and abortion while at the same time founding the modern world by preserving literature and educating generation upon generation. As the Roman Empire collapsed and barbarians descended, it was the Irish monks who took up the tedious, difficult chore of copying all Western literature and serving as channels through which the cultures of Rome, Greece, and Palestine were offered to the tribes of medieval Europe. "Without the Mission of the Irish Monks, who single-handedly refounded European civilization throughout the continent in the bays and valleys of their exile, the world that came after them would have been an entirely different one," writes Thomas Cahill, who notes that later historians, for the most part Protestants, would over-look "a tremendous contribution in the distant past that was both Celtic and Catholic, a contribution without which European civilization would have been impossible."

No institution had as much long-term effect and certainly no king, no nation, had such a beneficial one. It was incredible how that little cadre of persecuted Christians, the faithful followers of the first century who had prayed with Mary, the martyrs who had so valiantly struggled under the hatred of pagans and suffered so egregiously around the Mediterranean, had now bloomed like the great mustard seed into a Church that out of necessity had both political and military clout; a Church that dominated the continent; a Church that took back what the Muslims had stolen and built for its faithful the greatest of monuments to the Almighty in timeless stone.

Nothing secular, nothing built by kings, could match the Church's art and architecture nor its spiritual cachet. Catholics prayed and fasted. They took the New Testament literally. Like Jesus many of their leaders chose the transcendental life of celibacy and believed what Christ said about His being present in the Eucharist (Matthew 26:26). The Church faithfully kept alive rituals rooted in Abraham and its spirituality was seen during the eleventh century with the erection of the first austere Cistercian monastery. The very establishment of that monastery in Citeaux, France, was greatly affected by the Virgin, who appeared to one of the founders, an abbot named Alberic, and presented him with the idea for a white habit with black hood. She pre-dicted to another monk that the Cistercians would last until the end of the world, and when Alberic died, it was said his face radiated as he repeated the words, "Holy Mary, pray for us!"

Bishop Fulbert of Chartres noted that "the Mother of the Lord rules everywhere in great magnificence" and "can easily send the holy angels to minister to us and cancel the pacts of hell according to her good pleasure," crushing the serpent's head through her own transcendence. Her force, her elevated status, convinced many that she indeed had been assumed into heaven, body and soul, that Christ had resurrected her in a unique fashion after His own, perhaps in the Valley of Josaphat where there was a legend of her empty tomb. Others believed she never really died but was simply taken up to heaven.

For more than a thousand years the Church had been given constant reason to view Mary as far more than a normal saint and while her role may have been secret during her lifetime so as to preserve her from the persecutions of Jews and Romans, that didn't diminish the unique spirit that God had imbued in her. The Church properly beheld Mary as a special figure whom Christ wanted specially honored. She was the mother of organized ministry, and the Church she helped her Son build was "catholic" because that word meant all-inclusive and universal. She was a unifier and a doorway to her Son, which meant she was a doorway to salvation. She was a co-redemptress. "God, Who has made all things, has made Himself from Mary, and thus He has recreated all He created," said Anselm, a doctor of the medieval Church.

Anselm argued that her surpassingly great force through the power of Christ gave her command of angels like those reported around Anselm's time in Belgium. In northern Europe at Basse-Wavre, about fourteen miles from Louvain, more celestial music wafted across the marshy flats with the gleamings of inexplicable luminosity when night fell during 1050.

"As these phenomena took place notably on the feasts of Our Lady, crowds were attracted to gain what they prayed would be her special blessings," wrote historian H.M. Gillett. "By the end of the year the phenomena were of daily occurrence and, owing to the increase of astonishing cures and favors, it was decided to build a Lady Chapel on a low hill, named Balloit, the nearest firm land overlooking marshes. Everyone took part; some brought stones, some gave labor, others money. Our Lady, however, according to the legend, had other designs. Each daybreak the good workers were disconcerted to find that their labor of the previous day had been dismantled and the materials moved to another spot, always the same spot in the midst of the marshes."

That was where Mary wanted the chapel, and that's where several priests saw her in apparition.

*"I shall dwell in this valley,"* she said simply, *"because I have chosen it."*

The chapel was moved there.

Similar phenomena were observed in England by a widow named Richeldis of Faverches. She was called to build a replica of the Annunciation House at a place called Walsingham. While she was trying to discern exactly where the construction should be, a frost covered the area except for two spots, both the precise dimensions of the planned house. Richeldis decided on one of the areas, but when workmen tried to erect the frame, they met with so many problems that the widow spent a night of prayer over the matter.

The next morning she discovered that the materials had been miraculously transported to the second spot a couple of hundred feet away, which is where the chapel was then constructed.

In similar fashion a noble in Puglie, Italy, built a chapel after being led by a dream to a thicket near the Cervaro River. Suddenly the nobleman, who may have been Count Ariano, saw flames or a beam of blinding light. Stumbling, he fell to his knees at the foot of an enormous oak. It was from the tree that the light issued and the rapt nobleman heard a voice that said, *"Do not be afraid, my son. I am the Mother of God. It is my desire that a little chapel be built in this place where I may receive the veneration of the faithful. In turn I will entreat from God many graces for them."* The light was extinguished and the forest returned to its normal hue but under the tree the nobleman discovered a little statue of Mary. The chapel he built became known as *La Madonna Incoronata* or "The Crowned Madonna."

There were many similar stories. It wasn't always clear why or how, but Mary's images were turning up in forests while others were found buried near places like Castellammare de Stabia just south of Naples where fishermen saw a strange flame or light for several nights. When the bishop had his men dig at the site, they found a cistern containing an ancient but well-preserved picture of the Virgin. Meanwhile there was a report that Mary appeared in Spain to Muslims as they approached to plunder a Mozarabic monastery. The appearance not only dissuaded the assault but also converted a leader named Prince Ali-Maymon, who saw the Blessed Mother above a fig tree. Another relic was found in Madrid on November 9, 1085, when a tower in the Wall of Almudin collapsed after Alfonso VI concluded a novena in search of just this relic. Mary was credited with so much intervention in Spain that every June 24 an image of her was paraded through the province of Alva and placed on a throne at the general assembly.

She came to resurrect her images. She came to help men like Count Rogiero fight Muslims in Sicily. If her appearances were hallucinations, they were experienced by the highest levels of society in the most curious and often momentous of circumstances.

As always, however, Mary was as concerned with the little guy, with the small crises of life, as with the major ones. When an infamous criminal named Diogini was about to kill a devout man in Sicily, she stopped the murder by appearing to Diogini. In 1096 near Trevisto she also materialized to a paralyzed woman named Lucretia Della Torre and healed her.

In Rome there were manifestations but of a different sort. I'm speaking again of the strange phenomena at Nero's tomb. During the late years of the eleventh century the poltergeists and unearthly shrieks grew so blatant that Pope Paschal II ordered three days of fasting and prayer with special invocations to the Virgin in churches throughout the city. Then he asked the faithful to assemble with axes and picks in order to chop down an infamous walnut tree that had grown on Nero's tomb and was supposedly the habitat for evil spirits. The pope assured his workmen that as they destroyed it they would be under the mantle of Mary.

Paschal himself took a swing or two at the tree and soon it was felled, along with every tree, bush, and shrub on that unlucky knoll. The hill was left barren.

And lastly they dug up Nero's tomb, casting its dust to the wind and the bone into the Tiber.

From what I can gather, that was the end of the haunting. The date was March 13, 1099, and soon after a chapel was erected there in Mary's honor.

# 12

## "The Bells Are Ringing"

In addition to erasing evil, as the new Eve Mary had come to give direction. As if to grant another secret, she indicated, she whispered that life on earth was one large test in which God yearns to see humans correct or at least avoid repeating the mistakes of the Garden.

Was life hard? Of course it was hard, especially in the Middle Ages. That was the test. As heirs of Christ, humans were instructed to follow His steps and reject the easy way, the lustful way, the road to hell.

Mary was a crossing guard. Her role was to help her children avoid the kinds of mistakes that had caused calamity for Egypt, Israel, and the early Romans. She preferred that the emerging nations of Europe not have to endure such a purification. She knew as the Old Testament said that calamities were to dismantle evil and they arrived in proportion to the wickedness. When a society sinned or when the Church needed cleansing God, in His wisdom, gave that society a glimpse of hell. He did this by allowing exposure to the demon. It was a simple truism: sin brought the devil. When a person was living out of line with the Commandments that person was especially exposed to both attack and deception—the false glamour, the self-importance, the shining elements.

Satan was a con. He could make night seem like day. He was the shining darkness. He sought to lead mankind into the same trap he used with Eve and when that happened, when mankind took a wrong direction, when it was in danger of damnation, God in His mercy had little choice but to allow certain events including warfare and natural calamities that tend to purge the poison.

He wasn't a vengeful God so much as a God of mercy and justice. Sometimes the best thing for a delinquent child is to simply let that child wallow in his or her doings. Sometimes it takes the deepest crises and most morbid depression as well as the assault of demons to make sinners realize the error of their ways. And so, just as the Virgin materialized, so did evil spirits, half human and half beast, mythical creatures with the upper bodies of humans and the hooves of a horse, or with the body of a wolf and the head of a hideous person. But mostly they attacked as invisible agents. Such was the case on a grander scale if whole nations were in error. When God drew back His protection, all sorts of negative events were possible. That's what had happened to Rome at the end of the Classical Age and now, nearly a millennium later, in the Middle Ages, evil regrouped; again it gained momentum. Men were brutal and selfish. There was materialism and a creeping coldness. Improvements in agriculture brought a better yield of crops, which caused the population to increase and commerce to revive and the old urban way of living, destroyed by barbarian invasions, to make a comeback.

Archaic towns were resurrected and new ones were born along trade routes, passing the wagonloads of lumber, wine, fine cloth, and spice to other centers of trading activity.

As change came, as complexity rose, so did the dangers. There was the need of direction. There was the need of truth. There was the need of Mary, who knew that if materialism and lust, evil and coldness, built to a high enough point, there would be horrifying events on the medieval horizon.

She had been sent to prepare the people and to lessen the chastisements, and so it was that the Middle Ages, the rough and tumble medieval times, an era when men were inhumane to each other, and rebellion sprouted everywhere, was *rife* with the supernatural. No one can calculate all the dreams and apparitions. No one could guess the number of visions.

During the first decade of the 1100s the Madonna appeared with special persistence in Italy, France, and Spain. On March 24, 1101, a young girl, a deaf-mute, was pasturing geese on a meadow in Borbiago, Italy, when she saw a magnificent lady in a light so bright that she had to close her eyes. The woman approached and placed her hands on one of the girl's shoulders, asking her as only Mary could to bring the local priest and dig there. If he did, explained Mary, he'd find a marble statue, which should be carried in a solemn procession to the church and enshrined. The girl apparently was able to complete the task and as in Castellammare de Stabia, the excavation was very fruitful and indeed miraculous. Volunteers soon struck something that gave forth a metallic sound. Digging deeper they uncovered a bronze bell. Within its cavity was the promised statue, which depicted Mary in a standing position with the Infant on her left arm, His little hands touching her right arm.

There were hundreds of lost or hidden images, all with stories, all with precious secrets, found during this intense period. In Tendilla, Spain, two knights from the St. John of Jerusalem Order were hunting in an area called the "Valley of Hell" when they were surprised by a terrific storm. Lightning flashed and thunder reverberated against the rocky cliffs. Accustomed though they were to danger, the storm in its fury scared even these knights, who took shelter beneath an overhang and invoked the Virgin.

Almost immediately a light shone forth from a nearby willow and, as it strengthened and grew brighter, the storm decreased in violence. When the knights approached, they were surprised to find an image of Mary in the crotch of the tree. They fell to their knees in astonishment.

Back near her first apparition site of Saragossa, Mary manifested at a mountaintop known as Villamayor to a humble shepherd named Gerardo, who discovered a wooden statue that *spoke* to him. As in so many cases, the Virgin's voice asked him to tell the people about her image and build a shrine on the mountain in her honor, which then allowed her greater intercession. Gerardo dashed off to the village and did as instructed but no one believed. Disheartened, he returned to the site and again Mary spoke, telling him to try a second time. Finally Gerardo found a believer in the bishop, who ended up building a chapel for the mysterious statue.

Mary beckoned across the old Empire. She beckoned from the farms. She beckoned in the woods. She beckoned from more trees. Devotion exploded. There were celebrations of the Annunciation, the Assumption, and even her birthday. Special prayers were said on Saturdays and, besides composition of the *Salve Regina* ("Hail Holy Queen"), the modern Rosary continued to take form. There was the increased practice of repeating the Angel's Salutation, which soon joined with the *Lord's Prayer*. New hymns were written to Mary, more chapels were dedicated, and in Paris the cathedral of Notre Dame was built. "I am sure that what I have been able to receive through the grace of the Son I can also receive through the merits of the mother," stated St. Anselm, who while differentiating between the power of Christ and the influence of Mary described her as the exquisitely admirable woman "through whom the elements are renewed, the netherworld is healed, the demons are trodden underfoot, men are saved and angels are restored." Anselm had a vision of Mary around 1100.

Bernard of Clairvaux also encountered her. Bernard's apparitions began when he was just a boy of seven. He had a vision of Mary praying in a stable, holding a radiant baby. *"Come, Bernard, dear,"* she said. *"The bells are ringing."*

When he was old enough, Bernard joined the hard life of a monk at Citeaux, where Mary had once requested the white habit and where the present abbot, an Englishman named Stephen Harding, had *also* seen the Virgin. Bernard's slogan was "all for Jesus through Mary." He was credited with supplying lines for the *Memorare* and promoting one addition of "O clement, O loving, O sweet Virgin Mary" to the *Salve Regina*. During a serious illness in 1125 the Blessed Mother appeared to Bernard with St. Laurence and St. Benedict, who rested their hands on Bernard (suffering from an incessant flow of phlegm) and caused a healing.

She appeared to devout priests and to those who were dying and to a thief in Turin who had stolen one of her images and was made to return it. If she had a bias it was toward the poor and lonely. She was drawn to peasants. She was drawn to the lowly. The vast majority of apparitions were to average people going through average struggles, those who labored with their hands as she and Joseph had. But she also appeared to kings. William the Good of Sicily saw her in 1114. One summer afternoon, wearied by a morning of hunting, the king lay napping in a forest. It was then Our Lady appeared and requested a church, which William promptly constructed.

She was a taskmaster but she was loyal. She never forgot her own. Not for a minute. When cholera struck Italy, not a single case occurred at the site of her apparition to the deaf girl in Borbiago, and when plague threatened Arras, France, Mary appeared on a church tower holding a candle. That was 1105 and just over a dozen years later she appeared at Monte Virgiliano, where there had been a temple to the supreme goddess Cybele. She was also reported in Thetford, England. So devout was Britain it was becoming known as "Mary's Dowry" although the main action, the most frequent visions, remained in France, where she appeared at Premontre to a man named Norbert whose father was the count of Gennep. His conversion had come while riding near the Westphalian village of Wreden, where, like the knights at Tendilla, he was nearly overcome by a thunderstorm.

Frightened by a flash of lightning, Norbert's horse had reared, throwing him to the ground. When he regained consciousness Norbert, a man known to enjoy his worldliness, experienced a locution: *"Turn from evil and do good: seek after peace and pursue it."*

As with the great apostle Paul, Norbert gave away all that had been his illustrious life and took up prayer, meditation, and fasting. He became a priest and eventually founded his own community in the forest of Couchy, a place which had been indicated to him by an apparition of the Lady during an all-night vigil. As at Citeaux she directed the use of white habits and left him rapt in prayer till morning. Norbert was often associated with prophecies of the Antichrist, indicating to his friend and confidante Bernard that the son of perdition would come during this period of time.

Bernard took Norbert's prophecy more as an indication of current problems in the Church than of the Final Judgment. At the time there were two popes, Innocent II and Anacletus II, who both claimed Peter's throne. Innocent won the struggle in 1137 and while neither was the Antichrist, Satan once more had shown his strategy of division. *That* was the spirit of perdition; *that* was how to frazzle Christians. And if not by internal divisiveness then by external hostilities. Contention between Church and state and the attempts by the king of England to exert authority over bishops were constant problems and took the life of Thomas Becket, the archbishop of Canterbury, who was not only a Church hero but a seer. On one occasion as a youth Mary had visited him with two golden keys. On another occasion she came with a mysterious little box containing a cape. I don't know what the keys meant, but if the cape, which was red, symbolized martyrdom, it was right on the mark, for on December 29, 1170, in an incident that reverberated with the same trauma and moment as the later assassinations of men such as Abraham Lincoln, Becket was confronted by four knights who burst into his cathedral. "Where is the archbishop? Where is the traitor?"

"Here I am," Becket boldly replied, "no traitor but archbishop and priest of God." He positioned himself between the altars of Our Lady and St. Benedict. The knights threatened him with an axe and sword. All Becket said was, "I am ready to die, but God's curse be on you if you harm my people."

A blow was struck, but Becket refused to give in. The blow was a glancing one which caused blood to run into Becket's eyes. He wiped it away and when he saw the red stain said, "Into thy hand, Lord, I commend my spirit." He was thrown to the ground and a sword severed his scalp, his brain flung by another action of the metal. As the great saint lay still and bleeding in the cathedral, a thunderstorm broke overhead.

# 13

## *A  Distant  Thunder*

There were also clouds across the rest of Europe. They were figurative clouds and they were still rather small. They hadn't formed into a major front, not yet. But the cumuli were numerous and there was a vague but growing darkness.

Wisps of darkness. Still no rain across the entire landscape but the calm before a storm. Although there were traumas such as the Becket assassination and, as always, tensions between emerging nations (France and England had fought a little war), overall there was a relative and at times eerie quiet, with only the hint of distant thunder.

It was heard on occasion from faraway lands. It was heard in the remote war cry of Mongolians, who were becoming a threat, and it was heard from China, which had just invented gunpowder. It was heard in Asia Minor where the Turks were developing into a world power. It was also heard from the Crusades, which started as a noble mission and ended with ignominious defeat. It was a dark and gritty time. Society had not yet organized itself to handle the return of urbanization. Narrow streets were often filthy and full of debris. Dwellings were wretched wooden affairs with earthen floors.

But people in the Middle Ages were courageously striving to look beyond the physical. There were good things about the Middle Ages. There were aspects that were deeply spiritual. Medieval society was not as ruthless and shallow as Roman times. The perspective of most people was *other-worldly*. There was great concern for the salvation of souls. The Church had developed a deep and moving spirituality. It touched a level no other religion had touched. If its doctrine could be summarized in one word that word was love. Nowhere was love more pronounced than among those who were serious Christians. Piety was at an unprecedented level. There were holy hermits and canonized saints whose holidays had now all but completely replaced those of pagan gods, and as I said, Christmas had usurped the sun holiday and Easter was fully instituted as a replacement for the pagan festival of Ostara, the spring goddess. Christianity had paganism backing into the corner and it had also corrected some of the loose morals. In many places sodomy was considered a practice among individuals whose wills had been enslaved by demonic forces and adultery was a matter for secular judges and Church tribunals. The standards had been severe since the seventh century. Incest and sodomy were ranked with murder, arson, and forgery. Transgressors could be excluded from Communion for thirty *years*. Even within marriage, sexual practices were regulated and an extramarital affair could cause expulsion of a woman from the matrimonial home, confiscation of her dowry, and separation from her children. In one canon dating back to the 600s, the penance for abortion was to fast for seven years.

These stiff penances had been born of a Church determined to help its members avoid the pains of hell and purgatory. Earth was considered a place of suffering—as truly it always had been—and a strict life drew the most merit from it. Everything had a spiritual side. Even the conferring of knighthood was a religious ritual. On the evening before his initiation, a knight kept vigil before the altar, praying for the intercession of Mary. The sacraments were highly valued, confession was frequent and the transubstantiation of bread into the mystical Blood and Body of Jesus was imposed as official doctrine.

But as we saw at the turn of the millennium, moral laxity was moving in, especially in the upper echelons, and many aspects of medieval life either contradicted Christianity or were outright hostile to it. And such aspects were soon rapidly growing. Prostitution was allowed or even institutionalized by many governments, and scandals were creeping in on the clergy. There was also the notorious medieval tendency toward violence. As an historian named Harry Elmer Barnes wrote, "Not only was the feudal noble a soldier above all else, and war both his profession and his function in society, but he actually loved war with all its harshness and butchery. For the feudal noble the clashing of arms, the burning and pillaging of a castle, and the killing of an enemy were not only pleasures, but a social need, filling out the meagerness of his life."

This tendency toward violence sucked in the Church during the Crusades. Initiated by Pope Urban II to Christianize the Middle East, the First Crusade was largely successful. The Holy City was recaptured from the Muslims. Sturdy foot soldiers and armored knights had traveled across Asia Minor and bravely fended off attacks by Turkish horsemen on the way to a siege of Antioch, followed two years later by the sweep into Jerusalem.

But the forays (backed by kings of nations such as England, Germany, and France) were not always under Church control and there were terrible abuses. In Jerusalem crusaders massacred their prisoners, including women and children, and during the Fourth Crusade, Constantinople was horribly sacked by greedy, treasure-grabbing soldiers who left the ancient city bereft of its heritage. Although most of the crusaders, fighting under the standard of the cross, had been brave and righteous, the Mohammedans reconquered Jerusalem and the Middle East remained Muslim territory.

Everywhere was the melee of shields, the breaking of lances, the clash of gleaming helmets and conflicts between feudal lords. Men like Becket were killed for bucking the secular world and there were many sackings of the Church. War was everywhere, and if violence wasn't enough to taint medieval spirituality, there was also the time-honored penchant for superstition or occultism. The predictions of astrologers carried inordinate weight and out of the Crusades evolved a cabal of knights, the Templars, who adopted certain arcane rituals and developed into major landowners. Their holdings spanned territories in France, England, Scotland, Spain, and Portugal. They started as ascetic knights and fearless crusaders but soon evolved into master builders, handling much of the capital in Western Europe, founding the modern system of banking, and at the same time rumored to possess rituals handed down since the fall of Rome by a cabal of architects.

Distant thunder. There were many such rumblings. If it wasn't the perpetual threat of the occult, it was the new threat of atheism. It was the threat of antireligion and nonspirituality. It was the devil's threat: if people wouldn't accept *his* kind of the supernatural, which of course was occultism, then he would negate any semblance of religion. He would dismiss all forms of the supernatural by promoting philosophical and scientific notions that excluded the spiritual element.

The real storm, the heavy thunder, was thus gathering on the spiritual battlefield. Christianity had established its undeniable power by forcing King Henry to do humiliating public penance (for the death of Becket), but there were new problems for Catholicism, spiritual troubles. Despite its supernatural foundation, the Church was becoming too secular. It was virtually a state. It was a governor, a rent collector, a giant landowner. It imposed taxes, produced material, employed labor. It was a tradesman as well as a merchantman, a mortgage-broker, a custodian of morals, but also a banker with influence over royal and worldly affairs.

Any keen bishop could see the weather vane. It was pointing to a looming battle between the physical and the nonphysical, between spirit and flesh, between spirit and "intellect." Creeping materialism. Creeping worldliness. Universities were springing up in Europe and while that was largely a positive development, it became clear almost from the outset that many of these institutions were going to take on lives of their own. They were going to become not just an instrument of knowledge but the definition of it, and they were going to separate from the cathedrals that originally bore them. Organizing like the guilds, teachers and universities were going to become religions unto themselves. They were going to replace spirituality with the new idol of rationalism (the brain-god).

If medieval society was still largely steeped in the supernatural, there were also now the swiftly germinating seeds of secularism. As the universities rose they were infiltrated by the old thoughts of Aristotle, whose works were being translated and thus resurrected in the West and who had wanted only physical, this-world explanations for everything that happened on earth.

There was thus a developing class of society that would be known as "intellectuals." To them the fortuitous events of life—the blessings—would soon be logically explained as mere luck, and the supernatural would become superstition.

# 14

## The Secret Presence

The problem was that logic was not the final wisdom. It wasn't God. It was only one tool of human intelligence—good for arithmetic and designing buildings and new inventions—but it wasn't the seat of the spirit. It wasn't the seat of discernment. It wasn't the highest perception. It was a limited faculty, limited to the physical, material side of life, and it did not equal sagacity. It didn't define wisdom. Logic was memory, the accumulation of facts, the fruit of deduction. It relied on the five senses. It was based solely on that which could be seen, heard, touched, tasted, or smelled. It was minor next to the perception, balance, and wisdom of an angel or heavenly being like the Virgin, who was the example of both mundane intelligence and transcending wisdom. Mary was enraptured with God yet also down to earth. She was both logical and spiritual. She knew sorrow and pain but she was full of joy and encouragement. She transmitted the perfect balance between intellect and spirituality and in that symmetry, heaven was united to earth.

That was a truth that could not be "deduced." It could not be "rationalized." It had to be felt through prayer. It was felt through the Salutation. It was felt in the Rosary.

*Hail Mary, full of grace... smarter than any philosopher.*

Smarter than anyone of the world.

The "real" minds, the "real" intellects, realized it. They recognized supernaturalism. They admitted there were many invisible and intangible forces.

Plenty of highly educated monks knew the supernatural reality through firsthand experiences. In England on March 8, 1150, a dozen friars headed by Abbot John Kingston were ready to leave from a Byland cloister for Joreval in Yorkshire, where they hoped to establish a shrine, when Kingston experienced the apparition of a woman "nobly dressed and of surpassing beauty." In her left arm was a Child so fair that His face was like the luminosity of the moon. The Boy plucked a bough from a little tree in the quadrangle of the cloister and then both figures vanished.

Soon after, losing their way in a thicket and surrounded by tall rocks and thorns and brambles, the monks stopped and decided to read the Gospel and say their Hours. It was as they finished praying that the same ephemeral woman reappeared with the Boy. "O fair and beautiful lady, what doest thou in this desert?" asked the abbot. "And whither art thou going?"

*"I am often in desert places,"* replied the woman, *"and I come from Rievaulx and Byland, where I have been speaking with the abbots, and with certain monks who are especially dear to me, and I am now going on to Newminster to console my beloved abbot there, and certain other of my monks."* When Kingston asked why she sought the company of others, the Blessed Lady said, *"Truly, I have One Who has chosen me for Himself and from Whom I am never separated, either in presence or in will, but it is good to also seek other friends who, next to Him, love me faithfully. Yet our ever-perfect love never decreases, but always augments."*

Kingston then asked the Virgin to guide them. She knew where they were heading without being told. She looked over to the Boy and said, *"Sweetest Son, for the love wherewith Thou hast ever loved me, be a guide to these brethren who are our friends, for I am called elsewhere."* And with that she left and the monks continued their journey guided by the youthful apparition Who held out the bough as if to wave them along and Whom the monks took to be a representation of the Christ Child.

And a lesson in intercession.

Also, a secret.

The secret of His Presence.

In all the paintings, in all the statues and other images that supposedly went back as far as the apostle Luke and the miracle of Saragossa, Mary had been pictured with the Infant or Child in her arms. He seemed always to be in the background, nearly part of the scenery, outshone by the adult figure of Mary, who was so often portrayed with great and towering flourishes. The pictures seemed always to focus on Mary and to credit her with the miracles, but as the Joreval case indicated and as I've tried to stress, Jesus was behind her. Mary herself said it was Christ *"from Whom I am never separated."* He was doing the secret blessing. He was the power and He was present whenever Mary was present. He gave her the Holy Spirit. Without Him she couldn't make her appearance. Without Him she had no power. He was the quiet and secret dispenser. Truly, as the Salutation said, the Lord *was* with Mary. Her presence was the secret Presence of Jesus. And the peace felt by those who encountered her, the peace painters and visionaries and those who prayed encountered—the peace that the rationalists could never know—was the calm that flowed from the Prince of Peace Himself. *"These are my most merciful eyes which I can incline in favor of all who invoke me,"* Mary said to St. Gertrude, pointing to the Infant's eyes instead of her own.

According to Scripture, Jesus would come in glory on the clouds (Matthew 24:30) but until that time, until that day, He would quietly and invisibly accompany His mother. He was subtle. He was playing it low-key.

He preferred that His mother come before Him. He liked Mary to precede. She had preceded Him in Nazareth. She had preceded His coming as she prayed in the Upper Room (Acts 1:14). Her visibility was the precursor of His. She was His forerunner. She stood the ground while He was at the right hand of the Father, King of all heaven, being careful about how He showed Himself and when. He was saving His special Presence for special intervention, and although He made Himself manifest in some cases, mostly to saints, it seemed, as at the Sea of Tiberius (John 21:1), that His major appearance was as yet in the future.

His moment was not yet and so He accompanied the holy Virgin as a silent babe. She was powerful against the enemy because Jesus accompanied her with *His* power. The mere whiff of His authority, His Presence, destroyed the lawless one (2 Thessalonians 2:8). It was no contest. Christ was in charge of the universe. When He wanted He could exert complete control. Satan had to flee. There was no choice. In Austria, at what is now called Maria-Eich, between Ried and Aurolzmünster, a legend was told of a Count Hunt who had been presented a wonderful image of the Virgin by the abbot of Admont. In the forest between the two cities Hunt was stopped by an armed knight who was dressed in black. The knight ordered him to throw away the holy image or engage in combat. Holding the image high, Hunt made the sign of the Cross and the dark "knight," actually a demon, vanished.

Although details of time and place are scant, there were similar legends throughout the Middle Ages, enough to fill several volumes, including a series of books entitled *Miracles of the Blessed Virgin Mary.* There was the case, for instance, of a woman who had lost her sanity due to the duress of Satan. After a year of seeking deliverance, the woman was finally freed on the annual feast commemorating the Purification of the Virgin.

There was also the account of an unnamed monk who had been devoted to Mary but who had strayed into drunkenness. After one alcoholic stupor the friar encountered not pink elephants but a great bull that sought to gore him. The fright occurred in the cloister on the way to church. The monk was nearly overcome when "there came to him a very beautiful maiden with long hair flowing over her shoulders and holding in her right hand a linen handkerchief, who rated the devil, and bade him depart from the household of God, then suddenly both visions vanished," said the literature from this period. And when the devil reappeared as an immense lion, Mary again materialized and made it vanish "like smoke."

These manifestations proved what Antony of the Desert once said, that depending on their mission devils could come in either human or animal form, patterning their phantasms after our thoughts. In another monastery was a brother named Hieronymus who liked to paint. His specialty was beautiful figures of the Virgin. Those images were contrasted in his art by foul and misshapen portrayals of the Adversary, whose images Hieronymus used to spit upon. Enraged at the affront, Satan appeared to Hieronymus as a very beautiful woman who got the artist into trouble by convincing him to steal precious objects from the church for her. Hieronymous was caught and punished until Mary, who was faithful to her devoted but deceived artist, released Hieronymus from a pillar where he was bound for the crime and instead bound the demon. *"Be comforted in the Lord and hereafter stand firm and beware of the wiles of the devil,"* she told him.

In another case, a certain matron, the wife of a knight, had committed adultery through the devil's prompting. After a while God inspired her to repent, grieve of the sin, and forsake her lover. "He, however, keeping watch on the house until the husband was absent then entered it, and, finding her alone, tempted her to sin as before and, when she refused, he tried to force her," said this account. "And she, seeing that she could not resist him, had recourse to the guardian of all chastity saying: 'I beg thee, Lady, by the sacred *Hail Mary* to deliver me.' At these words all the spirit went out of the soldier and withered, and so the woman escaped unhurt, the soldier not daring ever to say another word to tempt her or anyone else."

Satan had also sought to deceive a cloistered nun by coming in the form of an angel. Lacking discernment, the nun allowed these apparitions to continue for quite some time, until her confessor sensed the deception. "When the angel again visits you," he instructed, "you will say, 'My good sir, I beg you show me Our Lady, for if she has caused the vision, you will bend the knee and say, "Hail Mary,"' and if he remains, it is no delusion."

Next time the devil appeared, the nun did as directed. She cried out to Mary. And then came a startling woman, a "maiden of wonderful beauty," who caused the evil phantom to melt into a "whirlwind."

In the diocese of Cologne was another nun who, through a sin that caused her to seek refuge in a convent, had been exposed to a demon. The imp took the form of a young man standing near a well. Often she saw him from her window. The demon played all kinds of games with the nun, whose name is given to us only as Adelheidis. While holy water and the sign of the Cross helped, the demon continued to return.

Then a fellow sister "of riper years and wiser" instructed Adelheidis to hurl the Angelic Salutation in the devil's face. The next time he came around, she was to simply recite the beginning words to what we now call the *Hail Mary*.

And when she did the spirit was "stricken."

In Chartres was yet another case in which Mary arrived to dissuade a wife from killing a maidservant who was having an affair with her husband.

The cases went on. They were endless. As before, Mary appeared to deacons and bishops. She appeared to errant knights in order to convert them. There was a special flurry of reports from the monasteries. Since Saragossa, the graph line had been on an upward curve, but now the curve began to steepen. Apparitions rose at much more of an angle. The proliferation was largely due to increased devotion and population. But there was something else at work. There was something on the order of a secret. There was always a reason for the patterns of Mary and now, in the middle of the Middle Ages, the apparitions were a harbinger, an omen. Something was coming. There was both opportunity and danger. It smelled of chastisement. It was still the calm before the storm, but the thunder was closer. There was an upsurge in satanic activity and while demons were always around, while they were evident in every period, it was now one thousand years since the upsurge in Rome and Satan was again loose from the pit (Revelation 20:2). His rise paralleled the rising and perhaps skyrocketing immorality. St. Elizabeth of Schönau saw horrible goats in black fire, while others described unnatural creatures like the vampire or the werewolf.

If not wolves, if not bulls, then monsters. There was the beginning of what the German seer Hildegard of Bingen saw as the *tempus muliebre*, an era of decline that set the endgame, an apocalyptic scenario, into action and would lead up to that day when the Antichrist would arrive as "a monstrous and totally black head with fiery eyes, ears like the ears of a donkey, nostrils and mouth like those of a lion, gnashing with vast open mouth and sharpening its horrible iron teeth in a horrid manner."

Others thought the time was not in the future but right now. A prelate named Otto of Freising was convinced the end was near and the monk Joachim of Fiore believed the Antichrist was already alive and a teenager.

# 15

## *Pillar of Fire*

While once more the Antichrist failed to arrive, the fact that so many sensed his presence and that so many reported demons indicated a special hour. Change was coming. There was spiritual conflict. Such was the case at every historical juncture. The larger the coming change, the greater the conflict.

In the tangible world it manifested as turmoil. There were both natural and societal disruptions. Thus far there'd been only minor upsets, but they were arriving in a steady and growing pattern. In France there had been no less than *sixty* famine years between 970 and 1100, with the worst coming during 1086, right after a dispute between the pope and Henry IV. Another came in 1125. They were just local affairs but small trials often preceded larger ones. Or trials preceded heresies, the regularly occurring attempts of "reformists" to splinter the Church. Currently there were the Waldenses, a group who, like Montanists, claimed their goal was a return to "primitive" Christianity but who cast unwarranted doubt on Church dogma. Mary was clearly coming as an admonition of man's pretension and her apparitions, her manifestations, paralleled both the spiritual and natural trouble.

Once more, as at Pompeii, there were rumblings of the earth. On February 11, 1169, a major quake struck in Italy near Mount Etna, killing fifteen thousand, while at the spiritual level the tremors included a pretended Messiah proclaiming the Second Coming in France and Persia.

The quake didn't qualify as a world-stopping event and neither did the false prophet but they certainly seemed to be in the realm of admonishment.

So did flooding along the North Sea, especially in the province of Frisia in Scandanavia. There Mary appeared to a devout matron and explained that the inundation—which had destroyed whole villages—was a result of disrespect—blasphemy—against the Eucharist. In Caesarius an image of Mary was found to be sweating, as if to show her strain at holding off heavenly justice. There was also the story of a priest "to whom many secret things were revealed from heaven" and who in ecstasy was carried to the tribunal of Jesus. At Christ's right hand he saw an angel with a trumpet that sounded so loudly it shook the world "as the wind shakes a leaf." When the angel went to blow his trumpet a second time—an event which would have caused global disaster—the Mother of Mercy rose from her seat and threw herself at the feet of her Son. The priest said Mary begged Jesus to put away His wrath and spare the world.

At first Christ had hesitated. *"Mother, the whole world lies in wickedness and so vexes me with its sins that I ought not to hold my wrath or spare mankind,"* the priest heard Jesus respond during the vision. *"Not only laymen but clergy and monks offend me from day to day."*

But when Mary continued to plead, Christ was appeased and held off.

Those who realized such intercessory powers—and they *were* real—placed the Virgin above worldly authority. In Viseu, Portugal, a priest named Theotonius was preparing to offer a Mass of Our Lady when he received a note from the Portuguese queen, who was present in the pews. The queen, who apparently was in a hurry, requested that Theotonius shorten his Mass. The priest was appalled. And he let Her Royal Highness know it. Quickly he sent back a note saying that the Mass was for the Virgin, a woman who was greater than any royalty, and that if the queen didn't like it she was free to leave.

Mary's own queenship was expressed in the *Salve Regina*, which was introduced into the liturgical services at Cluny during the twelfth century. She was indeed a queen, but of peasant demeanor. She was indeed royalty, but crowned with poverty. She was a queen in heaven, the queen of motherhood. This was evident in a touching portrait from Ukraine known as Our Lady of Vladimir that showed Mary and the Christ Child tenderly touching cheeks. Such images were accompanied by phenomena. There were spectacular things going on in Ukraine, especially at Zarvanystya, about a hundred miles east of Lviv. There a monk discovered a miraculous icon of Mary while he was hiding from the rising Mongolian hordes known as Tartars. Sleeping near a brook, he had a dream in which the Mother of God appeared with a host of angels. When the monk awoke the next morning, he noticed an odd bright light near the brook. Approaching it he discovered a radiant icon of Mary and the infant Jesus. So powerful was his experience that he had a chapel built there. Meanwhile in England a famous church was dedicated in 1170 at Willesden, in a nation that would eventually claim at least fifty Marian shrines, while in Switzerland an apparition to a man named Conrad of Seldenbüren directed erection of a celebrated Benedictine monastery. At Norétable, France, Mary appeared to a fleeing murderer who then became a hermit, and at Durham, England, she visited a monk called Holy Godrick, teaching him songs that some say were the beginning of modern charismatic invocation.

In Spain a priest experienced an apparition of Mary before the high altar at the cathedral of Tortosa. She was wearing a queenly crown and accompanied by white-robed angels who formed a court and filled the sanctuary with hymns. *"Because you have served me untiringly, you have merited seeing me in this life, here among this choir of angels,"* Mary told the priest. *"And because this church was consecrated in honor of me and my Son and because the people of Tortosa have taken great delight in venerating and serving us, I present this belt with which I am girdled, fashioned by my own hands, and I place it on this altar as a token of my love."*

According to Charles B. Broschart, an American who conducted brilliant research into Tortosa and many similar visitations, the striking feature of such legends is how they appeared in accounts of people who were widely separated by language and distance. It was as if Mary manifested in certain styles, in certain motifs, for a period of time, then shifted either with the time or the culture. There were trends. There were patterns. There were flurries of nearly identical appearances. And while it could be argued that they were copycats, it seemed by virtue of the wide dispersion of such events at a time before mass media, when it could take an entire day to travel twenty miles, that the consistency between far-flung events could not be readily explained. In case after case, animals knelt prostrate at spots where Mary's images were then discovered, or little springs of water pooled into healing wells. In other cases wolves or similar beasts brought back lost children at Mary's behest or she would make a person invisible to a pursuing enemy. She was the source of rescue and calm. At Basse-Wavre and Brussels she was enshrined as Mary of Peace.

In 1190 in the town of Buschhoven, Germany, a sportsman named Ritter Wilhelm Schillings, Herr of Bornheim, was hunting with his hounds when they suddenly began to bark and point to a rosebush in bloom alongside the trail. Curious, Schillings dismounted and as he approached the bush, he discovered what Broschart described as "a lovely image of the Blessed Virgin together with two lighted candles and a small bell." Schillings took the image back to the castle and placed it in a chapel, but by the next morning it had mysteriously disappeared. The aristocrat remounted and headed back to the area of the rosebush and found the image there. Now sure that the Virgin wanted it enshrined at that spot, Schillings built a little shelter for it and soon crowds arrived, establishing a permanent refuge.

There was also an apparition of Mary seen by Abbot Peter Monoculus of Clairvaux banishing a pack of demonic dogs.

And in 1198 in Warwickshire, England, an apparition occurred to a man known simply as Sir Hugh.

On April 17 of that same year, a Ukrainian monk went to pray on

Mount Pochaiv when suddenly a pillar of fire materialized. Shepherds tend-ing flocks nearby saw the glowing phenomenon and joined the monk. As they prayed the fire died down and Mary appeared on the rise, leaving a miraculous spring where she had planted her foot.

Then there was the case of the anonymous fisherman. It too came as the century wound to an end and was possessed of special drama. We don't have his name, but we know the fisherman had been trapped in a terrific storm. It was near Marseilles. His boat had lost its rudder and developed a serious leak. We can only imagine the picture: lapping waves, frothing sea. In desperation the fisherman began to sing a mariner's hymn, the *Ave Maria Stella*, and while his voice could hardly compete with the roar of the wind, it was enough to reach heaven.

For as his eyes sought the solace of shoreline, there she was, at the top of a mount. Mary, a transparent apparition, extending her hand.

That was when the fisherman felt a powerful and unseen force and the boat began to move toward shore despite the forces of nature.

# 16

## Secrets of the Rosary

By 1200 the apparitions which had first come as drops of rain and then as a brook at the beginning of the Dark Ages were now a constant and strengthening stream. There were at least three major occurrences in 1200 and at least thirty-six major ones during the rest of the century.

Mankind was in the midst of a supernatural episode and it coincided with new dangers. In Asia the pagan warrior Chingis or Ghengis Khan began to conquer large parts of the known world; after defeating a rival named Ongkhan, Khan became chief prince of the Mongols and during the first two decades he invaded China, captured Peking, and conquered Persia before training his eyes on Russia and the already-menaced Ukraine.

Brave and loyal to his allies, Khan was horrible to his enemies. Whole garrisons were slaughtered as his men mastered a horsemanship that made them as invincible as the old Huns.

"A man's greatest pleasure," Khan once declared, "is to defeat his enemies, to drive them before him, to take from them that which they possessed, to see those whom they cherished in tears, to ride their horses, to hold their wives and daughters in his arms."

There was no denying Khan's many appalling butcheries, but he wasn't alone. Religious and political strife was all around, often accompanied by bloodshed. In Europe two terrible massacres occurred in southern France, and by the close of the century Edward I of England would slay more than seven thousand in the town of Berwick.

The Chinese leader Wan-yen Arin had approximately fifteen thousand people put to the sword in 1218, and there was a case in Europe where thirty thousand youngsters were marched off to Palestine (during a "Children's Crusade") and never seen again.

"The age was one of exceptional violence and bloodshed," noted historian Henry Desmond Martin, "and Genghis and his contemporaries, Asiatic and European, being products of the age, behaved accordingly."

The onslaughts of Khan terrorized China, as if all of that nation's superstition and spell casting had horribly backfired. There was a deep history of the occult in China and it bore startling connections. The wooden figures found in Chinese tombs were totem-like figures that brought to mind the Native American totems. Like the natives who were wandering about America, the Chinese buried their dead under mounds of earth and their gods, both human and animal, were based on nature worship.

China's preoccupation with the dragon brought to mind the Viking dragonships and mythic lake monsters and, as in Africa, there was also worship of ancestors.

No wonder China was prone to tremors. There were earth gods, wind gods, and thunder gods. There was blood sacrifice as with the Druids, and basic to China's wizardry was communication with the spirit world through shamans who let ghosts possess and talk through them.

The earth gods must have been angry, for one hundred thousand people were killed on September 27, 1290, during a quake in Chihili.

Those were China's "signs of the times." Those were its contribution to sorcery. There were others throughout Eurasia. In Sweden there were the Vargamors, "wise women" who communed with wolves. In other

Nordic regions there were altars with blood sprinklers, and in East Germany there were shamans known for trance possession.

These practices had been subdued by the spread of Christianity, but paganism had the lives of a black cat and in Essex, England, an image of Woden with his pet ravens was found with the swastikas of another "god." The English and Danes recognized a trio of goddesses known as the "weird sisters" (who were consulted for knowledge of the future and seemed a precursor for witchcraft) and other forms of paganism would soon spread from India by bands of gypsies.

That's what Catholics were coming against, that's what Christians faced, but they had a secret weapon. They had the Rosary, which was during the thirteenth century in the final stages of development. This recitation of potent words neutralized the power of pagans. In addition, a series of 150 psalters in honor of Christ, followed by 150 in honor of Mary, joined the previous psalters composed of the Lord's Prayer and the Angelic Salutation. In other words, there were now four different psalters combined into new forms with a meditation on the lives of Jesus and Mary. When a psalter of the Virgin numbered fifty or was broken into groups of fifty, it was commonly referred to as a bouquet or "rosarium." And its power should not have been surprising. It was an act involving the Bible. It was an act of invoking Jesus through Mary.

That powerful combination, that brilliant form of prayer, was brought to yet greater refinement by a Spanish priest named Dominic Guzman who was destined to become one of the most important men in Church history. Born in Castile and ordained a priest in Osma, Dominic ventured into southern France to combat the new and frightening heresy of Albigensianism. Named after the French city of Albi and known also as Cathari, the Albigensians had absorbed certain rebellious habits from the early Montanists and repeated the dualism of Manichees. Albigensianism believed there were two gods, a good one who created the spiritual world and a bad one who created the physical world. It was actually more like a new religion than a heresy, but like the previous heresies of Gnosticism and Montanism, the goal of Albigensianism was to divide and disrupt the Church. In that way they all bore similarities. While the Church agreed that men should disdain the world, and the Bible itself had called Satan prince of this world (John 12:31), Catholicism had at the same time made it clear that earth was originally good (Genesis 1:10) and every moment of life precious. The earth wasn't the devil's creation but God's. The world had become corrupt, but was *not* entirely evil. Its origin was no error. Satan was a prince but there were princes and a King—the triune God— far above him.

There was also the queen, Mary, and she was the secret weapon. She was something that neither heretics nor pagans could anticipate. They could never understand her because they could never understand humility. She was Dominic's secret as he sought to stem the tide of Albigensianism. We pick up the story in France at a tiny crossroads called Prouille. Not far from Toulouse, Prouille was nestled in hills verdant with vineyards in summer and tan in the fall, a countryside of gnarled trees that were often under clouds. In 1208, while praying there in a chapel, Dominic had an apparition of Mary that was implicitly or explicitly supported by thirteen subsequent pontiffs. Complaining one day of the scant success he was having with the Albigensians (he was as discouraged as St. James had been discouraged so long before at Saragossa), Dominic suddenly experienced an apparition of the Blessed Mother, who came with these words: *"Wonder not that you have obtained so little fruit by your labors. You have spent them on barren soil, not yet watered with the dew of divine grace. When God willed to renew the face of the earth, He began by sending down on it fertilizing rain of the Angelic Salutation. Therefore preach my psalter composed of 150 Angelic Salutations and fifteen Our Fathers and you will obtain an abundant harvest."*

As it would one day say in the Breviary Office for Rosary Sunday, Dominic "was admonished by the Blessed Virgin to preach the Rosary to the people as a singular remedy against heresy and sin."

The Church could sense an authentic resonance. *Something* happened to Dominic. Something was with him in a special manner. He became a wonderworker with the Albigensians. He could sit in the evening with a group of ardent heretics and convert them by morning. Somehow he was impervious. Somehow he had no fear. Love cast out fear and Mary brought love. The heretics couldn't reach him by pelting him with rocks. They couldn't stop him with their curses. He was working feverishly to save Christianity from the shipwreck of heresy, but he could not have done it without the *rosarium*, which inspired faith, charity, and humility.

Humility was a secret Mary bestowed on those modest enough and meek enough to seek her assistance. As I've stressed and as I can't repeat enough, humility was deadly to the devil because it took away his territory. As Prince of Pride he had no jurisdiction over the humble. He couldn't claim their souls. He certainly couldn't claim their allegiance. Humility, the antithesis of pride, disarmed the devil. He was bothered more by the humble than he could ever bother them in return. It was Jesus Who had humbled Himself on the Cross in the crucial victory over the Adversary, as Dominic told his followers, and with humility and confidence in God they would stand invincible under any persecution, any affliction. Humility was in the quiet handmaiden. Along with reliance on the Creator, it was the secret of the Rosary.

That brought up the next major factor—faith. One had to *believe*. Faith in Mary was all-powerful because it was faith in Jesus. It opened the heavens. It went beyond the power of Satan, for as Dominic knew, faith unlocked the force of the Creator. Nobody and no thing could defeat it! Faith was the shield of heaven (Ephesians 6:16). Faith was the great equalizer. Faith shrunk the leviathan down to the size of a goldfish. Faith unlocked bliss. Faith proved the fidelity of man. Faith allowed Mary to believe all would be well even though she was pregnant and unmarried. Faith got her past Herod and the other rulers of the day and faith let her know that despite the horrible trauma, her Son would rise from the dead.

Faith brought the person above the storm clouds. When coupled with humbleness, it transcended all evil. Although no human could really grasp it, life on earth was all a test of faith. As Dominic knew, God did not have to prove Himself. It was up to humans to prove themselves to God. He wasn't going to display Himself to the first rudimentary telescopes of the nascent scientific era nor to the groping and pretentious systems of rationalism. He wanted men and women to endure the greatest of challenges and do so for the most part by blind faith. It was faith and not logic, not philosophy, that led to peace. Logic had its function but was subordinate to belief. God showered more grace on those who believed too *much* than He did on those who believed too *little*. Even the quaint and apocryphal legends brought grace because God honored belief and wanted the eyes of humankind on Him and not on the minor details.

And so, Dominic carried his faith as far as the pagan strongholds of Scandinavia. From village to village, he preached Christ's mysteries. He distinguished the different kinds of meditation in the Rosary as taught by Mary during the apparition and after each short instruction recited ten Salutations.

The result was dramatic. There were conversions. There was a protection of Catholic turf. There was even military victory. In 1213 Christian forces led by Simon de Montfort prayed the Rosary and defeated the Albigensians at the Battle of Muret. "The belief that to this form of prayer a special power has been accorded by the Queen of Heaven is justified, because by her instigation and under her patronage it was introduced by the holy Father Dominic, and it was spread in a time hostile to everything Catholic, much like our own, and as a powerful means of opposing the enemies of the faith effectually," declared a subsequent encyclical by Pope Leo XIII.

Most important was the war the Rosary waged internally. It granted humility because it placed one in touch with the humble woman. It led to pureness. It led to charity.

The Rosary was the last testament of Dominic, who died in 1221 and was canonized on July 13, 1234. His death from fever occurred in another monk's bed, for Dominic had no bed of his own. Some believe he had a final vision of the Virgin before he succumbed and while we'll never know for sure, we do know that when he died there was a sweet smile on his face.

# 17

## The Omen

Sweet too was the grace descending upon a mountain village in Italy. The name of the place was famous but few realized the extent of its phenomena. There were more marvels than anywhere since Jerusalem. It was like a membrane between two dimensions. Located about one hundred miles north of Rome, Assisi was a fortified city-state. After the fall of the Western Empire, it suffered invasion by the barbarians, then steeled itself against Turks and closer enemies like Emperor Frederick II, who was moving against towns in the region and was so feared there were those who thought *he* was the Antichrist.

In that tense and chaotic time came an extraordinary monk named John Bernardone. Because his father, a wealthy merchant, spent much of his time in France, he was nicknamed Francis, which meant "Frenchman." Captured during a battle between the cities of Perugia and Assisi, Francis had borne both the captivity and a subsequent illness with precocious patience. They seemed to be a preparation for his conversion, which came when Francis heard a locution tell him to *"serve the master instead of the man."* Filled with the Holy Spirit, Francis had given away all his earthly possessions and replaced his worldly activities with prayer. A friend of Dominic, whom he met in Rome, Francis was also the receiver of locutions that seemed to fall on Assisi like pleasing rain. He had been praying in a tottering little field chapel one day when out of a Byzantine crucifix came a voice that said, *"Now go hence, Francis, and build up my house, for it is nearly falling down!"*

Francis had taken the message literally and set about rebuilding the little church. In time he also rebuilt the entire Christian Church by establishing the great religious order we know as the brown-clad, sandal-shoed Franciscans. They spread faith where there was doubt and miracles where there was rationalism. They renounced "self" and replaced it with service to God.

Here was a huge secret that the Virgin harbored: renunciation and detachment from self, setting self to the side and aiming only for what God wanted, brought permanent satisfaction. There was no other way to lasting inner calm but by attaining the deepest level of humility. Such detachment brought many consolations and Francis himself, a master of selflessness, was like a walking site of apparitions. Not since the first century had there been such a great mystic. Many witnessed the miraculous power of his humble prayer, his selfless prayer, or actually saw him in conversation with celestial entities.

Secretly following Francis into a woods, one young man suddenly heard unusual voices and was amazed to see Francis surrounded by a light which contained the forms of Christ, John the Baptist, and Mary. The same phenomena were witnessed by fellow monks, but most renowned was the stigmata Francis suffered, actual bleeding wounds in the feet and hands that resembled those of Christ. The stigmata had come at Mount Alverna when he was fasting in honor of Mary and the Archangel Michael. The wounds were imprinted by a seraph with six flaming wings, and during that historic event witnesses claimed Mount Alverna looked like it was on fire.

To those like Francis who meditated on Mary and knew her power it came as no surprise that her apparitions and her fire increased as the spiritual war continued to take an ominous turn. Francis had heard the enemy. He'd even seen the demonic face. In the evenings during lonely prayer, in the chapel or in a cave, it would seem like someone was lurking behind Francis or a horrid head was looking over his shoulder. "Then he would hear voices in the storms whistling through the mountain forests, the demons would laugh at him, while the owl screeched outside his cell," writes biographer Jöhannes Jorgensen. "But worst of all was the almost inaudible whispering which, in the deathlike stillness of the hours of the night, would sound in Francis' ears, as if whispered by hateful and spiteful lips...."

The world was a dangerous place, truly a testing ground. Every century had its evil, but there were centuries and times when the evil seems to reach a peak. It was just such a time. Events continued to build toward some kind of climax. Evil was in the wind and so was chastisement. "Out of the sea rises up the Beast, full of names of blasphemy who raging with claws of the bear and the mouth of the lion and the limbs and the likeness of the leopard, opens its mouth to blaspheme the Holy Name and ceases not to hurl its spears against the tabernacle of God and against the saints who dwell in heaven," wrote Pope Gregory in a nearly frantic encyclical when Frederick challenged the papal state and the pope himself.

Such upheaval made the tranquillity of Francis all the more remarkable and was itself proof that the friar was in touch with otherworldly force. His refuge was Mary, but he didn't make a big deal over every apparition. He treated such phenomena as nearly routine. He never sought to stand out. He was like his patroness, the Virgin. There was a hiddenness about him while he was on earth. "God has glory in what He conceals" (Proverbs 25:2). Francis taught that "when God's servant receives comfort from God in prayer, he should, before he ends his praying, lift up his eyes to heaven and with folded hands say to God, 'Lord, Thou hast sent Thy comfort and sweetness from heaven to me an unworthy sinner. I give them back to Thee again, that Thou mayest keep them for me!'" He was a mystic the likes of whom come only once or twice a millennium and holiness, self-denial, and strict adherence to religious strictures opened the portal of wonders. No one could come to the knowledge of heaven, taught Francis, but through humbleness. Heaven wanted a bowing of the head as Mary so often was seen doing, for humility with wisdom dismissed temptation. What each one is in the eyes of God, that he is and no more, taught Francis, himself a servant, a preacher, a little friar who thought himself unworthy of the priesthood and thus was never ordained. "I am the herald of the great King," he explained one day when asked who he was by a gang of robbers.

A herald, nothing more. A pure vessel. He was closely in touch with the spirit of the Virgin, who hovered all over Assisi, where a great basilica called St. Mary of the Angels would one day rise. She was seen in the old town, not just by Francis but by any number of his followers. One day after Francis had died when Peter of Montecchio was meditating on the Passion of Christ, the Blessed Mother appeared with both John the Evangelist and Francis. *"Do not be afraid, dear brother, because we have come to console you and to clear up your doubt,"* said John. *"Know therefore that the Mother of Christ and I grieved more than any other creature over the Passion of Christ, but that after us St. Francis felt greater sorrow than any other. And that is why you see him in such glory."*

When Brother Peter asked why Francis' raiment seemed more glorious than John's, the apostle supposedly replied that it was because *"for the love of Christ he wore plainer clothes than I."*

The same mysticism was experienced by a nun named Clare. When Assisi was besieged by Frederick's soldiers, Sister Clare positioned herself near the door of her convent and had a silver and ivory ciborium containing the Communion bread brought from the church. From it came a Child's voice that said, *"I will always be your guardian."* The siege stopped and Frederick's henchmen went elsewhere.

When Clare died there was a deathbed apparition of Mary. It was said that Clare saw a parade of heavenly virgins decked in white garments with golden bands around their luminous hair. One virgin was taller and more beautiful than the others, brightening the cell like the sun. It was Mary, who bent over Clare and covered her with a veil of light. It was under that veil that Clare passed into eternity.

Mary also appeared to monks like Conrad of Offida, who saw her with her Blessed Son in such dazzling splendor that they outshone all light. These were among the numerous appearances that never found their way onto formal lists. They were never considered official apparitions. But they abounded as the storm gathered. Once when a Franciscan priest from the Province of Marches approached the Preface of the Blessed Virgin during Mass, God's grace came in such a torrent and with such sweet consolation that when he reached the *Qui pridie* he could hardly endure it. By the time he got to the consecration, the priest was so rapt he kept repeating the first part over and over. His attention was focused on the vision of a throng of angels. Many attending Mass cried with a feeling of awe and joy. Still immersed in the sweet bliss, the priest finally uttered the *Corpus Meum* ("This is My Body") and the appearance of the bread seemed to disappear, replaced by a vision of Christ Glorified.

So taken was the priest that after finishing Mass, he fell into a blissful unconsciousness that lasted for hours.

There were similar accounts from France and Belgium. Throughout Europe, Communion hosts were the center of extraordinary phenomena. These were not fairy tales. There were times and dates. Sometimes there was verifiable residue. There were mentions of these miracles in papal bulls. In some cases light streamed from the consecrated bread or the Host actually exuded blood, as in Santarem, Portugal, where blood dripped from a wafer that a woman was trying to sneak out of church and give to a sorceress.

Such miracles multiplied during the twelfth and thirteenth centuries along with apparitions of Mary, who would one day be called Our Lady of the Blessed Sacrament. She visited Canterbury where Becket had died and Rostov, Russia, where she was reported by Prince Yurly Dolgoruky. In

Barcelona there had been an appearance to St. Peter Nolasco, and in Orleans, France, to a man named Dean Reginald.

There were also prodigies. In Portugal, north of Lisbon not far from Santarem near a place called Fatima (which had been named during the Muslim occupation for Mohammed's daughter) a girl from the village of Reguengo do Fetal, tending to her family's cattle, encountered Mary during a severe drought. Hungry and thirsty, the girl was crying one day as she led her equally hungry cattle on the desolate hills near Fatima when suddenly a lovely woman appeared to her. *"Little girl, why are you crying?"* asked the apparition.

"Because I'm hungry," replied the tearful youngster.

*"Go back and ask your mother to give you some bread,"* said the woman.

The child protested. "The bread box is empty. She has none to give to me."

*"Go,"* the lady insisted. *"Return to your home and again ask your mother for bread. Tell her you met a lady who sent you to say that in the box there is bread."*

The girl obeyed and hurried home and told her mother, who was naturally skeptical. But she was also curious. Going to the bread box, she opened a lid and was stunned to find it filled with bread of extraordinary excellence. The mother and daughter stuffed themselves with the inexplicable food. When the girl returned to her herd and became very thirsty, Mary again appeared and told her to sink her staff into the ground. When the girl did, a stream of cool water flowed outward.

Mary was the consolation and guidance in this time of drought and famine and war, in the *tempus muliebre.* When, after Gregory's death, the Vatican refused to lift Frederick's excommunication, the emperor went into a frenzy. War was waged and papal loyalists were blinded with hot irons, dragged by horses over stony ground, or sewn in sacks with poisonous snakes and tossed into the water. The conflict spread across Italy and then to Germany, shaking Christendom, letting it know it was somehow headed in the wrong direction, perhaps indicating that if it wanted to involve itself too much in worldly affairs it would suffer worldly consequences.

These were mere warnings. Much more was to come. Mankind in the Middle Ages needed purification. While Frederick was feared as the son of perdition, there were plenty of other "anti-Christs": the Mongolians who overran China, using the swastika as an amulet, or the Egyptians who recaptured Jerusalem.

All this commotion was concommitant with natural effects, quakes that struck again in China, Japan, and Asia Minor, which had been taken over by the Turkish Muslims.

There was also the scourge of leprosy. That horrible illness was brought back to Europe by the star-crossed crusaders and it was yet another omen.

# 18

## The Seven

Was something coming?

What did the omens mean?

There were also a ton of apparitions and the episode was only *beginning*. No longer were there only one-shot sightings. By now plenty of people were experiencing multiple or "serial" apparitions. As usual Mary seemed to favor the humble but also appeared to Pope Honorius III, Queen Helene of France, and Princess Ermesinde of Luxembourg.

The princess' occurrence took place near a clear spring or *clairefontaine* that gave the area its name. Clairefontaine wasn't far from Luxembourg and had been blessed six decades before by St. Bernard on a journey through the area. Apparently it was known even then as a place of sacred wonders, the sparkling water running past luxuriant foliage in a delightful stream.

It was in this charming valley that Princess Ermesinde, who was recovering from the recent death of her husband, had her vision while meditating under a tufted oak. It was an experience that would inspire erection of a convent dedicated to the Heart of Jesus. Some say the princess was dozing, others that she was awake and sitting. Whether a vision or apparition, what she saw was the sky "open" and a woman of incomparable grace descend on a fleecy white cloud. The woman was Mary, holding Jesus. She approached the princess and stationed herself by the stream. Around her was a flock of unearthly white lambs. As they gathered, she smiled at the animals and caressed them. On their backs they bore unusual and unforgettable black crosses, but the most striking feature was the Child, Who was of such beauty that Ermesinde felt there could be no equal in the world.

If Ermesinde's experience occurred with her eyes closed in a sleeping state, it was technically a "vision"—and a fleeting one at that. There were many other instances at this same important historical juncture, however, that were experienced in a fully wakeful state or that left physical evidence. Such was the case in Spain of a young shepherd named Francisco Alvarez who lived on the outskirts of Alcaraz. His case typified many of Mary's appearances during this particular period. One afternoon Alvarez, who had a badly crippled arm, was dozing at the foot of an ancient holm-oak when he awoke at the sudden rustling noise of his cattle, which were trying to flee the area. The same thing happened the next day. They were being spooked by something. When Alvarez finally saw why, it took away his breath: A strange and intense light was emanating from the holm-oak and stranger still was the sound of sweet music.

Overcome, Alvarez fell into sort of a faint. When he recovered he noticed that the light was gone, replaced by a statue of Mary nursing Jesus. The image, which may have been hidden in the tree during the Muslim invasions, spoke to Alvarez, requesting the townsfolk to build a chapel. When the herdsman expressed concern that no one would believe his story, he was told to extend his useless arm and it was immediately healed.

That case was the combination of locution and statue phenomena, which were by far the most frequent manifestations, but of most interest were the visions and apparitions. While visions could be symbolic manifestations or like a dream, apparitions were living images seen with the physical eyes and often Mary was not transparent or ephemeral but a corporeal apparition, meaning she had tangible aspects. She seemed physically present. She could touch a seer. She appeared to a man we know as

Blessed Reginald of Saint-Gilles while he was in Rome and anointed his eyes, ears, hands, and feet, bringing him out of a serious illness. She had also appeared to Anthony of Padua in 1221 encouraging him when he was challenged about her Immaculate Conception (*"My son, feel assured that I was born without sin"*) and her visit to Pope Honorius had come in 1226, when she told him to ignore a group of cardinals who were opposed to establishment of the Carmelite Order. In like fashion she appeared at least twice to Albert the Great, who as a youth had been an untalented, even "dim-witted" student but who, through the Rosary, through beseeching Mary and Christ, was granted the gift of intelligence and went on to become an authority on physics, astronomy, chemistry, and biology, such a natural scientist that there were those who would soon compare him to the great Roger Bacon. (He also excelled at philosophy and when he went to Cologne, Thomas Aquinas was among his pupils.)

In 1225 there was testimony that Mary had been seen at a grave accompanying a young deceased boy's soul as it sailed skyward. She also appeared to a Flemish woman named Lutgardis who experienced stigmata in the form of specks of blood as if from a crown of thorns on her forehead.

The standard apparition was to those whose names were lost to history or who attained the merest of footnotes. In Kiev there was a missionary known as Hyacinth who in 1231 was beginning Mass when word came of an attack by a tribe of Mongols. The Tartars had suddenly burst into the city and their mission was to destroy everything and everybody. There was no choice but to take immediate flight. Still dressed in his vestments, Hyacinth grabbed the Blessed Sacrament from the tabernacle and was ready to leave when he heard an inexplicable voice, which seemed to come from an alabaster statue. *"Hyacinth, my son,"* said Mary. *"Are you going to leave me behind to be trampled underfoot by the Tartars? Take me with you."*

"How can I?" protested Hyacinth. "Thy image is too heavy!"

*"Take me nonetheless,"* beseeched Mary. *"My Son will lighten the burden."*

Somehow Hyacinth grabbed the large statue with one arm while carrying the Blessed Sacrament with the other, and in that way escaped the raging flames of Kiev.

We see then that Mary spoke several ways, sometimes while she was seen, sometimes in a pure locution, sometimes in a nonverbal fashion, and sometimes through statues. Her very presence said that mankind was in great need and again hinted at chastisement. Flame. Fire. Disease. There were already so many warnings. They indicated big trouble as the Church stumbled into worldliness and as society as a whole headed toward the error of materialism. All of this was underscored by Mary's tremendous appearance to seven wealthy merchants in Florence.

This rare simultaneous apparition to a group of people occurred on August 15, 1233, as the merchants, devout albeit caught up in money, were in thanksgiving after Communion. It was at that time that each saw a bright light encompassing the Queen of Heaven and her angels. *"Leave the world and retire together into solitude in order to fight yourselves,"* said the Blessed Virgin. *"Live wholly for God. You will thus experience heavenly consolations."*

After another apparition in May of 1234, the seven men set up a crude hermitage on Monte Scenario. Then on Good Friday, April 13, 1240, coincidentally also the Feast of the Annunciation, Mary appeared a third time bearing a black habit, a book, a scroll, and palms. *"Beloved and elect servants, I have come to grant your prayers. Here is the habit which I wish you to wear henceforth. It is black that it may always remind you of the keen sorrows which I experienced through my Son's Crucifixion and death. This scroll bearing the words 'Servants of Mary' indicates the name by which you are to be known. This book contains the Rule of St. Augustine. By following it you will gain these palms in heaven, if you serve me faithfully on earth."* That was the start of the Order of Servites.

There was also the Order of Mercy, which was likewise inspired by a simultaneous vision involving three men: Peter of Nolasco, Raymond of Pennaforte (the most competent authority on canon law at that time), and

King James I of Aragon in Spain, who all saw Mary on the same night but in different places. According to the literature, she instructed them to work together to form an order whose purpose would be the ransoming or rescue of Christians who had been captured by the Moors. The three men heeded her request and one evening as King James sought a location to house the order, he was astonished to see seven unusually bright stars hovering over a hillock. It brought to mind the seven stars representing angels in Revelation 1:16. All the countryside witnessed it. This was a place called Puig. When James directed workmen to the site, they found another hidden image of Mary, shielded in a bell!

Then there was the great revelation to Simon Stock. This was a classic, corporeal apparition. A holy hermit whose father had been Lord of Kent, Simon at age forty-seven had entered the Carmelite Order, and was sent to the order's very root, Mount Carmel in Israel.

Located in the northern part of that country between Megiddo and Tyre, Carmel stood as a testimony to many generations of mankind. There, along the sparkling Mediterranean, its caves had been the habitat for ancestors who began with the prehistoric forebears known as *homo erectus* and went through the Neanderthal phase and then a phase linked to the emergence of modern *homo sapiens.*

Mount Carmel was a treasure trove for archeologists, but more important was its spiritual history. Elijah called down the fire there and ordered death for the prophets of Baal. He then went up to the top of the mount, telling his servant *seven times* to look out to the sea. When he finally did, the servant saw the unusual sight of "a cloud as small as a man's hand" rising from the water (1 Kings 18:44) in a way that reminds us of the puffs or billows of cloud associated with the Virgin. Indeed, the Carmelites would later claim that the cloud (which of course was seen many centuries before her birth) was Mary's forerunner or "prefigurement."

Whether or not that's true, it was a very holy place and dedicated to Mary by ancient hermits. Simon was so impressed by the holy men, whose existence was uncovered by the crusaders, that he joined the order and was soon their leader.

But more than an administrator, Simon Stock was a visionary. His most famous apparition and one of the most important in history came during a night of prayer on July 16, 1251, when his cell was flooded with a great light bearing the Blessed Mother. Mary held the Infant as well as a sleeveless brown outer garment that was to be known as the scapular. A broad piece of cloth that went around a monk's head, it became the Carmelite habit. It was later modified for laymen as a string with cloth squares. And it too indicated special times. It too indicated the need for protection. It was the protection that Mary promised. As Simon himself recounted, "She appeared to me with a great company, and holding the habit of the order said, *'This will be for you and for all Carmelites a privilege. He who dies in this will not suffer eternal fire.'*"

# 19

## The Foreboding

For fire was always the greatest danger. The fire of hell. It existed, Mary told her seers. It existed despite wishful thinking. It was a place for those who ignored or disdained God and it was Mary's fondest wish to help her children avoid it. That was her wish! She knew that life was a test and those who chose the wrong way, who chose lust over love, lies over truth, disbelief over faith, fell into a trap that brought them in danger of what Christ had described (Matthew 8:12) as "the outer darkness."

Right now the world was in a special period. The clouds darkened. Man was approaching the High Middle Ages. A new era was on the horizon. There was going to be change. There was going to be another great chastisement. For a while society had been heading in the right direction, ridding itself of immorality and paganism, building the Church, honoring the one true God. There were many good things about the Middle Ages. It had been an age of much spirituality and faith. There had been the Christianization of Europe.

But God chastises those He loves and society was now taking a wrong turn. Morality was shrinking. Materialism was growing. Far too much bloodletting was occurring in the form of duels and battles and executions, some in the name of Jesus. The lust for blood was a *tremendous* danger!

There were also the Church problems. There had been great laxity in the liturgy (which had been turned into stage dramas instead of the Eucharist) and the Church was becoming secularized. There were sex scandals. Religious and societal problems often fed off and coincided with each other, and when they did—when they dovetailed and augmented each other, and when there was cruelty and no respect for human life— there was need of a leveling; there was need of purification.

The number seven stood for the seven sorrows of Mary but also could be related to Leviticus 26:28 where it says, "I, also, will meet you with fiery defiance and will chastise you with sevenfold fiercer punishment for your sins."

If Leviticus, which foresaw "deserted cities," "desolate countryside," and "corpses," was indeed the relevant passage, something was coming that, in its acute nature, might be many times or at least "seven" times as bad as what had hit Pompeii and Rome.

Right now it was a time of tests. They were God's mercy. Instead of sending men to the outer darkness He first sent indications and precursors. It was an opportunity for entire countries to come back to Christ or face tougher and tougher tests. Since the beginning of time there had been warnings to sinning nations followed by castigation if they didn't heed the warnings. Right now the world was at the stage of admonishment. The quakes in China and the explosion of Mount Etna and the spread of leprosy were clues and warnings. Like any good mother, Mary came when her children were in danger. It was her time. It was a special time. She'd been given the role of advocate and that's what she was doing. She was an intercessor at the right hand of Jesus and she was interceding to prepare the world for what God had to send. *"I give thee My sweet mother as thy protectress,"* Jesus said to Gertrude the Great, who had visions for twenty years. *"I confide thee to her care."*

In ecstasy a German nun named Mechtilde heard Jesus say to Mary that it was only for His mother's sake that He was so indulgent and patient.

But something was going to happen. It was in the wind. There were so many phenomena that the thirteenth century was becoming known as "Mary's Century." Everywhere was heard the *Angelus*—there was much prayer—and such devotions had parted the veil, had opened a doorway, had already afforded mitigation of punishments, but couldn't hold them off forever.

As her apparitions intensified, the Blessed Virgin appeared to many religious. She manifested to friars, hermits, and Princess Margareta of Hungary, who spent her life in a cloister. She showed herself to several men and encouraged them to join the Servites. She came to heal more of the infirm, to save souls from hell and free others from the flames of purgatory. Saints and sinners were both taken under her mantle. All it took was repentance. All it took was devotion. She appeared to Blessed Benvenuta in northern Italy and revealed to her that the devil would appear under a most horrible form to tempt her with vain fears but that Mary would hasten to her assistance.

From the woods of Depedale to the streets of Cambridge and Oxford, Mary was honored and her statues exhibited. All the devotion was terrific and continued to keep intercession alive. But her example of gentleness was not being followed. The aftereffects of the Crusades continued to bear hardship. The faraway wars had left fields without laborers and made countless women widows. As the economy faltered, they could no longer buy bread and could find little comfort in a society that was turning cold and cerebral. "For God's sake, give us bread!" shouted women in every marketplace. "Bread for the love of Jesus!"

There was a foreboding in the air and the errancy of mankind also brought to mind Jeremiah, who had warned in the Old Testament that without repentance and obedience, death would cut down "children in the street" and "young people in the square" and enter even palaces (Jeremiah 9:16-21). It was no coincidence that at this very time King Louis IX of France brought an ancient statue from the Holy Land of a woman believed by Muslims to be a prefigurement of Mary carved by none other than Jeremiah!

It was clearly a time of special retreat to the heavenly mother. At Chartres penitents came beating their breasts and pleading mercy as if they knew that they faced a miniature judgment. The frequent visions and assault by demonic spirits indicated that spiritual warfare was still heightening. In Spain Mary's presence was chronicled in a collection of essays compiled by King Alfonso X, who presented no less than 353 wonders performed by the Virgin. The book became famous as *Las Cantigas* and according to a footnote, twenty-three of the miracles occurred to the king or his friends and relatives.

Such intensity marked a special intervention. It came to save men from heresy and armed conflict, from the battles erupting in Germany, where legend says a platoon of godless soldiers had tried to plunder a hermitage near Zweibrucken but ran in horror when the arrows they shot at an oak statue of Jesus and Mary caused the actual flow of *blood*. When news of the wonder spread, many came to see the damaged, bleeding statue and more miracles began to happen. It was said that a blind man who put his eyes to the blood regained his sight. The Countess Elizabeth von Blieskastel was also healed of an ocular affliction. There were pilgrims from Alsace, Luxembourg, and even Switzerland. There were also throngs visiting a miraculous image in Hal, Belgium, while in Italy a young shepherd was pasturing his sheep just beyond the walled town of Lucca when he found a rose blooming in a thicket near a watchtower that contained a little painting of Mary. A rose blooming in the middle of winter!

About four years later, in 1269, a nobleman named Lucian Herr von Sernau was hunting near Ostro, Germany, when he spotted a strange and lovely "matron."

It was exactly where the Blessed Mother had been seen centuries before by Charlemagne's soldiers.

Curious, Sernau spurred his horse to overtake her and find out who she was and he saw her go to the top of a hill overlooking the village of Rosenthal.

By the time he got there, however, the woman had disappeared into a huge linden and in her place was now a statue of Virgin and Child in the crotch of the tree.

# 20

## *Signs and Curses*

Those were the signs. Those were the consolations. There were also indicators in the climate. Europe was getting colder. There were two freezings of the Baltic Sea followed by storms and an unseasonable cold that ushered in a period we now call the "Little Ice Age." Glaciers were to advance for the next four hundred years, severely reducing agriculture and eradicating pagan settlements. Greenland was losing its green, while in central Asia sirocco winds from the Sahara blew hot dry air onto already hot parts of the region causing Mongol and Turkish nomads to move their flocks and also causing a migration of rodents carrying various agents of illness.

These environmental signals accompanied the economic downturn. According to historian Robert S. Gottfried, the robust growth of the medieval economy had stopped around 1250 and now there were severe agricultural problems. Because commerce was not yet able to distribute grain to inland cities, towns away from the ports saw their supplies dwindle and their inhabitants face starvation. Whole districts of corn and pasture lapsed into marsh. The Crusades had dragged away able-bodied farmers, and if war didn't get them, if they hadn't succumbed to the sword, they died from a strange Asiatic pestilence contracted in or on the way back from Palestine.

Warnings. Signals. Failed crops. Across Europe an endless interminable, rain pelted the continent. The subsequent shortages of food left many communities hungry and prone to dysentery. There were livestock epidemics that again raised Jeremiah 9:9 ("unheard is the bleat of the flock") and as always there was war. As always, men killed men. As always, newly formed nations fought each other. There was also strife between territories *within* each country as Europe turned into a military cauldron. If France wasn't fighting England it would fight the Germans while the English would turn against the Spanish or the Spanish against French. Italian cities like Genoa would scrap with Venice when they weren't fighting with Pisa. There was also the Inquisition, which had started as a righteous purge but had since degenerated into brutality.

There were skirmishes and battles and wars between kings. Men liked to torture men and such sadism was ill-fated and tempted God's wrath simply because it was evil. There had been no Antichrist in 1260 as so many again expected but Mary warned a young widow in Foligno, Italy, that mankind was falling away from virtue, and the implication was that such a falling away would bear its consequences.

When she spoke to the Flemish stigmatist Lutgardis, the Virgin was dressed in black. *"The cause of my affliction is those heretics the Albingenes, who crucify my Son afresh,"* Mary told the saint. *"In vengeance of this great crime God will send unheard-of evils on the earth. To avert this wrath, Lutgardis, fast for seven years, taking no nourishment but bread and water, and for all those years let your eyes never be dry of tears."*

It was said that at the end of the fast Christ Himself appeared and requested yet another seven years *"for the sins of the world."*

The violence, the feuds and battles, the loosening morals even among clergy, the trend toward fashion and narcissism and vanity, all these tempted divine chastisement. The "enlightened" age had begun. Europe was in the midst of a great burst of development, with leaps in commerce, art, and building. This period brought into use the mechanical clock and spinning wheel but it was also a time, wrote historian Barbara W.

Tuchman, of great corruption. Fashion became all-important and even servants began wearing long pointed shoes and hanging sleeves. Surcoats were embossed with gold, velvet was lined with ermine, and the vanity mirror had entered the scene.

The word "live" turned into the word "evil" when seen in the reverse of a mirror.

"There was so much pride amongst the common people in vying with one another in dress and ornaments that it was scarce possible to distinguish the poor from the rich, the servant from the master, or a priest from other men," wrote an English chronicler named Henry Knighton.

Yet in reality the gap between rich and poor was widening. So was the gap between those whose faith was in God and those whose faith was in their own brain. Colleges continued their spread across Western Europe and began to think themselves equal to the Church when it came to theology. It was said that because of its grand university Paris was home to the "goddess of wisdom." It was the successor of Rome and Athens. And the more intellectual Europeans became, the more disdainful they became of religion. In what was known around Christmastime as the Annual Feast of Fools, satirists installed their own "bishops" or "abbot of fools" in ceremonies that included ribald acts and obscene language. During a sacrilegious liturgy participants ate black pudding and tossed dice on an "altar" as those playing the role of priests wore inverted vestments and pagan animal masks. A "censer" made of old shoes vented an obnoxious smoke and there were hoots and satirical cries as a mock pope went through a mock benediction.

Neither the "intellects" of that time nor subsequent ones understood the implications. It was the onset of what some like to think of as an "enlightenment" but which was really spiritual regression. If mankind was gaining in certain material ways it was doing so too often at the expense of its spirit. In its debauchery, in its drunkenness, in its pleasure seeking, it resembled not some brave new world but rather ancient Rome.

At the same time that Mary was appearing as a humble servant to nuns in places like Proceno, Italy, or to young mystics such as Bridget of Sweden, the rest of the world was caught in what seemed like an inexorable move toward arrogance and secularism. The obsession with the physical at the exclusion of the spiritual would go beyond satire. Many lashed at the clergy and destroyed Church property. There was a burst of clerical assaults and according to Tuchman a mob in London beheaded the bishop and left him naked in the streets. They called it "anti-clericalism" but it could also be called demonism.

As for the economy, it was back to usury and excessive profit taking. Merchants got what they could and what the market could bear to satisfy their avarice, despite the fact it violated Church tenets that said no one should profit at the detriment of another. It was Catholic teaching that prices should be put at fair levels, which meant the expense of labor added to the expense of raw materials rather than profiteering and gouging. It was also in canon law that buying something wholesale and selling it at a higher price with no change or further labor, resulting in profits beyond what were needed to support the merchant, was evil. Yet that was precisely what was happening as we neared the conclusion of the High Middle Ages.

It was this quest for power and control, the superiority, and the greed that brought in Satan. "In the name of God and profit" was one ill-considered and self-contradictory motto of the period.

There was nothing wrong with making a living but there *was* most definitely something wrong with evaluating a human by the number and quality of material goods he had horded.

And it was totally at odds with the recent discovery near a road in Loreto, Italy, of a mysterious little house that materialized as from nowhere. It was made from limestone and cedarwood, and greatly resembled the structure where Gabriel had visited the poor woman named

Mary. It represented the place of Annunciation and it beckoned the Church. It beckoned Catholics back to a simpler mission. It beckoned humbleness.

At that time matters were all but simple. The Church was a massive and increasingly mundane complexity. While it was fine for Christianity to build grand monuments to glorify God, it was not fine to be swept into the vortex of temporality. Papal esteem plummeted because the popes had engaged in political struggles with emperors or had become involved in revolts like those that swept Sicily. This was the Church's Vietnam. It was a time of disarray.

There was a rift between cardinals, and in a clumsy attempt at solving the problems they elected a holy but uneducated mountain hermit as pontiff. Celestine V was so out of his element that he resigned the same year, replaced by a strong-willed man named Benedict Gaetani who became Boniface VIII and promptly imprisoned Celestine, who died soon after. Boniface repeated the recent mistakes and dove into secular contention. He boldly moved against King Philip IV when the French king wanted to tax clergy. The pope not only forbade clergy to pay taxes, but demanded that all kingdoms and all creatures be subject to the papacy.

His declaration, called *Unam Sanctam*, was perhaps the strongest assertion of papal power in history. It threw down the gauntlet at a time when even the clergy didn't know whether to put their allegiance behind the pope or kings, and Philip retaliated by kidnapping the pope in 1303. He accused the pontiff of everything from heresy to murder, and while Boniface was released after just three days, the old pontiff died a month later from what was probably sheer trauma. He was replaced by Benedict XI, who also died soon after assuming Peter's throne, possibly by being poisoned. *Then* came a Frenchman from Bordeaux known as Clement V. He was known as a pope who bowed to the pressures of King Philip and whose papacy never made it to Rome. He was crowned in France and detained there by the cunning and vicious king.

Soon Clement would transfer the papal court to the French city of Avignon, a move that was supposed to be temporary but, through the predominance of French cardinals, the feebleness of a number of popes, and the constant turmoil in Italy, became permanent.

The turmoil and uprooting, a remarkable mess, was the Church's reward for secularism. It was its reward for its own evil. And as usual, the mess was accompanied by prophecies of the Antichrist, who many now expected to come as the pope himself. Such sentiments were even aired by writers like Dante. Instead of the Antichrist being secular, he was increasingly anticipated as an ecclesiastical leader. This prediction seemed in line with 2 Thessalonians which said the son of perdition would take his place in the Temple. There was a growing obsession with "good" and "evil" papacies. It was the idea of an *orthopontifex* (a correct pope) versus the *pseudopontifex* (or false one). If the Antichrist was going to be the ultimate in deception, then the most likely pinnacle of deception was the papacy. Such fears had been growing since A.D. 1000 and now were in full swing. It had gotten to the point where St. Bonaventure complained of hearing to "satiety" prophecies dealing with the Church's troubles and the end of the world. There was falsity and overexcitement.

The Church was a mess. The hens were home to roost. Christ had warned that those who raised the sword would perish by the sword (Matthew 26:52) and now the Church and society were both in danger of perishing. Christianity had become too involved in secular power. While the Church and not kings took care of the helpless, the orphans, and cripples and used man's resources to build high and spiraling cathedrals glorifying God (as opposed to palaces glorifying only human power), the Avignon papacy draped itself in royal splendor. Popes lived in a residence that had banquet halls complete with gold plates. The walls of one study were covered by panoramas not of saints but of stag hunts. "These Avignon popes—rightly or wrongly—put great faith in the efficacy of external pomp," wrote the historian Bokenkotter. "In an age of increasing wealth, they felt it necessary to display a magnificence on a scale equal to their claims. A massive palace was built whose forbidding parapets still dazzle the eye of the tourist. A crowd of courtiers—knights, squires, and chamberlains, their ranks swelled by an army of hungry benefice seekers—filled the spacious rooms. The palace's luxurious furnishings were the talk of Europe."

Perhaps that was why Mary appeared twice in Avignon between 1313 and 1316, once to a monk named Peter Favier and then to Pope John XXII. Pope John's apparition was recorded early one morning while the pontiff was on his knees. During the visitation Mary tenderly reminded John that it was as a consequence of her solicitations to Jesus that the pope enjoyed his level of honor as well as deliverance from enemies. In return she wanted him to confirm the Carmelite Order. *"John, vicar of my Son, it is to me you are indebted for your exaltation to the dignity which you enjoy, in consequence of my solicitations in your behalf with my divine Son, and as I have delivered you from the snares of your enemies, so do I expect that you will give ample and favorable confirmation of the holy Carmelite Order,"* Mary said. *"And if among the religious or brethren of the confraternity, who depart from this life, there should be any who have been detained in purgatory for their sins, I their glorious mother will descend on the Saturday after their death and deliver those whom I find there and take them up to the holy mountain of eternal life."*

There were also apparitions in Mühllacken, Germany, not to mention the ongoing miracles at Montserrat and an apparition to a patriarch named Holy Peter in Zargrad, Russia. Such immaterial manifestations should have shaken the Church from its material course but unfortunately scant attention was paid to a remarkable mystical revival. Society remained on a precipitous course. The city of Avignon was rife with thieves, astrologers, and prostitutes. Even St. Bridget would decry the new papal city as "a field full of pride, avarice, self-indulgence, and corruption," and it served as a metaphor for what threatened the rest of society. It was a metaphor for the way that debauchery entered the Church. It was a metaphor for the clergy who began to dress in the sleeve and silk of laymen and certain priests who lived with mistresses or spent their time in search of one. There were cases of confessors selling absolution or officials garnering much-needed income by selling indulgences. In some instances, abbots and bishops gave money under the table to obtain their nominations. Priests with illegitimate children could buy dispensation.

If that wasn't enough, there were also unconfirmed but always tantalizing rumors that Christendom was threatened by that cabal of mysterious knights known as the Templars. While begun as ascetic and fearless crusaders, they were now a pan-European organization with a "temple" that controlled much of the money in Europe. While the original knights had been approved by the pope, their extensive financial stranglehold, their sponsoring of their own guilds and their patronage for craftsmen and stonemasons, along with their hidden ritualism (rumors that they practiced pagan worship) caused all sorts of hearsay.

And it gave King Philip of France the opening he needed. When Philip ran out of money, he turned on the Templars and under the pretext of the corruption seized their wealthy Paris temple as well as every one of the two thousand members that his men could find.

This took place on Friday, October 13, 1307. Among those arrested was Jacques de Molay, the grand master himself, with his retinue of sixty knights.

King Philip spared no calumny in justifying the arrests. He accused Templars of idol worship, selling their souls to Satan, and requiring initiates to spit three times, urinate, and trample on the Cross.

It's hard to say whether (or how much) the king was trumping up the charges since similar things had been slung against his papal adversary, but the accusations of dangerous ritualism were taken seriously. Philip pressured Pope Clement into authorizing trials of the Templars, who were then tortured into giving spectacular confessions.

According to Tuchman, many of the Templars "were racked, thumb-screwed, starved, hung with weights until joints were dislocated, had teeth and fingernails pulled one by one, bones broken by the wedge, feet held over flames."

The issue came to a head in March of 1314 when, despite ardent protests of innocence, Jacques de Molay and his chief lieutenant were condemned to be burned at the stake.

It's said that among Molay's last words was a curse upon the ruthless king and his descendants to the thirteenth generation.

As he burned, Molay also cursed the king and pope to meet him before the throne of judgment.

Coincidentally or not, Pope Clement died a month later and less than a year after, so did King Philip.

# 21

## Horrible Wonders

Away from all the pomp, in the hilly terrain southwest of Madrid, near the river called Guadalupe, a humble cowherd named Gil Cordero of Cáceres was searching for a lost cow when something very strange happened. It was 1326. He'd been searching three days. Thirsty and fatigued, Cordero was heading for the sound of a mountain stream when he spotted the cow motionless on a mound of stones.

Figuring the animal was dead, Cordero pulled out his knife and prepared to take the animal's hide, which he then could sell. As was the custom, he pressed in the knife and made an incision in the form of a cross on the cow's breast.

The cow suddenly moved. Not just moved but sprang up on its hooves as if restored to life.

Cordero must have backed away. He was astonished and terrified. The "dead" animal was abruptly standing!

At the same time Cordero spotted someone coming from the woods. It was no normal woman. There *were* no normal women out here. It was a female "of marvelous beauty" who spoke in a kind supernal voice. *"Have no fear, for I am the Mother of God, by whom the human race achieved redemption,"* she told the speechless herdsman. *"Go to your home and tell the clergy and other people to come to this place where I appear to you and dig here, where they will find a statue."* As was her custom she also asked that a chapel be built.

Cordero had to have stood there staring. Whether the Virgin left in a flash of light or faded into the backdrop is not in the records. Once he got hold of himself, Cordero turned his attention back to the cow and, as instructed, headed into Cáceres. There he informed the clergy and anyone else within earshot that the Virgin had appeared out near the Guadalupe and she wanted them to dig for a lost relic and build a chapel.

Looked upon as an uneducated and ignorant peasant, Cordero's account was immediately mocked. The ridicule left him in a state between depression and desperation. "Friends, do not dismiss these things!" protested the lonely cowherd. "If you will not believe me, then believe the mark the cow bears on her breast!" Cordero insisted that the Virgin had promised to work many miracles and that people would come from many regions because of her wonders.

Seeing Cordero's despair and knowing that many images had been hidden during the Arab occupation, which was about to end with a final expulsion, officials in Cáceres relented and paraded with the entire village to the precise spot where the animal had been found. Knights, noblemen, and priests pushed small boulders and removed stones. They dug into the earth until the ground collapsed into a small cave.

Inside was just what Cordero promised: a statue along with an ancient bell. There was a document explaining its origin as well as the relics of St. Fulgentius and St. Florentina.

The statue is what drew the attention. As the document explained, it was the long-lost image of Mary that Pope Gregory the Great had given the bishop of Seville. It was the one that may have been paraded around Rome in 390. Moreover, the unstained, oriental wood seemed in perfect condition despite six centuries in the earth. Buried when the Muslims had first attacked, it was now coming out of seclusion at a time when the last Muslim holdouts were being expelled!

A hut was hastily built and a humble altar of stone was mounded. Soon that was replaced by a chapel. The bell was melted and mixed with other metal to form two bells which called the faithful to prayer and were rung during severe storms to preserve the crops. A subsequent and enlarged shrine was attended by dignitaries from many parts and visited a century later by a devout explorer named Christopher Columbus, who would carry a replica of the statue with him on his voyages and who would name an island in the West Indies "Guadeloupe," a name that would also spread to Mexico.

But we're getting ahead of the story. We're still in the 1300s, and the Guadalupe account, incredible as it was, was only one of a multitude. There were other apparitions. Mary not only brought relief to blind beggars and crippled shepherds but gave guidance to an entire civilization that was about to face a stunning series of chastisements.

The miracle of Guadalupe was at the crossroads of history and catastrophe.

Right now there were just warnings, but they were growing increasingly severe. From 1310 to 1314, wheat yields had dropped 50 percent in France, creating famine. Huge numbers of barefooted people, their bones poking out, paraded to shrines hoping for any kind of relief or encouragement. In Rhineland troops had to be posted at execution sites because "ravenous people were rushing the gallows, and cutting down and eating the corpses." Horsemeat, usually scorned by all, was now too expensive for all but the aristocracy.

Something was coming. Something *big* was coming. It was unwinding slowly, it had been threatening for a while now, and it was starting piecemeal, but as in ancient Rome the famines were joined by war and contagious disease. There were plagues in the Gobi Desert and battles all over, wars between the Swiss and Austrians as well as between the English and French. There were uprisings in Japan and China.

The Chinese were especially mysterious, steeped in a zodiac based on dragons. That kind of public idolatry mirrored the days of Pompeii and, like ancient Rome, invited disaster. News filtered from Asia to the West of droughts and earthquakes. "Then had come floods in which 400,000 were said to have died, as a result of which, presumably, the mountain Tsincheou 'fell in,' causing great chasms in the earth," wrote historian Philip Ziegler. In true apocalyptical fashion the earthquake was followed by more drought followed by swarms of locusts and famine.

As for tremors, wrote Ziegler, "An earthquake in the mountains of Ki-Ming-Chan formed a lake more than 100,000 leagues in circumference. In Tche the dead were believed to number more than five *million* [my emphasis]. Earthquakes and floods continued from 1337 to 1345; locusts had never been so destructive; there was 'subterranean thunder' in Canton."

Five million dead! There were also reports of terrible sickness that had been carried by migratory rats and the roaming Mongol horsemen from Burma, Yunnan, and the Gobi Desert.

An epidemic of some kind broke out in the province of Hopei, killing 90 percent of the population!

The same was true in India, the land where hymns were sung to snakes. This pagan turf was likewise the turf of horrible wonders. A Flemish cleric who based his report on a letter from a friend in the papal curia of Avignon recounted (with what had to be some metaphor) that

in the East, hard by Greater India, in a certain province, horrors and unheard of tempests overwhelmed the whole province for the space of three days. On the first day there was a rain of frogs, serpents, lizards, scorpions, and many venomous beasts of that sort (see Exodus 8:2). On the second, thunder was heard, and lightning and sheets of fire fell upon the earth, mingled with hailstones of marvelous size; which slew almost all, from the greatest to the least. On the third day there fell fire from heaven and stinking smoke, which slew all that were left of men and beasts, and burned up all the cities and towns in those parts.

There was a sense of miasma and malady, of a corrupted atmosphere. Some insisted that an evil and noxious smoke, a foul blast of malignancy, had descended. There were many omens: falling stars and strange clouds. The stars were interesting because in A.D. 79 during the eruption of Mount Vesuvius there had also been reports of the stars rearranging themselves in the sky. Other events were closer to the earth. A column of fire was spotted above the papal palace in Avignon and a ball of flame was seen above Paris. In Venice the rumble of a violent tremor set the bells of St. Mark's Basilica ringing.

These signs increased in direct proportion to the evil, which was expressing itself not only through war but also through crime. Europe was now a place where rape was so common that lower-class women were abducted from their very homes. Drunkenness and lechery were also commonplace. Society was out of whack. There was no spiritual wellspring. The Church was now more of a bureaucracy. As in earlier times, men from noble households were appointed bishops and there were priests who couldn't read. Pardons, indulgences, and absolution were handed out like commodities. Men like Henry of Hereford, a chronicler of this time period, shouted for their fellow men to take heed of the "dangerous situation"—at the evil in high places, which was always part of chastisement (Proverbs 28:28)—and so too were the mystics shouting. There was an epidemic of doomsaying. There was the predictable talk of the Antichrist, soon in an extremely big way.

Many were false prophets but there were also authentic seers like St. Bridget. As a result of a vision, she wrote an outspoken letter to Pope Clement VI urging him to abandon Avignon, return to Rome, and bring about peace between Philip IV of France and Edward III of England. When that didn't happen, the great mystic kept harping away. She sensed the peril. She had a vision of the Passion. She saw Christ wounded by the sins of man, those who scorned Him. In her vision the Savior told Bridget that while mankind had followed His lessons for a long time, *"Now impiety and pride grow strong."*

All of heaven was burdened. The Virgin was seen by Blessed Angelo of Foligno praying for the human race.

These were serious times that seemed to have come precipitously close to disaster. There was a veering in favor of Lucifer, and with that came a prevalence of spirits who were often described as a combination of man and animal, precisely as portrayed in the more hideous images of idolatry. Now they again seemed *rampant*. Demons were on the loose, released from the pit. It was the thousand years, or maybe a simple result of poor morals. Devils were allowed to test men and even harass holy souls like Elizabeth of Schönau. It was a time of every diabolical illusion, not just societal temptation but also spiritual temptation in the way of false visions. One always had to be on guard against Satan coming as a seductive, beautiful person or even an angel of light (2 Corinthians 11:14). A stigmatist named Christina Bruso of Stommeln, Germany, had legitimate visions of Jesus but also experienced deceptions by a demon who disguised himself as St. Bartholomew and tempted her with suicide.

Mysticism was heavy traffic. Only those who prayed and fasted, only those of true humbleness—those who had died to spiritual pride—could be confident of discernment. When tempted by impure thoughts, Bridget was taught by Mary to say, *"Jesus, Son of God, Who knowest all things, help me to take no pleasure in vain and sinful thoughts."* When tempted to talk too much or say the wrong thing she was to say, *"Jesus, Son of God, Who was silent before the unjust judge, restrain my tongue till I have considered what and how to speak."* And when inclined to work, rest, or take refreshment, she was to seek guidance by saying, *"Jesus, Son of God, Who was bound with cords, guide my hands and all my limbs, so that my works may be all done according to Thy good pleasure."*

Security came only by abandonment to Christ and detachment from self but society was heading in the opposite direction. There were yet more fashions and vanity mirrors. Men wore long pointed shoes called *poulains* which were supposed to represent their sexual prowess. Fashion was a statement of the carnal self. It glorified the body and tempted lust and as such was an *enchantment.* Dressing nicely was one thing; idolizing the body was another. Mary worried enough over body idolatry to have warned about both fashion and the wrong kind of dancing to Bridget. Fashion took the eyes off what was spiritual and focused on what was carnal, which could lead not only to adultery and fornication but also to deviant practices like sodomy, long linked to witchcraft as a deliberate and willful challenge to the natural order. These practices were so hateful to the Creator that many believed they provoked disasters.

The Middle Ages did not seem to be overrun by abortion, for it was forbidden in the Latin text of the Hippocratic Oath, but there was plenty of other sin and sin attracted demons and demons brought accidents and illness. As long as there was sin in the world, Satan had a hold. God allowed that. It was part of free will. The greatest chastisement was the evil that man invited through his own sin. When man was in sin, there was tribulation. There was smoke. There was the scent of disease. It took faith and humbleness to purge it. Faith and humility. Those were the cleansers. Those were the secret antidotes. Mary couldn't repeat them enough, nor could she overstate the power of Mass, which was another secret: *Satan could not bear up to it.* No matter how powerful he seemed, he was the incredibly shrinking devil when a person went to Confession and Mass. But people were forgetting devotion in the High Middle Ages, they were forgetting the truths of the Savior, and so something was coming, something so grave as to defy prophecy, something like Pompeii or Jerusalem.

# 22

---

## The Chastisement

That something was called the Black Death.

Born in the Asian hinterlands and spread by Mongol horsemen, the disease, similar to what had stricken Italy in the time of Gregory the Great, made its way to China where it caused horrible desolation. Marked by fever and huge swellings the size of eggs, the disease was actually a combination of several bacterial agents that thrive in rats and their fleas. Most prominent was a bacterium called *Pasteurella pestis,* the cause of bubonic fever. It was often accompanied by yet more lethal bacteria that caused pneumonic and septicaemic illness, diseases that attack the lungs and cause dark skin blotches.

Perhaps that or the fact black rats were carriers was why they called it the "Black Death," but more likely it was simply its lethality. The utter darkness of its effect, coupled with the fact that once introduced into an area it could spread by human contact and kill within days, made it a "black death" indeed. It preyed especially on populations like China's (where ironically the zodiac included a "Year of the Rat" and where the droughts, locusts, and floods had weakened the population in the 1330s), and although we don't know exactly how many died from the plague, the Chinese population would be reduced from 123 million in 1200 to a mere 65 million by the end of the fourteenth century.

In 1339 the first record of the plague's westward movement showed in mortalities near Lake Issyk in the Tien region. From central Asia it moved on overland routes or through merchant shipping to the Middle East and then Europe. In 1345 the plague was at Sarai, a major trading center on the lower Volga in what is today Russia, and within a year it was in the Caucasus and Azerbaijan. Dead bodies littered territories from Armenia to India, the infirm no doubt fleeing to Vedic gods as this mysterious and awful ailment, which could be spread by merely breathing near or touching someone or by contact with contaminated clothing, depopulated much of the subcontinent and found its way around Yemen to the Red Sea.

Kurds fled in vain to the mountains. Hardly anyone survived in places like Caesarea, the current-day Iran-Iraq region. Syria and Egypt were hit, and so was Mecca, despite Mohammed's belief that disease would never reach the Holy City. Within two years the entire Islamic world would lose from a third to 50 percent of its population. As the disease made its way over commercial routes, the Christian parts of the eastern Mediterranean were likewise devastated. After ravaging Constantinople, the plague was carried on Italian ships to Cyprus in 1347, the same year that Cyprus suffered an earthquake and several tidal waves. The water swept over large parts of the island, destroying olive groves and fishing fleets. Islanders murdered many of their Arab slaves for fear they would take advantage of the chaos, and then fled inland but couldn't avoid what one chronicler called "a pestiferous wind" that spread "so poisonous an odor that many, being overpowered by it, fell down suddenly and expired in dreadful agony."

Earthquakes also did severe damage in Rome, Naples, Pisa, and Venice just before the plague arrived. Its entrance into Western Europe came at least in part through the Sicilian port of Messina, where residents insisted demonic entities transfigured into dogs wreaked the harm on humans.

So aghast was the populace that few ventured from their homes until by common consent and at the wish of the archbishop they gathered their courage and marched around the city reciting litanies.

According to a scribe named Michael of Piazza, "While the whole population was thus processing around the streets, a black dog ... appeared
among them, gnashing with his teeth and rushing upon them and breaking all the silver vessels and lamps and candlesticks...."

It was a terrifying and prodigious vision. Artists portrayed the plague as
spread by demons or avenging angels who shot arrows tipped with sulfur
or poured forth a deadly censer, as in Revelation 8:5. Some like Pope
Clement VI declared the plague a "pestilence with which God is afflicting
Christian people." It seemed indeed like the stench of hell, a plague so dis-
gusting, so unbearable in its sweat, excrement, and spittle, in its black or
red urine, in the fetid respiration, that it inspired less pity than detestation.

Many theorized that poisonous fumes were rising from cracks in the
earth, claiming it was sulfur from the netherworld. Noxious clouds
indeed! In desperation the residents of Messina fled by foot and horse six
miles outside of town to get an image of the Madonna said to have special
power. As the horse carrying the image approached Messina, the animal
suddenly stood motionless, fixed like a rock.

That was interpreted as a sign that what was occurring was God's
requital of an unrighteous, bloodstained people and that Mary was not to
intervene.

In the words of Michael of Piazza, the Blessed Mother judged the city
to be "so hateful and so profoundly stained with blood and sin that she
turned her back on it, being not only unwilling to enter therein, but even
abhorring the very sight thereof."

In truth, Mary never turned her back, but the protection of heaven did
seem absent. There was a lapse in the Virgin's apparitions, a relative silence
during the 1340s, except at a Ukrainian monastery called Pochaiv, as the
scourge continued to cause wreckage. It was the same casualty count—
one-third—as prophesied in Revelation 9:15. Aimless ships were spotted
with dead crews and by December of 1347 the disease had spread to

much of southern Europe, entering through various ports and fishing villages. From there it coursed into the central and northern parts of Europe through harbors like Genoa, where three galleys which had put to port after being driven by fierce winds from the East were found to be laden not just with the sought-after spices but also with *Pasteurella pestis*.

Terrified residents had attacked the ships with flaming arrows "and diverse engines of war" in hopes of keeping it out, but it was already too late. The plague had found its way ashore. It also entered Venice and Pisa. In hard-hit Florence an estimated one hundred thousand died. The stately homes and the grand palaces were all evacuated. Brothers abandoned brothers; uncles their nephews; parents their children. As the classicist Giovanni Boccaccio phrased it,

> There came the death-dealing pestilence, which, through the operation of the heavenly bodies or of our own iniquitous dealings, being sent down upon mankind for our correction by the just wrath of God, had some years before appeared in the parts of the East, and after having bereft these latter of an innumerable number of inhabitants, extending without cease from one place to another, had now unhappily spread towards the West.

It was devastating. It was eerie. As the plague arrived church bells were silenced and black flags flapped in the quiet breeze. While conservative estimates say 33 percent of Italy succumbed, many scholars would put the mortality for that particular nation at 40 or even 50 percent.

From Italy the plague made its way to the western Mediterranean with the same deadly results. In lust-ridden Avignon eleven thousand were buried in a six-week stretch. Soon a third of the cardinals died along with *half* of the lay population. Indeed, along with Florence, Avignon was most severely affected. Mortality among priests was particularly high and hundreds who worked at the luxurious papal palace were counted among the deceased. In a short time Pope Clement VI had to flee the city. No one could be sure exactly how the Black Death was spreading, but at least one of its three forms was fantastically contagious. Astrologers tried to find an explanation in the stars, but there was precious little to go on. The disease spread northward along the river valleys and arrived in Paris by 1348, with more than five hundred corpses carted each day out of the main hospital. In that city the sick were tended by courageous nuns who, in all humility and selflessness, gave no thought to their own imminent expiration. In that horrid year, 28 percent of Europe's cardinals and 207 bishops succumbed.

In Spain the plague had reached Saragossa and other areas in this nation. At that time a certain image of the Madonna and Child, said to have been used by Gregory the Great during the scourge in Rome, resurfaced from the cavern at Guadalupe to help men against this new and more awesome plague.

Throughout the continent, towns were special targets. The sick were ruthlessly deserted and turned quickly into cadavers that were simply left in the front of homes or piled like cordwood. Eventually the bodies were disposed in huge communal pits, while neglected crops withered and livestock roamed untended. Jeremiah indeed! As if repulsed, wolves shied from scavenging the dead and at one hospital in Montpellier nearly every doctor died. In Marseilles each of the 150 Franciscans was counted a fatality. In some locales the plague was believed to descend like a ball of fire. "One such ball was fortunately spotted while hovering above Vienna and exorcised by a passing bishop," wrote the historian Ziegler. "It fell harmlessly to the ground and a stone effigy of the Madonna was raised to commemorate this unique victory...."

But such triumphs were temporary. Many more were the defeats. Vienna suffered as badly as Avignon and the whole of Europe was the picture of emptiness: cattle without herdsmen, widows without children. In England the plague made its way along the coast to Bristol, killing with the same vengeance as on the mainland. The poor clergy who bravely ministered to the dying were especially hit. County Dorset was struck in 1348 and 44 to 50 percent died at manors in Suffolk and Worcestershire. Bath and Wells seemed to suffer their most devastating period between November 1348 and May 13, 1349. So bad was the shortage of priests that Bishop Ralph of Shrewsbury issued a letter declaring that a dying person could make his or her last Confession to another layman if clergy was not available. The same was true of the Eucharist, which could now be administered by a deacon if the vicinity was priestless.

The fact that Confession was open to laymen signaled an unprecedented emergency. Clement decided it was necessary to grant absolution to all who had succumbed because so many had no minister. Before the plague there had been 17,500 monks, nuns, and friars in English monasteries, but within two years there were about *half* that number. Many believed it was the end of humankind. In Kilkenny, Ireland, a friar named John Clyn sensed "the whole world, as it were, placed within the grasp of the Evil One."

That precarious position had been earned by lust and greed, by irreverence among knights, by lack of respect for life and God, by the astrology and crystal-gazing which had become so startlingly popular in Europe. The people had tapped into dark powers and, like Pompeii, were now reaping the result. "God for the sins of men has struck the world with this great punishment of sudden death," bemoaned King Magnus II of Sweden. "By it, most of the people in the land to the west of our country are dead. It is now ravaging Norway and Holland and is approaching our kingdom of Sweden."

While Germany was not hit as hard as southern Europe, the devastation affected places as far off as Greenland. There was no escape, no respite. Venturing to Rome in 1349 as the plague still raged, St. Bridget advised everyone to "abolish earthly vanity in the way of extravagant clothes, give free alms to the needy, and order all parish priests to celebrate Mass once a month in honor of the Holy Trinity."

If few in Rome were willing to heed such words no one could deny Bridget's impressive presence. Nor could they deny her miracles. One woman watching her son die said, "If only the Lady Bridget were here!" At that moment the saint walked in and laid her hands on the man's forehead. A few hours later the man was healed.

In other cases relief was sought at shrines like Willesden. There a statue of the Blessed Mother was carried in procession and healings were reported. The king of Sweden called for fasting on bread and 1350 was declared a holy year. Obviously it was ridiculous to blame the Church for all this woe, especially since the plague began in pagan land, but guilt was still felt by a hierarchy that had counted piles of money at the papal palace in Avignon and had turned the Church into a granite bureaucracy.

There was evil in that. There was evil in the legalism and pretension. There was evil that filtered down to the local level. The pope, traumatized by the disaster, criticized many of his clergy as "the proudest of the world, arrogant and given to pomp ... grasping ... covetous," wasting their money, he charged, "on pimps and swindlers."

The pope's tirade was no doubt magnified by stress and there was ample reason.

His agents calculated that the plague—this great chastisement allowed by God—had killed 23,840,000 in Christian Europe.

# 23

## *A f t e r s h o c k*

Between a quarter and a third of Europe had perished. At least twenty million died on other continents. It was right out of biblical prophecy. By sheer number it was greater than any disaster in documented history. The actual body count was almost surely higher than in the days of Noah, and while not to equate the two events, the medieval disaster fulfilled Revelation 6:1-8—"famine and plague"—just as Pompeii and Jerusalem had fulfilled predictions in Matthew 24. Whatever the numbers, it had all the earmarks of a judgment: not the Final Judgment, not the grand and fiery denouement many had expected, not the long-awaited finale, but a denouement nonetheless. It was a lesser judgment or "judgment in miniature."

An era was ending in the same way that an era had ended with the afflictions that followed Nero. And as had happened then, the afflictions persisted and lingered. The Black Death was not a single event. Its eruptions flared into the next century and were accompanied by other chastisements. The entire human structure was whipsawed. Plague was the most flagrant aspect but only one of many evils. Other punishment occurred at spiritual levels. It was the *tempus muliebre*. The burst of evil was sociological as well as medical. In the wake of bubonic death men turned cold and selfish. They were grasping and greedy. They were antagonistic and hard. There was a dramatic increase in suits, disputes, and brawls. Charity had cooled and as one chronicler said, "greater evils than before pullulated everywhere in the world." The physical plague was but an outward sign of a spiritual disorder. It was all part of the same judgment, the fruit of secularism. There was superficiality, extravagance, and a wild wave of debauchery. The plague had brought on a fatalistic demeanor: eat, drink, and be merry, for tomorrow you will die. That meant gluttony and drunkenness and morbid sexuality.

It also meant occultism. As the chastisement bore on, sorcerers and mind readers—drug vendors and witch doctors—rose like fungus. Men and women made pacts with the devil. In 1366 there were so many sorcerers that the Council of Chartres ordered they be denounced every Sunday from the pulpit. Into Eastern Europe came bands of Indian gypsies whose occultism was as old as Babylon.

On the civil front, crime increased with widespread corruption in government. There was no moral leadership. Institutions were devoid of manpower and shells of their former selves. There was no one to work. Those who had survived were emotionally disturbed. Shell-shocked, every man was for himself. Police and courts were crippled and to keep government operating inexperienced and dishonest men had to be appointed.

There was incompetence and gross negligence, and offices and influential positions were again subject to purchase in the Church. The sale of indulgences put the Church on the road to Luther and was already incurring the wrath of an Oxford "reformer" named John Wycliffe, who would take correction to the extreme and begin denouncing the sacraments and priesthood.

Mary as the *Madonna della Misericordia* was still there. She was still watching. But it was as if she had been told to step from view and let the purification run its course.

In devastated Avignon the papacy continued the scandal of detachment from Rome in what many referred to as the "Babylonian captivity." It was another aspect of chastisement. The pope was still in the south of France instead of on the "rock" or tomb of Peter. Complaints against the Church were matched in civil life by the disaffection of working peasants who would soon revolt and lead awful massacres. There were farm strikes and universal upheaval.

And there was a resurgence of the diabolical disease. In England new waves of plague struck in 1360 and 1369, then in 1375, killing between 13 and 25 percent in restricken areas.

The same was true of France and Italy. Wave after wave, epidemiological brushfires, minor but killing punishments.

There was also the fire of prophecy and it ran riot. There were feverish expectations of Church schism and a false pope or *antichristus misticus* to be followed by more disaster and the final beast or *Antichristus magnus.*

The schism turned out to be a true prophecy, but many had gone off and predicted that the Antichrist was currrently ten years old and living a hidden life "beyond the Tartars."

That was an illusion as in Nero's time but the *spirit* of antichrist (1 John 4:3), the spirit of evil, was indeed in the world, and with it all the devil's deceptions. The area of Lake Issyk—where the plague had originally been tracked—was to become a place of weird aerial or "UFO" sightings.

There was an unleashing of evil. There was demonic delusion. There was sensuality in the form of indecent new fashions. Women appeared in public wearing artificial hair and low-necked blouses with breasts laced so taut it was said a candle could be placed on them. Jewels abounded and the nouveaux riche had an infatuation for garish colors.

Blasphemy and sacrilege were commonplace and there was the passing of courtesy.

Gentility was gone. Consideration was gone. There was a coolness of mind and heart. There was a precipitous decline in manners. Speech became lewd and slang-ridden.

There were also waves of anti-Semitism. Jews were accused of charging exorbitant interest, blaspheming Christian rituals, and desecrating the Eucharist. While there was truth to some of those charges, the Jews were also blamed for spreading the plague by poisoning wells. It was an absurd claim but it was especially prevalent in German and French regions. The result was slaughters in Freiburg, Augsburg, Nürnberg, and Munich. Sixty Jewish communities were exterminated in 350 separate massacres. About two thousand were killed in Strasbourg alone. Pope Clement officially threatened anyone who persecuted the Jews with excommunication, and he gave Jews refuge in Avignon, but the damage was done and the seeds were sown for future disaster.

And so there was prophecy. The Antichrist was expected between 1360 and 1370. He was so well described by visionaries that some said even a child could recognize him.

We had seen the same thing in previous centuries, but now the fervor was overwhelming. These were not prophecies from the Blessed Mother but rather from independent locutions or decipherings of Scripture. As with ancient Montanists there were millenarian expectations. Many believed there would be a period of peace before the Antichrist arrived, a break from all the horrors. Others set forth a scenario that saw catastrophes like the Black Death culminating in the reign of Antichrist and then the victory of Jesus, which would be followed by a millennium or one thousand-year period of earthly perfection. During this period swords would be beaten into ploughshares and unprecedented justice, peace, and spirituality would reign until a final eruption of evil and the end of the world in the year 2370.

In the meantime, there would be more mayhem and death. The devil would become incarnate. Such were the predictions that circulated on single sheets of paper from Ireland to lower Austria.

Tribulation. Chastisement. Among the doomsayers were bands of fanatical Christians known as "flagellants" who roamed from town to town in two-column formations preaching penance and the millennium. They atoned for the world's sins by whipping themselves.

Bells rang as flagellants entered town to "save" the Christians. While the message of prayer and penance was good and the flagellants caused many to convert, their extremes and vehemence led Pope Clement VI, who initially had been favorable, to issue a condemnation.

There were cases where flagellants arrogated themselves above the local clergy and took over their altars and pulpits. Iron-tipped whips were used for the mortifications and some even drove nails into their flesh. Of most concern was the fact that a number of flagellants, who were convinced that Jews kidnapped Christian children and were also responsible for the plague, participated in the massacres.

# 24

## Where Devils Trembled

That was the horror. That was the bewilderment. It seemed like the light of heaven had gone out, that confusion reigned, but now Mary was posed for re-entry to prevent yet greater disaster. She had been told to step out of view but she was about to return and save her children. She came when her people asked her to come, and the lonely nuns and monks, the lonely and faithful devout, the lonely priests who had not succumbed to scandal were doing just that. They prayed new prayers with fervor. In the midst of depravity, they were islands of holiness. A precursor of the Angelus had been officially approved by the pope on October 13, 1318, and in the 1360s a Carthusian named Henry of Kalkar grouped the 150 *Angelic Salutations* into decades and placed an *Our Father* before each decade, thus edging yet closer to the final version of the Rosary.

If, in accordance with divine Will, her protection had its limits, Mary's grace had not lessened. In fact her presence was growing. The endgame was in play. She knew the final Antichrist was not yet alive, but she also knew what John had said concerning the Antichrist spirit (1 John 2:18). She wanted it recognized as the filth it was. Against it, in stark contrast, was her Immaculate Conception, which had been unofficially celebrated since the seventh century and fully explained by a Franciscan theologian named Duns Scotus just before the cataclysm in the last part of the 1200s.

Mary was back, and you could see that in the rise of the miraculous accounts. In Italy she appeared to three people in different places on the same night asking for a church in Pozzuoli, and she was to come to the aid of St. Vincent Ferrer when Satan whispered to him and tried to entice him out of monastic resolve. At Chartres, France, Mary intervened on Monday, April 13, 1360, when King Edward III of England tried to attack the devout city and take over the region. Encamped just outside town, the king's army was besieging Chartres when suddenly it was hit by a hailstorm so violent it was described as a cyclone. The storm felled both men and horses. Realizing it as a portent, Edward dropped to his knees and with arms stretched in the direction of the august church promised Mary he'd stop the assault and make peace if she would spare them. Even secular accounts report that the storm immediately stopped. Within a month there was a treaty in Brétigny that ended the first stage of a war that had been in progress for two decades. In the face of Mary, Edward had relinquished.

Ten years later, on March 25, 1370, there was another storm and another miracle. A ship traveling just off Sardinia from Spain to Italy was buffeted by what was described as a hurricane. With the ship in immediate danger of sinking, sailors set about throwing cargo overboard. The last piece was a chest. As soon as it was tossed into the sea, the waves calmed and the storm broke.

Curious as to what might be in the chest, a small boatload of sailors set about chasing it. The chest drifted up the Gulf of Cagliari, but finally they caught up with it as it washed ashore near a church run by Mercedarian priests at the foot of a hill called Bonaria.

The sailors went to take the chest but oddly it was too heavy to budge. A crowd of onlookers watched as the sailors struggled. That was when a boy ran to fetch the priests, who had no problem carrying the chest to their church (where Mary obviously wanted its contents enshrined). Upon opening it, their eyes were riveted to a gorgeous five-foot statue of Mary in blue mantle, crimson skirt, and a long tunic.

More prodigies were also reported back near Fatima in that anointed area where the bread and miraculous spring were revealed to the hungry girl from Reguengo do Fetal and where around 1380 another spring in the neighborhood of Aljubarrota was associated with a poor woman named Catarina Anes. According to Charles Broschart, one day Catarina went to the forest on a mountain called Vale de Deus to search for firewood. As she gathered bits of wood, a lady appeared and said, *"Catarina, do you want me to help you with your work?"*

Catarina declined the offer because she didn't know the woman, but when she was ready to leave the lady made another offer to lead Catarina through the forest.

Again Catarina declined. She knew the way. But the woman kept appearing, and one day she came with St. Marta, whose hermitage had been nearby and to whom Catarina had a devotion. *"Catarina, follow me!"* said the woman. Again Catarina paid no heed. *"Come here, Catarina, for I wish to give you a key that you lost."*

That got Catarina's attention. She indeed had lost a key. "How could you possibly have it to give to me?" she asked.

The woman then handed over the key and now when she asked Catarina to follow her, Catarina went with her to the top of the mountain. The woman asked her to dig a hole and almost immediately Catarina struck a spring of crystal-clear water. *"Now go and tell the people of your village that here they will find a remedy for all their infirmities,"* said the woman, obviously Mary.

Catarina did as directed and although the bishop, D. Pedro de Castillo, was inclined to reject the story, he changed his mind when a blind man washed his eyes in the spring and regained his vision.

In the same vicinity around the same time a third marvel was recorded as a knight named Nuno was headed for the hamlet of Aljubarrota. He spotted a small church dedicated to the Blessed Mother in what is today the county of Ourem. Dismounting, Nuno entered the church and knelt before the altar, invoking Mary one last time before heading into a great struggle between Portugal and the Castillian army, which outnumbered his force. His prayers said, the knight then marched to battle. He was passing through the village of Fatima when he and his men felt a heavenly presence and their horses lowered themselves as if to kneel on the ground. There was indeed a heavenly presence. The knights swore they saw angels, including the Archangel Michael, in the sky, just as Michael had been seen in Rome at the end of *its* great plague. Invoking him, the knights then finished their mission and went to victory on August 15, feast of Mary's Assumption.

These were crucial signs. These were important definitions of who Mary was and how she operated. Her connection with Michael accented her role as demon-chaser. Those who feared she was herself a "demon" were like those who thought Christ was casting out devils in the name of Beelzebub (Matthew 12:24). Her image caused devils to tremble, to flee and tremble, to scream in agony. There would soon be a case near Riardo, Italy, where a lovely painting known as the Madonna of the Star was found in a forgotten subterranean chapel. The image, along with a painting of Michael, was used to cure a woman from Versano who suffered periodic bouts of possession. As the woman neared a wayside shrine, she wailed with strange terror, "No, no, no! I do not want to go to the Madonna of the Star!" But in that moment the demon left and the woman was cured.

The Virgin also came to the aid of Catherine of Siena. Once when Satan appeared as a handsome young man offering Catherine a silk gown glittering with jewels, Catherine had thrown herself before the crucifix seeking help. That was when Mary appeared and instead gave Catherine a heavenly vestment.

It was Catherine who, like Bridget before her, tried to get the pope back to Rome. Imploring Gregory XI in person and prodding him through prayer, she finally helped convince him to return to Rome, but a year later Gregory died and that was when real trouble started. Fear that the predominantly French College of Cardinals would now move the papacy back to Avignon caused a frenzy among the Romans. A mob assaulted several cardinals, warning them to elect an Italian, and in the ugly mood the protesters even invaded the Vatican and seized the papal wine cellars. An Italian named Archbishop Bartholomew Prignano was indeed elected as Urban VI, but he seemed to undergo a radical personality change after his election. His harsh manner led thirteen of the cardinals to declare his election invalid and denounce him as a tyrant, apostate, and antichrist.

On September 20 the breakaway cardinals elected their own pope, Robert of Geneva, who took the name Clement VII and set up shop back at the fortified palace in Avignon.

Thus there were two popes: one in Rome and one in France. Thus began—as prophesied—the Great Schism.

The Church was split apart. The "minor judgment" was now to include a Church in pandemonium.

Some nations supported Urban and others Clement. The two were soon going to war against each other. Urban proclaimed a crusade against Queen Joan of Naples, who supported Clement, and the English invaded France to break its allegiance to the papacy at Avignon.

Suspecting certain of his own cardinals of plotting against him, Urban reportedly put them to torture. Five of them soon died, perhaps thrown from the papal warship.

It was a tragic time for Christianity. The rupture brought papal prestige to a new low. Once more Church problems were paralleled by the continuing surge of mysticism. Seers arose on all sides and their visions gained an influence not known before. One such man thought he was Elias and foretold an earthquake that would precede the end of the world, while others were equally dubious and sucked in the clergy. "In some of the gravest sermons reliance was put upon these baseless predictions," wrote Professor L. Salembier of the Catholic University of Lille, "and certain compilations of the day present a singular mixture of prophetic insanities, astrological forecasts, and doctrinal statements."

But once more the rise of seers was a sign of the times and so was renewed discussion of the devil. Special treatises including at least one by a bishop were written on the Antichrist. Parts of Italy seemed all but overtaken by mournful processions of the devout. Parades of up to thirty thousand carried crucifixes that flowed with sweat and blood—miraculous exudations.

No one would ever really know when the end was coming and, as Augustine had said long ago, it was difficult to tell which signs would precede the Final Judgment because the signs in the Gospels referred not only to Christ's Coming and the end of history, but also to events such as Pompeii, Rome, and the destruction of Jerusalem *which already had happened.*

Now they also pertained to the plague and Great Schism.

Bridget had a vision in which Jesus explained that world history had three parts: the period between Adam until Christ's Incarnation; the roughly thousand years after His Coming; and now a third period that would precede the Last Judgment, a time no one but God knew, a time when iniquity would abound and impiety grow to a degree even greater than that which had been seen thus far.

# 25

## Secret Martyrs

I f Bridget was correct it was confirmation that the endgame had now been engaged. There was the beginning of the long and great and final battle. Would it last one thousand or five thousand years? There were no time frames. Those would come later. On these matters Mary seemed silent. She spoke of such things in secret. She preferred signs to speeches, action to words. She began a special intervention as the Turks—different blends of the savage Asian tribes—attacked Delhi and slaughtered one hundred thousand.

By 1390 the Turks had completed a conquest of Asia Minor and from there moved to Damascus, Baghdad, and Eastern Europe.

It was now the Turks' turn to challenge the world as the Huns, Muslims, and Goths had once challenged it. I can't recount the entire history for it comes at us with ferocity. So does the mysticism. The Byzantine image thought to have been painted by Luke and brought from Jerusalem to Constantinople and then Ruthenia was now in Poland. It was in danger from marauding Tartars who repeatedly besieged the castle of Prince Ladislaus, where it was kept in a special chamber. Although it had been struck in the throat with an arrow, Ladislaus took the painting and headed for the secure city of Opala to preserve it from further damage. On the way he stopped for a night of rest at the knightly village of Czestochowa and placed the image in a small wooden church until morning. When Ladislaus tried to continue his journey the morning of August 26, 1382, his horses refused to budge. They wouldn't pull the wagon. Ladislaus took that as a heavenly sign and decided the image should remain in the chapel, where it would become world famous as Our Lady of Czestochowa.

Four years later there were also phenomena near the quiet hamlet of Dorschhausen, Germany, where a man heard the strange sound of music and tracked it to a cavity in a fir tree. In the cavity was a hidden image of Mary.

You could track phenomena from Pisa to Segovia. The war was indeed engaged and heightening. The Blessed Mother, sweet though she was, was a relentless warrior. She was still taking back pagan trees and bolstering her Church with her appearances. As turmoil engulfed the papacy, her music inspired great composers and the *Angelus* was recited with the ringing of bells in many parts of staggering Europe. If there were those who resisted the doctrine of her Immaculate Conception because they had allowed hyperrationalism to infect what was supposed to be a spiritual institution— if they were trying to take the Church down an intellectual road, which Christ, a mystic, had clearly never intended—such attempts were foiled by Mary's miracles and by a deep, ineradicable instinct in the faithful. Whatever the new academics might argue and however they might want to phrase it, there was something extraordinary and transcendent about the very name Mary. When the faithful prayed for her help, she answered.

The people knew that mysticism and not theology was the basis of Christianity. Mary was there to teach lessons. She was there to help the common people who lacked guidance from a divided and intellectualized Church. She was bringing her Son's memory as a constant reminder and with it the Holy Spirit, Who was sadly missing from the sensuality of Avignon and Rome, where as *Butler's Lives of the Saints* recalled "open robbery and violence were rife, vice no less open and unashamed, the churches falling through neglect, and the people uncared for except to be exploited."

Mary also manifested in Toledo, Spain, and a statue of her "spoke" in Ireland at Cell Mor in Tir Briuin.

In Holland Mary appeared in a dream to a woman who had mocked a statue of her and asked, *"Why do you call me ugly whom am beautiful and dwell in eternal heaven? I tell you to have recourse to me so that you may overcome your sufferings and gain heaven also."*

She gave a number of such personal lessons. She taught what the Church was not teaching. She appeared to a noblewoman in Rimini, Italy, who had just lost her wealthy husband and reminded her that material things were in the end worthless. *"Of what avail to your first husband, whom you loved so well, were his honors, his fortune, and his youth,"* she asked, *"since death has taken him from you and from them?"*

Those kinds of personal lessons mattered more than any treatise. She helped the lame, the blind, the dumb. There were reports of her healing a withered hand of paralysis. On the eve of the Assumption in 1395 a young shepherd saw a bright light illuminate a yew near Garaballa, Spain. When he investigated he found an image of Mary in the branches. It was similar to subsequent reports at Santa Gadea del Cid in the province of Burgos, where on March 25, 1399, two shepherd boys, Pedro, son of Yñigo García de Arbe, and Juan, son of Juan de Enzinas, found an oak tree with a beehive. They returned the next evening, Wednesday of Holy Week, to gather wax and honey. That was when they were met by a sight stunning even by Marian standards. According to testimony documented on parchment and signed by a notary in Santa Gadea, the boys saw an entire group of ghostly people gathered around a huge hawthorn. At the top of the hawthorn, like the burning bush in Exodus 3:2, was a lady brighter than the sun, so bright they couldn't look at her without being blinded.

"And then they heard a voice from the people there calling out, 'Come to matins,' and at this call there appeared from the direction of Santa

María de Guinicio a great number of people as if in a procession in white garments," said the notarized statement. "And most of them wore red garments with white stripes on top, and many other colors. They carried in their hands branches like palms and two torches that lit up the entire procession as if it were daytime. This procession came to join the people around the lady; and the brightness went up as far as the sky; and around her were three torches like big candles, so powerful they lit up all of the landscape; and it seemed that they went up as far as the sky. And they heard singing, like priests chanting the hours, and frightened by the voice they stopped gathering their honey and fled toward town. When they reached the flat place that is halfway, they looked back and saw all the lights join in one; and the singing went up to the heavens, so much that they did not dare go back."

The following Thursday Pedro was keeping his father's sheep near the same spot and suddenly a resplendent lady appeared to him. Again he could not look at her directly. She told Pedro to tell the local priests of his vision so that all should know that "she who he had seen on the hawthorn tree was the Virgin Mary glorified in person; and the people he had seen around her were the angels of heaven, that very pure company. And that they should know that her coming was willed by her precious Son, the Redeemer of the human race."

It was explained by the woman that the other apparitions were angels and martyrs as described in Revelation 6:11. The woman explained that at the time Spain was destroyed by the infidels there had been a town there called Montañana la Yerma and a church at this spot in her name. She told the boy that the people fled to the church during an onslaught and were beheaded when they refused to convert to Islam. The entire area was awash in their blood. She said Christ wanted the place kept holy by construction of a Benedictine church and monastery *to revive the memory of this secret.*

Those who came as pilgrims or sent alms would have remission of sins and would be helped and protected whenever they gave themselves with great devotion to her.

Whoever carried a picture of the apparition would be freed from the power of the devil. It would *"ward off pestilence and all disease."*

She said the three torches represented the Father, Son, and Holy Spirit.

*"Just as God the Father came to Moses in the briarbush, which was not consumed by fire for the good of his people, so I was sent in the hawthorn for the good of souls and bodies of the faithful of the human race,"* she said. *"The voice you heard calling to matins was that of the Archangel Michael."*

Interesting was the fact that the two shepherds were named Pedro and Juan—Peter and John—in recollection of the drama of Holy Week. It's also interesting that Mary said Juan should take up the arms of St. Catherine of Alexandria, the ancient saint who had been converted by a vision of the Blessed Mother around A.D. 306 and whose relics were now in a monastery at the reputed site of the burning bush.

Was that a sign to restudy Exodus? Was it a sign that martyrdom was again at hand? Or was it in response to the grave Church malady?

Mary always stepped up appearances during Church trouble and trouble there was. There were still two popes, Benedict XIII in Avignon and now Gregory XII in Rome. While the pontiffs agreed to meet to discuss the possibility of mutually resigning and letting a single pope take over, that denouement never took place. On March 25, 1409, an assembly of churchmen met at Pisa and declared *both* popes heretical. Their images were burned in effigy and a new pope—a *third* pope—was elected but he died in Bologna on May 3, 1410. *His* successor was Pope John, an unusual man who'd had the reputation of an ecclesiastical conquistador and who seemed to suffer slander and other continuing papal misfortune.

It certainly didn't look like he was the man to reunite the Church. The omens were any but good ones. When John called for a council on the schism and asked for descent of the Holy Spirit during the opening invocation, it was reported that a screech owl settled on his head.

# 26

## *The Secret of Obedience*

B ut the council settled the issue, forcing out the three popes and electing a single one. The other popes didn't go easily, and certain abuses remained, but Christendom was once more a single unit. The terrible schism that had divided the Church for more then seventy years had come to a grinding end.

So too did the great Medieval chastisement, which like other chastisements paralleled problems in the Church and lessened as mankind returned to piety. While bubonic plague would menace regions of Europe for the next several centuries, just as barbarian attacks had menaced Rome for a long while during the Classical chastisement, the way was now open for divine grace. The way was open for Mary to stop the disease from resurging. In village after village, in town after town, she came imploring prayer so the disease would fade into memory. In case after case communities that responded to her call were spared. While the tribulation had taken a horrifying toll, its destruction could have been apocalyptic. It could have exterminated all of Asia, Africa, and Europe. Even without disease, the Church had come close to extinction. This had always been the worry of prophets—that the devil would destroy the Church, that the pope and cardinals would be dispelled from Rome through schism or exile, that priests would be persecuted and stripped of their possessions, that one day Church property would be seized, that clergy would become perverted, that there would come a time when theological upheaval would mirror the rebellion, and that fury and warfare would pave the way for Antichrist.

Some thought he was ready to appear as the Middle Ages approached its last stage while others mentioned that he would come sometime after the twentieth century. "When the Feast of St. Mark shall fall on Easter, the Feast of St. Anthony on Pentecost, and that of St. John on Corpus Christi, the whole world shall cry woe," was one prediction. It was an apocryphal prophecy but the connection between the Church and society as a whole was unquestionable. As the Church had diminished, as it got caught in a materialistic web, as it had become involved in war, money, and politics, so had society diminished and so had it suffered from the spider's venom. Church and society were always intertwined. While society suffered politically and economically, while it suffered the fire of bubonic fever, the Church saw the hellfire of division. When there was division there was the devil. He inspired division by inspiring pride, self-will, and rebellion, which led to disobedience. Where there was pride, there was schism. Where there was arrogance, there was hatred. Where there was hatred, there was disease. As men drifted from God they drifted from His protection. It came down to obedience. Whatever its periodic faults, the Church had fourteen hundred years of collective discernment and that wisdom was worth obeying. Obedience had force. It brought grace and Mary was a demonstration of that powerful secret. She had obeyed God's Will when she conceived a child despite her unmarried condition and she was obedient right up to watching her only Child die on the Cross.

That was the power of submission. That was obedience. It said in 1 Peter 5:5, "In the same way, you younger men must be obedient to your elders. In your relations with one another, clothe yourselves with humility, because God 'is stern with the arrogant but to the humble He shows kindness.'" Obedience was submission to rightful authority like the Church. Scripture said it was better than sacrifice (1 Samuel 15:22). Obedience was selflessness, the highest form of humility, while ego and selfishness were the great spiritual inhibitors. They were very dangerous, the essence of pride. Where there was selfishness there was a separation. Where there was self there was a parting from God. Where there was self there was focus on the creation instead of on the Creator. Where there was self there were greed, rebellion, occultism, and paganism, because according to the Bible rebellion is "as the sin of witchcraft" (1 Samuel 15:23, KJV).

No one had been more of a rebel than Satan and no one had been more obedient than Mary. That was the bottom line, the unbridgeable difference. He was the prince of pride while she was the symbol of salvational humility. She was called Queen of Peace because her detachment from self brought serenity. It was galling beyond galling to the devil that a peasant woman—a lowly human—was being used until the Second Coming to strike evil down and alleviate human pain.

But that was the reality. Until Christ returned for the final denouement He was sending the Mother of Obedience. She came as the stopper of the Black Death and the beacon of hope, but above all she came as ambassador of submission, which is why she chose humble and obedient shepherds as her seers. They now saw apparitions just as shepherds had seen the angel during Christ's nativity (Luke 2:9). Heaven idealized little shepherds like those in and around Fatima, Portugal, where the girl from Reguengo do Fetal found the bread and spring in the 1100s and where the deaf girl from Casal Santa Maria, a hamlet about a mile and a half from Fatima, saw Mary. The deaf seer saw her over a cluster of ortiga bushes. Mary smiled and made an odd request. She asked the girl, who could suddenly hear, for one of her lambs. It was a test of obedience.

Suddenly the girl spoke as if deafness had never afflicted her. "I would have to have permission from my father," she said. And Mary smiled as the girl scurried off to do just that.

Naturally, her father was flabbergasted, awestruck, and overjoyed at her ability to speak. He told his daughter that the Blessed Woman could have the lamb and anything else she wanted. We can only imagine his joy. News of the miracle swept the village and far beyond in the era before mass communication.

Numerous townsfolk went to see the "mute" child and, after hearing her account, followed her to the site of appearance. To their further astonishment, there they found a wooden statue in the midst of the ortigas.

Mary was holding the Christ Child, this time in her right arm. Her cheeks were rosy; her stare was intent and straightforward. Full of fervor the townsfolk took the statue to the village but that night it disappeared. It was found back in the bushes at the spot Mary had chosen for a chapel.

That was the hinterlands of Portugal and from here on there was a great rise in Mary's appearances. Images of the Virgin were found in chestnuts and alden trees or buried in the ground and wrapped with silk, often in mint condition. Strange wisps of cloud were seen as in the time of Elijah and as predicted in Revelation 1:7. Although there were certainly cases where one legend spawned or informed another, it was remarkable how such similar events occurred at the same time in Spain, in Austria, in Italy, and in Germany (even though, for the most part, this was still before the first printing press and at a time when it took an entire day to travel thirty miles, indicating the supernatural nature of such inexplicable consistency).

As devotion increased, as the *Memorare* came into use, as the Scapular continued to spread, and as a psalter of fifty thoughts which would soon become 150 meditations on the lives of Jesus and Mary was attached to the Rosary, so did the phenomena, the consistent miracles, head for a new summit. There were teary statues and bleeding statues and a statue spirited away from invading Turks and paraded around Italy. There were statues discovered by more strange activity by animals and images that refused to burn even when tossed into fire.

At Siena an evangelist named Bernardine Albizeschi begged the help of Mary and a globe of fire descended, curing him of a speech impediment.

When Bernardine preached in the city of Perugia, many saw the Sorrowful Mother in the sky.

There were apparitions on the island of Madeira four hundred miles out in the Atlantic, and in Florence Mary appeared to a widow in 1420 to announce that her prayers had been answered and that the city would be spared another outbreak of plague.

In Bohemia a statue was credited with saving a church from enemy attack by the Hussars while in Valencia there was the account of a beautiful and intricate statue sculpted by mysterious strangers.

If some of the events, especially ghostly processions, raised questions of discernment, overall there was the feeling of the Holy Spirit. The true test of the good Spirit, noted Catherine of Bologna, who had both good and evil apparitions, was the feeling of peace, love, and burning charity. With the exception of righteous conviction, anything that disturbed, anything that caused persistent unease, came from the evil one. Vanity caused just such unease and those seers who were authentic shed their self-will. They were not narcissistic. The secret to union with God was selflessness. Anything that lacked humility lacked the Holy Spirit. Pride was the flag of warning. No one could truly call themselves "Christian" while infected with egoism. Pride puffed up "self" whereas humility gave glory to the Creator. When the Lord was glorified, heaven pierced the veil. There were miracles. There were intercessions. In Spain the Virgin was reportedly seen on June 10, 1430, at a place called Jaén. That same year in Czestochowa robbers tried to carry off the famous dark icon of Mary but suddenly found it too heavy to transport!

On May 26, 1432, the Blessed Mother manifested in Caravaggio, Italy, to a poor family called the Vacchis. Due to Mary's efforts in calming tensions between the city-states, she became known there as the "Queen of Peace."

She was also the Queen of Healing because in 1438 she stopped in Bologna to save that town from pestilence.

Many were the cases where the Blessed Woman came to halt recurrences of the Black Death, but she also tended to emotional ailments. In 1442 in Cordova, Spain, she stopped a sick and destitute man named Gonzalo from killing himself. As the desperate father went to hang himself, a soft light shone suddenly in his room and a beautiful woman appeared, healing him and his equally ill family.

In Saluzzo, Italy, Mary was seen above the flames during a major fire in 1447 and soon the stubborn and terrifying blaze which engulfed homes was extinguished.

A famous incident occurred at this same time about thirty miles southwest of Madrid. At Cubas a twelve-year-old girl named Inés Martínez had a total of six apparitions over a seventeen-day period. Mary was dressed in a snow-white *abrochada* and wore golden slippers. She warned the people to confess their sins because an epidemic was coming.

There was also a miracle during the 1450s in Betharram, France, where a statue of Mary turned luminous.

While such occurrences had become so frequent as to barely merit mention this one is important because Betharram is in the Pyrenees just a few miles from a place called Lourdes in a nation that one day would try to obliterate Christianity.

# 27

## The Secret of Faith

T
he Virgin also appeared at least twice during the next fifteen years in Hungary, where fog drifted off rolling forests and gray rain blurred the outline of castles. There in Transylvania lived a sadistic nobleman whose father was called *Dracul* for "dragon" and whose own nickname *Dracula* meant "son of the devil." Thousands were impaled on stakes or otherwise massacred by the tyrant.

That such evil could exist was a societal barometer. There was great peril. The plague had not spelled the end but Satan still wanted to destroy the planet. It was still the endgame and it was the reason apparitions of Mary rose to a new unforgettable height, with the greatest outpouring of phenomena since Pentecost.

It was why an image of Mary shed blood in Görgsony, Hungary.

The message was repent or face death, repent or the plague would repeat itself. That was the indication from apparitions that now swept the continents. I can't discern each claim and there were instances that were strange and puzzling, but there were points to be made with certain cases. In the Spanish town of El Miracle two young boys named Jaume and Celedoni saw a beautiful girl obviously not of the earth. It was on August 3, 1458, during another outbreak of bubonic fever. Jaume, who himself died from plague a week later, reported that the girl was blonde and perhaps eight years old, which was also his age. She was carrying a beautiful crucifix, which she handed to the boy for a moment, warning townsfolk to convert.

*"Tell the people to make processions, and make them devoutly, and to confess and convert and return to the side of God, and that if they do, God will forgive them,"* said the apparition, which was bedecked in a red cape. *"Tell them if they do not believe you, my Son will make them believe, and that there will be neither small or big, four years or older, whom my Son will not reap."*

At the other end of Spain, in Jaén, the phenomena had been somewhat eerie. Witnesses looked from the doorways in the middle of the night to see ghostly men in white carrying crosses before a woman who was also arrayed in white but much brighter and carrying an infant, accompanied by a man they swore was St. Ildefonso, the bishop who had experienced an apparition of the Blessed Mother in Toledo nearly eight hundred years before.

Why Spain and why such ghostly processions was a mystery but it brought to mind Revelation 3:5, which said, "The victor shall go clothed in white. I will never erase his name from the book of the living, but will acknowledge him in the presence of My Father and His angels."

In Loreto, Italy, Mary reportedly appeared to a seriously ill cardinal and informed him that he would not only be cured but would soon ascend to the throne of Peter. The cardinal, Enea Silvio Piccolomini, became Pope Pius II. In 1465 Mary also appeared at the University of Paris, stronghold of rationalism, to a Dominican named Alanus de Rupe.

Two short years later, there was a very spectacular case in Genazzano, Italy. On April 25, 1467, at the rundown church that had been dedicated to Our Lady of Good Counsel, unusual music was heard by a crowd assembled at the Piazza de Santa Maria for an annual festival.

The angelic music seemed to be coming from the sky. The crowd turned quiet and stared upward. "Soon, far above the highest houses, above the church spires and the lofty castle turrets, they beheld a beautiful white cloud, darting forth vivid rays of light in every direction, amidst the music of heaven and a splendor that obscured the sun," wrote a later missionary named Monsignor George F. Dillon. "It gradually descended, and, to their amazement, finally rested upon the furthest portion of the unfinished wall of the chapel of St. Biagio.

> Suddenly the bells of the high campanile, which stood before their eyes, began to peal, though they saw and knew no human hand touched them. And then, in unison, every church bell in the town began to answer in peals as festive. The crowd was spellbound, ravished, and yet full of holy feeling. With eager haste they filled the enclosure. They pressed around the spot where the cloud remained. Gradually the rays of light ceased to dart, the cloud began to clear gently away, and then, to their astonishment, there remained disclosed a most beautiful object.
>
> It was an image of Our Lady, holding the Divine Child Jesus in her arms, and she seemed to smile upon them and say, *"Fear not. I am your mother, and you are and shall be my beloved children."*

The image appeared to have been painted on porcelain or plaster. It was as thin as eggshell. No one could figure what was supporting it. It was just sitting there on a narrow ledge a few feet above the ground with not so much as a crack on it. In the painting Mary's dark green dress was trimmed with a gold collar, and a bright blue mantle covered her head. Her eyes were partly downcast, as if listening. The expression of both Mary and Jesus was one of rapt attention. At times the Madonna's cheeks seemed to turn from red to pink, and while she looked sad from one angle, she appeared to smile when the observer stood directly in front of her.

Even skeptics had to admit that the preservation of the image's texture and colors wasn't easy to explain, and even the hardest of hearts had to feel the fondness of Jesus for His mother as one little arm wound around her neck and the other held her neckline. Nothing actually touched the encased image, which though painted on such thin material seemed to stand of its own strength. Even today we can almost hear the cries of *"Evviva Maria! Evviva Maria!"* as whole neighboring towns emptied of their inhabitants, who came immediately in joyful but solemn procession.

Within four months, from April 27 to August 14, 1467, 171 cures and other miracles were recorded there.

Most remarkable was the subsequent discovery that the image of Mary was identical to one missing from a church in Scutari, Albania. It vanished before it could be destroyed by the invading Turks, and dumbfounded officials were to note an empty space on the wall that was 15-by-17 inches, corresponding precisely with the image that found its way to Genazzano.

Eventually the case was documented by the Vatican's Sacred Congregation of Rites and at least one later pope, Urban VIII, sought help there when plague again threatened.

The same year as Genazzano there was a less visible but no less powerful intercession in Viterbo. Like so many towns afflicted by recurrences of illness, residents decided to head that July for what was known as "Our Lady's Oak." There they solemnly invoked Mary's intercession and by the end of that month the plague had ceased, provoking another emotional outpouring.

A crowd of forty thousand gathered before Mary's picture in thanks for a nearly instantaneous deliverance. "On the first Sunday in August an immense procession, including fourteen religious communities, visited this new sanctuary of the Madonna," wrote historian and college president Father James Spencer Northcote, adding that among the miracles was the account of a man who had fled to the oak as robbers or enemies came after him. While he was near the portrait, he was invisible to his pursuers.

According to Northcote when a series of quakes hit Viterbo the Blessed Mother was again implored and there was "immediate cessation of this scourge."

In 1480 she also helped besieged knights in Rhodos, Greece, as thousands of Turks attacked. After five days the infidels were gone.

That same year she appeared as an indescribable beauty—not Hollywood beautiful, not model beautiful, but beautiful of soul—in a town called Locarno, Switzerland.

Clearly Mary was making a stand at another historical confluence, a crunch time for this century. It was the end of the Middle Ages and the start of the Renaissance, a change of era that had come when the Turks captured Constantinople. The new period saw new negatives as philosophers and artists fled to the West along with astrologers, cabalists, and alchemists who joined the Templars and gypsies in wielding esoteric power.

Europe was in renewed jeopardy. The times demanded prayer. In an incredible spectacle, a man named Miguel Noguer of El Torn, Spain, came upon a young girl praying heartfelt lamentations in a locked chapel. The incident occurred on October 25, 1483, when Noguer went to ring the *Angelus* bell at the church, which had been closed through official Church interdict either because it had failed to pay ecclesiastical duties or because it had been profaned in some manner.

Praying at the door, Noguer was surprised and disturbed by the sound of someone weeping. The cries originated right in front of him, on the other side of the closed doors, which miraculously opened when he rose to ring the bell.

There, just three or four paces before him, was an extraordinarily beautiful girl of seven or eight dressed in pure white and wringing her hands as she cried to Jesus.

Her voice was very sweet but she was weeping loudly. When Noguero summoned the courage to ask what the trouble was, the apparition addressed Noguero as "*son*" and identified herself as the Virgin Mary. She requested him to spread word that those in the parishes of Milleras, El Torn, El Salent, and San Miguel de Campamior must immediately stop using blasphemous language, keep Sunday holy, pay up their tithes, *charitas*, and duties, and *"restore other things that they hold covertly or openly which are not theirs to their rightful owners within thirty days"* or face chastisement. She was most serious about these matters. She asked Noguero to get the priests to promote fasting and processions every Friday once the prohibition on the church was removed.

"Unlike either a pietà or a Mary at the foot of the Cross, Mary at El Torn was not weeping for her Son, but rather *to* her Son for her symbolic children, the human race," wrote historian William A. Christian. "Her weeping was part of her intercession."

Mary's tears came from knowledge of the punishment this area warranted. She said the Lord was going to send mortal epidemics of bubonic plague over the land if there wasn't conversion. She told Noguero to inform the bishop she wanted piety and the interdict lifted. Then she vanished and the doors of the church closed as miraculously as they had opened.

The manifestations continued to span the miraculous spectrum. A year after El Torn, an image of Mary in Prato, Italy, was observed to change its expression, open and close its eyes, and shed tears. In Trevi on August 5, 1485, tears flowed from another portrait of the Madonna. It was the anniversary of the Mary Major Basilica. These were not ordinary tears but like Görgsony consisted of blood. And when blood appeared something was very wrong, something fatal was threatening. Pope Innocent VIII ordered an image of Mary paraded through Rome and as it passed the plague-stricken homes, women brought their ill children to the doors and windows, weeping and imploring the touch of Mary. There was also an incident on May 3, 1491, in the Alsace region of France near Morschwihr. The seer was a blacksmith named Thierry Schoere who was praying near a well when Mary appeared holding a stalk of corn with three heads as well as an icicle. *"My son, the people of the country around have aroused the anger of God by their sins, and if they do not repent, many scourges will come upon them,"* she said. *"The ice you see in my hand is a symbol of the hail ready to fall in all seasons and destroy the harvests, whereas the stalk of corn, with its three ears, which I carry in the other hand, shows the time of fertility and the blessings ready to be showered on the country if the people repent."*

There was similar urgency in Monte Figogna Genoa on August 29, 1490, when Mary appeared to a shepherd named Benedict Pareto in an apparition that was later entered into the Genoa State Archives and approved by the Church. Pareto was taking a break from cutting grass for his flock when suddenly his eyes were attracted to a light described once more as far more brilliant than that of the scorching sun. In the midst of it was Mary with the Child. The shepherd knelt as she approached and he heard her say, *"Do not be afraid. I am the Queen of Heaven and have come to you with my divine Son, and for this reason: that through you there may be built a church on this spot, to be dedicated in my name."*

Pareto fumbled for words. He didn't know what to say. He remained on his knees and said only, "As you wish, my lady, though I do not possess the means and doubt if I can find them."

*"Trust me, Benedict,"* she replied. *"The money will not be lacking. All that is needed is your own good will. With my aid all will be easy."*

"Very well," said Pareto. "I trust in what you say, but it will be you who will build your own church."

The apparition left and Pareto raced down toward his house and told his wife but she reacted with disbelief and sarcasm. Her skepticism undermined Pareto's own belief and he began to think he had seen a delusion. He thought maybe his wife was right and the apparition had been brought on by the hot sun. For fear of ridicule he dropped the matter and resolved to say nothing further.

When Benedict returned to work the next day, he was climbing a fig tree when a branch broke and he fell hard to the earth, breaking several bones. He was in such pain that he thought he might expire. Carried home, he was given the Last Sacraments as he lay in agony, deeply sorry for failing to obey Mary's requests and pledging that he'd build that chapel if his life was spared.

No sooner had this thought passed through his mind than Mary appeared, upbraiding him for his lack of faith, but also healing him.

Faith was a great secret, and it was exercised to a spectacular degree by another native of Genoa named Christopher Columbus, who set out blindly across the Atlantic. His devotion to Mary was described as nearly mystical. Before beginning his journey Columbus prayed at the Spanish shrine of Guadalupe (taking that replica of her image with him), and each night as they sailed the uncharted seas on the *Santa Maria* he and his men sang the *Hail Mary*. Faithful to her, watching for signs, they knew they were on the right course when on September 15, 1492, a "marvelous branch of fire" or "prodigious flame" fell from the sky.

Once across the Atlantic this faithful son named the first island San Salvador for the Savior and the second Santa Maria de la Concepción. Others were given names like Guadeloupe, Montserrat, and of course the Virgin Islands. Most intriguing is the fact that at landfall they prayed the *Salve Regina*.

Thus the first Christian prayer ever recited in the New World was an entreaty calling Mary the great advocate and Mother of God.

# 28

---

## "*I Await You*"

Clearly Columbus' voyage was Mary's voyage and just as clearly the mission was more than appeared on the surface. It wasn't a simple discovery. It wasn't a standard excursion. In one stroke the Blessed Virgin had brought Jesus to the Western Hemisphere. Although agnostic scholars would later try to downplay Columbus' accomplishment, it was one of the great accomplishments in history and it was won by invoking the Virgin.

Through the power of Christ and under the direction of His mother, the world was suddenly and dramatically larger. Instantly history had taken an entirely new course. The future was irrevocably transformed and the endgame had just shifted in a way that would counterbalance much of the disarray in Europe, where, among other things, Martin Luther was dividing the Church. No land had figured into history, no kingdom, empire, or land had attained the kind of global and eventually interplanetary reach— no land had ever changed the very way life was lived—like this new one would.

It was a hemisphere that included a nation which would become known as the United States, and while the Norsemen and perhaps even ancient Carthagenians had brushed along its coast, the true discovery came through the Genoese admiral who sang the *Ave* and operated under what he believed to be direct messages from God.

A cross was planted at Santo Cerro in the Dominican Republic at a shrine that became known as Our Lady of Mercy, and from there the Virgin's sanctuaries spread like wildfire. Soon her images were to be found from Quebec to Tierra del Fuego. They stood as a palladium, a tool of exorcism, in a world seething with idols. While scholars have sanitized the evil present in America just as they have tried to erase the accomplishments of Columbus, and while many of the Native Americans were good, friendly people, the fact remains that the Western Hemisphere was suffering from a level of paganism comparable to that of ancient Rome, Egypt, or Babylon.

During his very first trip Columbus had encountered the Taino religion that featured gods of sun or moon. If Tainos were friendly, the same could not be said for the Caribs, cannibals on the isle of Guadeloupe who hung human heads in ritual (or at least for decorative purposes). In ways stunningly similar to the practices of the Old World, Native Americans also practiced totem magic and trance mediumship or summoned their gods by beating drums. There were rattle-shaking "medicine men" just as there were chanting shamans among the Huns and Mongols. There were nightmarish ritual masks as in deepest Africa. If many tribes were monotheistic, accepting the "Great Spirit," there was also reverence for the serpent, which put one in mind of China's dragons and India's snake worship. The superior gods of the Zuni were similar to Neptune or Poseidon, and tribes like the Navajos were steeped in dark conjuring, which stretched to the Eskimos far north.

Whether as a spiritual symbol or a mere ornament, the swastika was to be found in the Yucatan as well as on rattles made from a gourd which the Pueblo Indians used in their religious dances. Swastikas or sun signs were also to be found on a calabash from the Lenguas tribe in South America, just as they had been an ancient symbol in Asia and Europe and just as they were to be found on bronzes from Africa.

The fact that such diverse and separated peoples could all have identical symbols and similar beliefs pointed more to a spiritual than anthropological source. I stress that most Native Americans were good, altruistic people with an admirable affinity for God's creation and for the precious environment, but I must also stress (as historians no longer care to mention) that often Indians fell into violence and sorcery.

Most glaring were rituals among the Aztecs, who were astonishingly similar to the ancient Egyptians in construction of pyramids and who seemed to have an unquenchable thirst for blood. Between twenty thousand and eighty thousand captives were sacrificed to the gods when Aztecs dedicated a great temple called Tenochtitlán near Mexico City around the time of Columbus. There was also the cult following of Quetzalcoatl, god of the air, who was also the "Morning Star" and "Feathered Serpent." On a hill called Tepeyac was a major temple to the goddess Tonantzin, "little mother" of the corn and earth.

It was at the hill of Tepeyac the same year as Halley's Comet that one of the greatest events in spiritual history was to occur. On December 9, 1531, just a dozen years after Mexico was conquered by Hernán Cortéz, a poor Aztec peasant from Cuautitlán once known as "Singing Eagle" but recently baptized as "Juan Diego" was walking by that hill on the way to Mass and early errands when at daybreak he heard a mellow sound atop the hill. The sound resembled that of scattered bird choirs and yet was different, surpassing any birdsong. So wondrous was the singing that immediately Juan questioned his state of mind and wondered whether he was dreaming. There was the quality of a terrestrial paradise. When the chant had suddenly ended, Juan looked to the east on top of the hill. There was an odd silence. Then he heard someone, a woman, say, *"Juanito, Juan Dieguito."*

It seemed to come from where the birds were. He couldn't see. A mist, a brightening cloud, hid the top of Tepeyac. When Juan, still spry although he was in his fifties, climbed to investigate, he saw a woman beckoning him to come closer. A woman! This was no goddess. There was a different quality about her. There was an immediate feeling of reverence and comfort. Juan had no fear. He was full of joy. She looked to be about fourteen and gold rays formed her person.

Around her the landscape transformed in a way that brings to mind the description of heaven in Revelation 4:3. There was an otherworldly, celestial quality about her. "Approaching her presence, he marveled at her superhuman grandeur," wrote an author in the 1500s who went by the reputed pseudonym of Antonio Valeriano. "Her garments were shining like the sun; the cliff where she rested her feet, pierced with glitter, resembling an anklet of precious stones, and the earth sparkled like the rainbow. The mesquites, nopales, and other different weeds, which grow there, appeared like emeralds, their foliage like turquoise and their branches and thorns glistened like gold. He bowed before her and heard her word, tender and courteous, like someone who charms and esteems you highly."

The apparitional woman asked Juan where he was going and after he explained he was on his way to pray she said,

*Know and understand well, you the most humble of my sons, that I am the ever-virgin Holy Mary, Mother of the True God for Whom we live, of the Creator of all things, Lord of heaven and the earth. I wish that a chapel be erected here quickly, so I may therein exhibit and give all my love, compassion, help, and protection, because I am your merciful mother, to you and to all the inhabitants on this earth and all the rest who love me, invoke, and confide in me; listen there to their lamentations, and remedy all their miseries, afflictions, and sorrows. And to accomplish what my clemency pretends, go to the palace of the bishop of Mexico, and you will say to him that I manifest my great desire, that here on the plain a chapel be built to me. You will accurately relate all you have seen and admired, and what you have heard.*

It was an apparition of enormous importance. One day this place would be the second most visited shrine in Christianity (after the Vatican) and it was here that Mary again began displacing the pagan goddess, wresting

Tepeyac from Tonantzin just as she had supplanted Venus at Genazzano. Juan returned after seeing Juan de Zummárraga, the bishop-elect, and Mary was at the same spot. He indicated to her that although the bishop was a very nice man, he didn't seem to believe the account. The poor Aztec urged Mary to pick someone of higher esteem so Bishop Zummárraga would listen seriously to the story.

The Virgin would hear nothing of it. She told Juan he was the one chosen as the intermediary and so he had to try again, which Juan agreed to do the next day, a Sunday, heading back to the chancery.

If not as doubtful as before, the bishop wanted more proof. He requested a sign. He also sent some men to trail Juan Diego and see what he was up to. Inexplicably they lost sight of him near the bridge to Tepeyac, where Juan again met with the Virgin and told her the bishop still didn't quite believe and wanted some kind of evidence.

*"Well and good, my little dear,"* replied Mary. *"You will return here tomorrow, so you may take to the bishop the sign he has requested. With this he will believe you, and in this regard he will not doubt you nor will he be suspicious of you, and know, my little dear, that I will reward your solicitude and effort and fatigue spent on my behalf. Lo! Go now. I will await you here tomorrow."*

The following day, Monday, December 11, Juan did not show up because his uncle, Juan Bernardino, had become gravely ill with a form of the plague called *cocolistle*. On Tuesday Juan went to summon a priest for last rites and tried to round the hill instead of crossing its slope so the Virgin wouldn't see and detain him. His uncle needed a priest and he was in a hurry.

However, as Juan tried to circumvent Tepeyac, there was the Virgin. She descended and approached at the side of the hill. When she asked where he was going, Juan explained that he needed a priest to give his uncle absolution. After considering his story the Virgin replied, *"Hear me and understand well, my son the least, that nothing should frighten or grieve you. Let not your heart be disturbed. Do not fear that sickness, nor any other sickness or anguish. Am I not here, who is your mother? Are you not under my protection? Am I not your health? Are you not happily within my fold? Do not grieve nor be disturbed by anything. Do not be afflicted by the illness of your uncle, who will not die now of it. Be assured that he is now cured."*

Thus confident, Juan stayed and followed the Blessed Mother's instructions on proof for the bishop. As directed, he climbed to the top of the hill where he had first seen her and looked for flowers she told him would be there. She had said to cut them and bring them back. When Juan got to the place he was astonished to see a whole array of Castilian roses in bloom despite the harsh terrain and the wintry season, which had left frost on the ground. The roses were fragrant and covered with an impossible dew. Juan cut them near the petals, placing them in his *tilma*, a burlaplike cloak draped in front of his body, and folded up to form a large pouch. Never had Juan seen flowers up there, only thorns and thistles on the barren and arid hilltop. Yet now he was bringing back beautiful roses! When he returned to the Virgin she asked to see what he had. She then took each flower and rearranged them one by one in his *tilma*, telling Juan to bring them for the bishop to see.

Holding his *tilma* tightly, Juan set out for town, engulfed by an incredible fragrance. When he got to the chancery, the bishop's assistants demanded to see what he was carrying and when Juan lowered the *tilma* they witnessed the unusual roses and tried to pluck them out.

They couldn't. Each time they reached in the flowers seemed suddenly painted, stamped, or embroidered on the cloth instead of existing as actual roses. Taken aback by the seeming miracle, the assistants allowed Juan to see the bishop one more time. He entered with reverence but wasted little time in announcing the sign and untying his *tilma*.

Zummárraga's jaw had to have dropped. We know he rose from his chair and fell to his knees. Others in the room did the same. As the flowers tumbled from the *tilma*, which dropped to Juan's ankles, they saw an incredible life-size image of the Madonna on the coarse cloth, an image of an olive-complected woman with her hands folded near her heart, her head bent slightly to the right, looking down somberly. Mary's face was a bit plain but also somehow beautiful. She was dressed in a salmon-colored tunic with a blue-green mantilla. Her hair was dark before the veil, with a sash which seemed like the Aztec signal that she was pregnant.

The effect of this prodigy on the entire region was nothing less than miraculous. Knowing on first sight that it was something completely out of the ordinary—that like Genazanno it seemed to change expression or color, but more importantly knowing it was impossible for something so detailed and exquisite to have been painted on a coarse piece of burlaplike cloth made from agave cactus—the bishop agreed to build a shrine. Immediately it drew Aztecs who were converted by the thousands. During the next seven years, from 1532 to 1538, an estimated eight million Mexicans became Christians. Upon Mary's request to Juan's uncle, whose cure was announced during the uncle's own apparition of Mary, the site became known as "Santa María de Guadalupe"—connecting it to the apparition site in Spain—and for the next four centuries Church officials and scientists would puzzle over the incredible image and the fact that it never deteriorated nor did its brightness dim although the burlap itself should have lasted only twenty or so years (maybe somewhat more with ancient preservative). The coloration seemed to be of no known combination of pigments or dye, and the colors changed when viewed from various distances, seeming more like the "surface sculpting" of a bird's feather or a butterfly's scales than any artificial coloring that would depend on absorption and reflection from molecular pigments. Like the Shroud of Turin, there was no rational explanation of how the image had *gotten* there. There were no undersketch marks, no brush strokes on the main image, no flaws. The colors never cracked, peeled, or bled through nor did they fill the spaces between fibers. Instead they seemed an integral part of the cloth. Mary's rose-colored robe was of the type worn in ancient Palestine and there was somewhat of a Byzantine look to the image that bore some resemblances to Czestochowa, the image thought to have been painted by Luke, even though this was a world away in sixteenth-century Mexico. Later investigations would show that peripheral images were added later, including an angel with a crescent at the Virgin's feet and perhaps also the pattern of fleur-de-lis on her robe, which was also like the Czestochowa image. But where these later additions showed signs of age, the original image, inexplicably, did not.

Moreover, computer-enhanced images would one day show incredible portraits in the Virgin's eyes, portraits of what seemed like Juan Diego, a bearded Spaniard, a woman, and possibly Bishop Zummárraga on the cornea of the painted eye precisely as they would distort with the curvature of an actual living eye, in a way that could not have been fraud.

# 29

## The Spirit of Rebellion

I t was a miraculous sign not only to the Aztecs but to all the Church, which had come out of the schism only to face its gravest crisis. For at the same time that Mary was claiming the New World, dissension was ripping at the Church in the Old World. A cataclysm was in progress and it had spun into play when the brilliant but emotionally wrought Martin Luther had posted his ninety-five theses on a castle church at Wittenberg, where he was known as a testy professor who rejected the authority of Rome, and who ultimately cursed those who followed it.

To be sure, the Church had great failings. It was still selling indulgences as if the pope could control purgatory—something with which Luther had taken special issue—and its worldliness subjected it to worldly judgment. Many complained that greed and simony, the act of selling ecclesiastical positions, had continued and that the Church was much too involved in civil affairs, often in a harsh fashion. After what was known as the "Evil May Day" riots in London, the cardinal there had ordered sixty of the rioters hanged.

But the catastrophic division worked through Luther went far beyond what was deserved, and there were elements in Luther's life that hinted at unbalance. A sincere enough Christian, endowed with rhetorical skills and knowledge of Scripture, Luther was often prone to drastic and bizarre mood swings. According to biographer Erik H. Erikson, three of

Luther's contemporaries claimed that in his early or middle twenties, Luther had suddenly fallen to the floor in the choir during a reading of Mark 9:17, screaming for no apparent reason in a way that was foreign and frightening. Such torment followed Luther to the grave, as did his conviction that the Church was somehow to blame for his spiritual anguish.

Luther's theses had been set forth on October 31, 1517, causing the spirit of dissension to spread across all of Europe. Though once devoted to Mary, keeping a picture of her in his room and believing that she was "holiness personified," "the purest adorer of God," the highest woman and "noblest gem in Christianity after Christ"—describing her in his own formal theses as a woman who should never be criticized but instead deeply venerated, one he had himself called upon in moments of need or crisis, and acknowledged as the "Mother of God"—Luther began to attack many things associated with Catholicism, and others following his lead began a terrible assault upon celibacy, priestly graces, and the sacraments. They argued that the sole source of authority should be the Bible, and while no Christian in his or her right mind would ever downplay Scripture, this flew in the face of what Christ had said about sending the Holy Spirit upon His followers (Acts 1:8), which left the door open for tradition, doctrine, and private revelation.

The protesters or "Protestants" would have none of that, and so fifteen hundred years of wisdom, fifteen centuries of tradition and revelation, were being dismantled. Most radical was the dissension spawned in Switzerland. So intense was the crisis that Mary appeared twice there in 1531, once near Lucerne, in a stream of light on Pentecost Sunday that shocked a group of reformers who had smashed an image of her, and in Gubel on October 11, 1531, during an actual battle between Protestants and the traditional Roman Christians.

The spirit of division was like a virus which went well beyond the control of Luther. Protestants quarreled among themselves and split into smaller factions of Quakers, Calvinists, Baptists, and Anabaptists. The Church was one big divided mess and so was society, which saw the

Church of England formally separate from Rome in 1531 when the pope would not grant Henry VIII an annulment.

Society also saw a peasant uprising in Germany that led to the raping of nuns and vicious attacks on 132 monasteries.

That assault was joined by the intellectual assault of rationalists whose power grew as the achievements of mankind grew. Impressive new discoveries puffed men up and indicated to the arrogant that there was no need for *any* church; that the highest form of intelligence was man, not God. Instead of considering new inventions a gift from heaven, men let such discoveries undermine belief in the spiritual. God was taking a backseat because many things once attributed to the supernatural were now explained by science, which was making impressive strides in astronomy, biology, and chemistry. There were cubic equations and there was the study of blood flow and there were new chemicals made of sulfur. There was an understanding of the planet and how it revolved around the sun as well as discovery that it was round, not flat. All it took to resolve such issues was observation, logic, and deduction. Men would be able to resolve things like weather and the seasons and draw maps of a once-mysterious and seemingly magical earth without involving anything transcendental. In the frenzy, in the euphoria of discovery, men would stray to the extreme of accepting only what could be seen with the physical senses and would squelch faith just as scholasticism had created doubts in Luther. Faith was knowing beyond the senses. Faith *defied* physical logic. It focused on God. Faith was rising above the human condition while scientism and hyperrationalists thought everything should revolve around humans and believed that man, not God, controlled his own fate, just as the writings of ancient Greek and Roman philosophers, now revived, had indicated.

Thus there was a schism between Protestants and Catholics, but there was also a yet greater division between those who believed in the spiritual and those who solely accepted the physical. It was a split that would grow with each passing year. Humanism. Self-worship. While men like Michelangelo who weren't afraid of religion had great, sweeping vision, creating masterpieces like the Sistine ceiling, others edged toward godlessness as the Renaissance glorified man.

At the Royal College of London, scientists were authorized to carry out human dissections, and Dutch opticians were ready to invent the modern telescope. There was zoology and even the study of embryos.

No longer was there the need for fantasy.

No longer was there the need for myth.

No longer was there the need for God.

# 30

## *Mercy and Justice*

And if it wasn't attack by atheists, it was attack by witchcraft, which was also being conjured throughout Europe. Based largely on Druidism, witchcraft was a synthesis of many evils dating back to the oldest pagans. But now it was crystallizing. Now, like atheism, it was mocking Christians. Now it was especially notorious in southwest Germany and the Basque region of Spain but was also prevalent in France and Italy.

Perhaps that was why Mary was stepping up her appearances, why she established a chapel at the site of a previous apparition in Heiligenbronn in the Black Forest, and why she came to Spain in the way of an apparition to Ignatius of Loyola—at the same time an earthquake, which seemed like another sign, rattled his castle.

Earthquakes also shook Portugal and then Shaanxi, China, where the most devastating tremor in history claimed 830,000.

In Llojeta, Bolivia, the only structure left standing after a similar quake was one that had given shelter to a *mysterious female stranger.*

These were hints. These again were signs of the times (Matthew 16:3). To a great extent they could be scientifically explained (earthquakes, after all, were shifts in tectonic plates), but in the larger picture they were part of a pattern. They were a series of warnings. The more man moved from

God, the less was His protection and the less firm was the *terra firma*. Without God things spun out of control or simply lapsed into nothing. All energies were subject to God because His power was the ultimate energy. That's why so many things went wrong at the end of the Middle Ages. That's why Mary was such a presence during the subsequent Renaissance. There was yet more danger coming. A new period, the modern era, was beginning and how it transpired, how it was handled, and whether the evils that still persisted after the Black Death were dispelled or remained and even increased would one day determine how the era would end— smoothly or by chastisement.

Right now it didn't look good. There were wars. There was demonism. There was carnage. "That part of mankind which escaped the plagues did not repent of the idols they had made," Revelation 9:20 had correctly observed in the chapter which had so explicitly predicted a third would be slain as happened during the Black Death and now went on to warn of a great coming evil.

Locusts. Scorpions. There had been two major chastisements—the Classicial Chastisement of the first several centuries and then the Medieval Chastisement associated with the plague. With every cycle the chastise-ments had grown in strength and promised to do so with a third major chastisement at some point in the future. As it said in Revelation 11:14: "The second woe is past, but beware! The third is coming."

A third chastisement was somewhere in the future, a number of cen-turies down the road. The more evil there was, the more the Lord would eventually have to purify. Right now the devil was prevalent anywhere there was idolatry. Men like Hernán Cortés sensed as much and marched into Aztec temples waving images of Mary. These were not perfect men, but they had a mission and when images were planted in the Old or New World, conversion took place and evil fled the area. It was a cosmic battle and also a cosmic teeter-totter. Mary was constantly countering demonic imbalance. She did this with miracles that bolstered faith because faith took humans from under the devil's oppression.

There were miracles from the Americas to Italy. In Breschia a fresco of the Nativity came alive in front of many witnesses including Bishop Paolo Zane who gave it the memorial date of June 24, while in Frascati it was said an image of Mary on the wall of a vineyard not only came to life but spoke words to Lutheran troops sent by German Emperor Charles V to pillage Rome because the pope had sided with his enemies.

As the eighteen hundred infantrymen approached Frascati, it was said Mary's lips parted and she sent them away by saying, *"Indietro, fanti! Questa Terra e mia!"* or "Back, soldiers! This land is mine!"

The warnings were for all Christians. The admonishments were for all believers. On March 18, 1536, a man named Antonio Botta was walking near Savona, Italy, when he heard himself called by name and saw a beautiful woman standing on a stone encompassed by a dazzling globe of light in the midst of a stream.

*"Be not afraid, Antonio, it is me, Mary,"* said the woman. *"Go to your confessor and bid him tell the people in church that they must fast for the next three Saturdays in honor of the Mother of God. You must go to Confession and receive the sacrament instituted by my Son and then, on the fourth Saturday, come back here because I have more to say to you."*

Antonio hurried back and told the priest. So wide did the news spread that he had to give an account to the mayor and vicar-general. His testimony was collected in a legalistic manner and when he returned to the brook on April 8, the Queen of Heaven appeared again in a splendor whiter than snow and crowned with jewels, her eyes raised to heaven.

*"Go to Savona, to those to whom you have already announced my former visit, and renew my instructions with even greater insistence, calling upon them to leave their sins and their vices,"* she said. *"Bid all and especially the religious and members of the confraternities to make three processions in penance, because my Son is greatly stirred in anger toward the world due to its iniquity and their lives will be short unless they do these things."*

When Antonio asked the lady to give a sign so others would believe, she said only, *"Go! Go, and I will give them an inward sign so that when they hear these things they will believe them without other signs."*

As if blessing the stream, Mary then raised both of her hands above the water and said, *"Mercy and not justice, my Son!"* three times.

That was Mary as advocate. She was also the heavenly teacher. *"Live quietly and without worrying,"* she would tell a sixteenth-century mystic named Victoria Fornari-Strata. *"All I ask is that you will trust yourself to me and henceforth devote yourself to the love of God above all things."*

She was the protector and exorcist. When a demon assaulted St. Alphonsus in Spain, the Blessed Virgin materialized to give him peace. *"Alphonsus, my son: where I am,"* she said, *"thou hast naught to fear."*

She had the same message when she manifested to a woman named Nicoletta on a storm-tossed ship en route from Rhodes to Messina. *"Do not be afraid, Nicoletta, this ship is under my protection and not one of these people who have already suffered so much for the faith will perish. Let them be unafraid for I will be with them always."*

Invocation of Mary was also credited with saving two fishermen caught in a storm on Lake Titicaca in South America. Storms and thunder continued to play into both biblical (Revelation 11:19) and Marian phenomena. In Spain there had been strange thunder during a putative apparition near Matamargó, and there was a clap of thunder before an apparition in Santa Maria de los Llanos.

The Virgin came with the sounds of a storm but was actually there to *stop* ill acts of nature. During a terrible drought that hit parts of France in the 1500s many dressed themselves in white sackcloth and walked barefoot to the barren slopes of a holy hill at Fourviere, where they could be heard crying, *"Sire Dieu!* Mercy! Holy Mary, Mother of God, pray for us. Water! Water!" and water came. There was rainfall.

One could no more deny Mary's intervention than one could stand before Mount Everest and deny there was a mountain. In Zapopan, Mexico, where Mary was making such headway with the Indians, luminous rays issued from one of her statues.

Quite a story had unfolded in another Mexican place called Xiloxostla, a village badly afflicted with smallpox.

The year was 1541. The territory was Tlaxcala. And it involved another man named Juan Diego, or more precisely Juan Diego Bernardino. This Juan had sick relatives in Xiloxostla and had gotten permission from his employers at a Franciscan convent to obtain water in a stream called Zahuapan that was said to have medicinal qualities.

The situation had turned desperate. Terror reigned. There was a catastrophic loss of population. In some areas nine out of ten people had succumbed to the illness and so, late one afternoon, an urgent Juan had walked down a mountain to the stream, filled his jar, and was making his way across the western slope of Cerro de San Lorenzo through a dense grove of ocote trees when suddenly his path was blocked by a beautiful woman.

*"May God preserve you, my son,"* she said. *"Where are you bound for?"*

Juan was speechless for several long seconds. Finally he said, "I'm taking some water from the *rio* to my sick ones, who are dying!"

*"Then follow me,"* said the woman. *"I will give you water to cure the disease. It will heal not only your family but all who drink of it. My heart is ready to help those who are ill, for I cannot bear to see their misfortune."*

Although Juan was initially afraid, the gentleness of the Lady's voice and the way she looked at him was most reassuring. Juan felt a huge weight leave his shoulders. He didn't know what she was talking about—as far as he knew, there was no spring in the ocote grove—but Juan followed anyway and after a slight break in the rise the woman indicated a vigorous spring of unclouded water.

*"Take as much as you wish of this water,"* said the woman, *"and know*

*that those who are touched by even the tiniest drop will obtain not merely relief from their illness but perfect health."* The woman instructed Juan to tell the Franciscans they would find an image of her at the place of the spring. *"It will not only manifest my perfections, but through it I shall generously bestow favors and kindnesses,"* she said. *"When they find the image they are to place it in the chapel of San Lorenzo."*

And so it was that Juan gave the water to the sick and watched the impressive, astounding cures. Many were the recoveries, and shortly after the plague ground to a halt.

The Franciscans didn't know what to think. There was no doubt something mysterious had helped the people of Xiloxostla. The priests cross-examined Juan three times, finding nothing inconsistent. They decided to follow him next time he went for the water. As they did a small crowd from the village spotted them and tagged along.

When the crowd rounded the eastern slope of Cerro de San Lorenzo they were met by an extraordinary and inconceivable sight.

The ocote grove seemed to be burning.

Or at least part of it was. There was a fire. In particular they noticed a large ocote shooting red into the dark.

The friars watched for some time and then, knowing there wasn't much they could do, returned to the monastery. After Mass the next morning they walked back to the site with another curious crowd and were perplexed at the grove's condition. The flames should have consumed the trees like a tinderbox for they were resinous and it was the dry season. But there was little damage. The fire apparently had extinguished itself. Burn marks were seen only on the lower branches, except for the large ocote, which was blackened from top to bottom.

One of the friars had brought an axe and was ordered by his superior to chop down the damaged tree. As he did, according to a Mexican chronicler, "a new marvel met their eyes: within the trunk of the fallen tree was visible the image of the Holy Mother of God, representing the mystery of the Immaculate Conception."

Somehow a fifty-eight-inch statue of Mary with hands clasped in prayer had found its way into the tree. The image showed a young woman with her brows slightly arched. Her mouth was small, her nose straight and narrow like Czestochowa but not as Byzantine. It also bore similarities to Guadalupe but was facing frontward.

Heeding Mary's request, the friars took the image to the chapel where it replaced a statue of St. Lorenzo in the center niche.

When a sacristan tried to remove it, preferring Lorenzo there, the statue kept moving back to the center in a way that was inexplicable.

# 31

---

## *The Prophecy*

Any question that mankind was heading into a new and more dangerous era was dispelled by the serious attention Mary gave the onset of the era and the breathtaking rate of her manifestations. Up to now no century could match them. She appeared to so many saints that we lose reckoning. She came to St. Cajetan Gaetano when he was on his deathbed and the same was true of St. Stanislaus Kostka. She was seen one day at the beginning of the *Salve Regina* by the great St. Teresa of Avila.

This is not to mention the obscure visions encountered by hundreds of others. Some were false. Some were deceptions. There was a nun in Cordova, Spain, who had demonic ecstasies and stigmata that fooled even cardinals for thirty-eight years. There were so many seers, especially young women, and so many political and religious predictions that Leo X had published a Bull prohibiting his clerics from publicly preaching on them. By the next century there would be a period in which the Holy Office would issue twenty condemnations.

But there were also great saints like John of the Cross who saw Mary in all her true splendor. And there were so many wonders, including one witnessed by Pope Pius V, that it seemed nothing less than a massive spiritual censorship could have prevented the large number and wide range from having reached us.

Mary manifested a brilliant flash of light from a statue on April 23,

1544, stopping a Turkish pirate named Ariadeno Barbarossa from plundering Italy, and she also appeared in places like Kazan, Russia, during the reign of Ivan the Terrible. In Aberdeen, Scotland, a heretic was stricken after throwing filth into a miraculous well, while in Austria Protestant troopers raiding a monastery at Garsten were unable to chop up a statue of her. At Chartres her image survived Protestant cannons that destroyed surrounding walls, and there were other accounts of her sightings during quakes in such countries as Peru and Bolivia. In Lima, Peru, a statue at the Chapel of the Blood would be seen to animate during a violent earthquake by turning itself to the main altar and joining hands in prayer. In Quito Mary came to bring rain that precipitated volcanic ash which might otherwise have suffocated the people. She came to Casalbordino, Italy, to explain a chastisement of damaging hail *("because of the sins they committed daily")* while in the Mediterranean there was the remarkable "miracle of Lepanto."

Lepanto was the case involving Pius V. It came as Christian Europe was under severe threat from the invading Turks, who had besieged Vienna, declared war on Venice, and threatened to make a mosque out of St. Peter's Basilica. If Islam was to be stopped from taking over Europe it had to be done now. Pius enlisted the aid of Spain, Venice, and smaller Italian states in forming a fleet of 208 galley ships and six huge oar-driven boats to defend the continent. As all of Christendom prayed, the allied fleet assembled at Messina and set out to confront the Turkish fleet near Lepanto (now Corinth) in the Gulf of Patras. One of the squadrons was commanded by Admiral Giovanni Andrea Doria, who carried an oil-painted copy of the Guadalupe image with him.

The stage was now set. The stake was Christianity. From the minute the expedition started Pius had fervently prayed and there was a huge Rosary procession. As Catholics recited the *Hail Mary,* as the pope implored heaven, as cardinals gave Communion, the allied fleet boldly positioned its forces. The battle was engaged on October 7, 1571. Doria's squadron moved to a position north of the gulf but was outmaneuvered and in great danger when Doria went to his cabin, knelt before the Guadalupe image, and implored the help of Mary.

By nightfall the momentum began to miraculously change. A Turkish squadron was captured and a wind drove the smoke of combat in the faces of Muslims, who panicked. In one of the greatest maritime conquests of all time, the Christian fleet captured 117 galleys, liberated fifteen thousand enslaved Christians, and sank or burned about fifty Turkish galleys while losing only twelve itself. At the very hour of triumph Pope Pius, conversing with some of his cardinals, suddenly turned from them, opened a window, and as if approached by an invisible messenger remained standing for a long while with his eyes fixed on the sky. Then, closing the window, he turned back to his cardinals and said, "This is not a moment in which to talk about business. Let us give thanks to God for the victory He has granted to the arms of the Christians."

Although it took weeks to confirm the victory, Pius' vision was correct and in appreciation he instituted the Feast of the Holy Rosary.

Galloping through history now, we do so because Satan was galloping knowing his time was short (Revelation 12:12). Lepanto was but the opening battle in an expanding war. The devil was attacking the remnant of Mary's seed and Mary countered with so many phenomena that by the time of Lepanto every nation of Christian Europe had not one but dozens of places where miracles occurred. Had Protestants known the extent, authenticity, and good fruits of the phenomena, they not only would have stopped blaspheming the Virgin but in Christian faith would have joined in devotion to her.

There were unusual stars seen in the sky (including a new one discovered on the day of Pius' death) and countless were the cases of woodsmen finding mysterious images in trees, sometimes embedded in the very bark. Protestants and Turks would find that they could neither burn nor discard her images. The one from Garsten somehow returned *upstream* to that village after it was dumped by frustrated Protestants in the Enns River.

It was a momentous century for Mary as the battle with Lucifer entered the modern era, as the conflict took on yet larger proportions, as the door of hell continued to creak open. Now the battlefield had been expanded to include South America. On January 21, 1577, just a few years after Lepanto, a group of Immaculate Conception nuns in Quito were gathered in the choir for vespers when extraordinary rays of light pierced the dark and shone on the main altar, on the images that decorated it, and particularly on a statue of Mary holding Jesus and a scepter. The nuns also heard the sound of singing and smelled the odor of sanctity. The supernatural nature of the light was beyond questioning because there wasn't a single lamp in the chapel. The nuns were too poor to afford one. There wasn't even a light for the tabernacle and yet the altar was all lit up, the illumination such that villagers noticed it.

As the light played on, the Blessed Virgin seemed to increase in brightness. Then she appeared to move and take on the appearance of a living person. The figure of the Infant she had been holding in her left arm vanished and the statue transformed itself into a representation of the Immaculate Conception with numerous angels around her. The villagers stopped in to see what was going on, knowing the chapel should have been dark. They too witnessed the phenomena.

These events were recorded by Church officials and so were other cases witnessed by crowds in Chile and Paraguay. Signs appeared in the sky, and deliverance from plague occurred in 1604 when an image of the Madonna was credited in Arequipa, Peru, with stopping the "black vomit." Other epidemics were halted in Venezuela and there were also instances of radiating images or more apparitions, as in the Peruvian city of Orcotuna.

The seer there was a humble Indian woman named Rosa Achicahuala. One night while mending by candlelight, Rosa heard a dog bark. Peering outside, she saw a beautiful girl bathed in the light of a full moon. The girl's face was framed by golden hair and her dainty feet rested on a flat rock in the middle of a flowing stream, as at the site half a world away in Savona. She was washing a baby's tiny shirt. When she finished she squeezed the last of the water and shook the garment, then spread it over the twigs of a bush to dry.

Rosa tried to approach, but when she did the apparition disappeared. This happened night after night, sometimes with the addition of angels and their melodious song. Finally one night Rosa was able to draw near and raise the nerve to ask, "Why do you wash at hours so late? What is your name? Who are you?"

Softly the lovely young woman replied, *"Listen, Rosa. I have chosen you as my faithful servant. Do not be afraid. I am Queen of the Heavens. I will take care of your every need."*

Immediately Rosa fell to her knees and kissed the hem of the Lady's robe. "My little mother, what do you want me to do?"

*"I wish only to entrust you with the building of a little chapel close by this spring where I will be venerated under the name of 'Virgen de Cocharcas,'"* said Mary. *"I came from Copacabana, crossing Titicaca and forests and mountains that I might pour my blessing here."*

Why South America was chosen as such a center of activity remains a mystery. But a center it was. There was St. Rose of Lima experiencing daily visions of Mary and missionaries encountering her in prayer, in dreams, or through statue miracles. *"Have confidence, my son, your fatigue will take the place of purgatory for you,"* she told a missionary named Father Michael De La Fontaine who was prostrate and so exhausted he couldn't rise. *"Bear your sufferings patiently and on leaving this life your soul will be received into the abode of the blessed."*

The spiritual war was especially apparent on February 2, 1605, in the frontier region near Ráquira, Colombia. There, hermits and priests were holding a festival in honor of the Most Holy Lady of Purification. As Mass began, a frightful thunderclap resounded through the valley and as recounted by Charles Broschart,

The sky obscured by dark clouds [was] ripped repeatedly by lightning flashes. Then winds of hurricane force blew up, cataracts of water coursed down the hillsides, and soon the Gachaneca River overflowed with a roar like that of wild beasts. All this happened in a very few minutes and was accompanied by voices of the devil that threatened death to all. The crowd attending the Mass began to cry out in terror and many fled up into the hills. Those who remained quiet although not without fear were those within the chapel and they had faith in the power of the Virgin. The voices of the demons could be heard more and more horribly and at times the frame of the chapel creaked and shook on its foundations.

But the Mass proceeded and as the priest prayed for deliverance the rain suddenly stopped and a fire started by lightning was likewise extinguished.

Such dramas led to conversion. Most dramatic was the appearance of Mary in Quito to another Immaculate Conception nun, Marianna Torres of Jesus, on February 2, 1634. Sister Marianna was praying before the Blessed Sacrament when the perpetual lamp was suddenly and inexplicably extinguished. As before, the chapel was totally dark (although by now they could obviously afford lamps) and, like the earlier event, there was a soft heavenly light. This time Mary was in the light. I call her appearance dramatic because she allegedly spoke a long prophecy that if authentic is one of the most impressive in Church annals.

"*My heart-loved daughter, I am Maria del Buen Suceso, your mother and protector,*" Mary said. "*The sanctuary lamp burning in front of the Prisoner of Love, which you saw go out, has many meanings. The first meaning is that at the end of the nineteenth century and for a large part of the twentieth century, various heresies will flourish on this earth, which will become a free republic. The precious light of the faith will go out in souls because of the almost total moral corruption. In those times there will be great physical and moral calamities, in private and in public. The small number of souls keeping the faith and practicing the virtues will undergo cruel and unspeakable suffering.*

"*The second meaning is that my communities will be abandoned. They will be swamped in a sea of bitterness, and will seem drowned in tribulations. How many true vocations will be lost for lack of skillful and prudent direction to form them! Each mistress of novices will need to be a soul of prayer, knowing how to discern spirits.*

*"The third meaning is that in those times the air will be filled with the spirit of impurity which like a deluge of filth will flood the streets, squares, and public places. The licentiousness will be such that there will be no more virgin souls in the world.*

*"The fourth meaning is that by gaining control of all the social classes, the sects will tend to penetrate with great skill into the hearts of families and destroy even the children. The devil will take glory in perfidiously feeding on the hearts of children. The innocence of childhood will almost disappear. Thus priestly vocations will be lost. It will be a real disaster; priests will abandon their sacred duties and will depart from the path marked for them by God. Then the Church will go through a dark night for lack of a prelate and father to watch over it with love, gentleness, strength, and prudence, and numbers of priests will lose the Spirit of God, thus placing their souls in great danger.*

*"Satan will take control of this earth through the fault of faithless men who, like a black cloud, will darken the clear sky of the republic consecrated to the Most Sacred Heart of my divine Son. This republic, having allowed entry to all the vices, will have to undergo all sorts of chastisements: plagues, famine, war, apostasy, and the loss of souls without number. And to scatter these black clouds blocking the brilliant dawning of the Church, there will be a terrible war in which the blood of priests and of religious will flow.*

*"That night will be so horrible that wickedness will seem triumphant.*

*"Then will come my time: in astounding fashion I shall destroy Satan's pride, casting him beneath my feet, chaining him up in the depth of hell, leaving Church and country freed at last from his cruel tyranny.*

*"The fifth meaning is that men possessing great wealth will look on with indifference while the Church is oppressed, virtue is persecuted, and evil triumphs. They will not use their wealth to fight evil and to reconstruct faith. The people will come to care nothing for the things of God, will absorb the spirit of evil, and will let themselves be swept away by all vices and passions."*

# 32

## Past the Edge of Knowledge

lready the prophecy was unfolding. Not since Roman pagans had the Church been as challenged by the occult. Not since the Dark Ages had there been as much political contention. Venice fought Austria and Russia fought Sweden. Germany was caught in the Thirty Year's War while England, having fought France for a *hundred* years, was now in the mood to go at it with Catholic Spain. Their colonialists, the settlers at Plymouth and Virginia, as well as the French near the Great Lakes and the Spanish in New Mexico, vied over chunks of North America at the same time they battled Native Americans.

In 1625 in Santa Fe a famous statue of Mary was brought from Mexico City via wagon train. It would later serve as protection during a threat by the Comanches. She was known as Our Lady of the Assumption and had a hidden role in establishing America, which was about to be wrested from pagan control in reverse of what was occurring in Europe, where the Christianized continent was in danger of being taken *back* by pagans in the form of secret societies like the Freemasons, who seemed derived from the ancient Templars.

Witchcraft continued to spread and would soon sweep from the Black Forest to Salem.

In Germany a major witch hunt was in progress and at least 3,229 accused sorcerers were killed in the southwest of that troubled nation. The frenzied Germans blamed witches for a dangerous resurgence of plague. At the height of the frenzy and killing, a statue of Mary in the diocese of Freiburg cried and perspired as she urgently reached out to Catholics and non-Catholics alike. In 1614 she had appeared to a young Protestant girl in Nürnberg who converted back to the traditional Church and to a distinguished Hungarian Lutheran visiting Lublin, Poland, who saw Mary in a radiant light and was likewise converted.

Also converted was a Protestant baron named Ernst von Kollonitsch from Hoheneich, Austria, who became a Catholic after the gate on a wall he had built to stop Catholic processions to a Marian church mysteriously flung open when touched by the procession's Cross-bearer.

Around the same time Mary was reported thousands of miles away in the Philippines by a missionary named Franz von Otazo who was being attacked by heathens. Mary told him to *"fear not, I protect you."* Near Goa, India, another missionary named Antonio Andrade was healed by Mary after he was poisoned on his way back from Tibet. In Naples Mary was credited with protecting residents during another eruption of Vesuvius and she was seen in Japan by a persecuted Christian named Nikolaus Kegan Fucinanga.

She was also making her first appearances in North America. The same year as the Quito apparition Mary had shown herself to an imprisoned Jesuit named Jean de Brebeuf near Lake Huron in what would become Canada, and in 1646 she appeared to two Huron Indians who had been imprisoned by the rival Iroquois, helping the converted Hurons find their escape.

In Europe her stepped-up appearances came as the continent was destabilized and as witches admitted to stealing Hosts and performing other sacrileges. During one trial, a witch recounted a *strange inability to recite the Rosary.* So widespread was demonism that it was blamed for everything from cattle deaths and an unusually severe hailstorm in the Würtemberg region (a storm said to have devastated the area as if a battle had been fought) to a bolt of lightning that struck Dornstetten in the Black Forest and reduced twenty-six homes to utter rubble.

"Many are the wonders which have lately happened, as of sudden and strange deaths of perjured persons, strange sights in the air, strange births on the earth, earthquakes, comets, and the like," wrote a seventeenth-century pamphleteer in London.

And while there were no comets now over England—at least not Halley's—a star of some sort, a metaphoric comet, seemed to have opened the abyss (Revelation 9:1). There were very strange reports of ghosts and demons, as in an English alehouse where, during 1641, a group of Catholics encountered what another pamphleteer described in old dialect as "the Devill in the shape of a Monster, all as black as pitch, as big as a great Dogge, which appeared in a most horrid shape, to the affrightment of all the company."

In the region of Avignon, France, a French ambassador named P. Riville reported an equally strange but far larger haunting February 8, 1641, on a mountain in Province where an odd mist had settled. According to the ambassador, three thousand residents were alarmed by the inexplicable noise of trumpets and drums, which were so distinct between 7 and 8 A.M. that the residents ran for their arms. As they prayed in church, a great number swore they heard the voice of commanders and the trumpets of calvary, some deeper, some shriller, all baffling and terrifying, continuing for an hour and a half.

A similar vision of a heavenly armada with great ordnance was also reported over Dublin in December of 1641, and the following year yet another was reported in Northamptonshire, England!

In Turk-held Constantinople it was said that a tempest had raged with "fearful" thunder from August 10 to 13, 1641. It was made all the stranger by the claim of "two comets or blazing stars with double tails, or forked posteriums."

In Italy it was said that between the Vatican and Castel Sant'Angelo—where Michael had once been seen with his sword—there was a shining light and the image of a flaming dragon.

Was this at all related to the three hundred thousand Chinese who died in floods during 1642 in the Land of the Dragon?

Back in England a haunting was experienced over the course of several nights in October of 1649 by a group of surveying commissioners staying near Woodstock in one of the king's manor houses. It was a terrific scare as doors knocked or flung open and sounds like thunder were heard. The noise of invisible chains was also reported, along with flying glass.

Was it all imagination, as the rationalists would have it? Could it all be "logically" explained? Materialism was quickly gaining as the explosion of radical rationalism rather than healthy logic cast doubt or at least confusion on everything. A new cosmology was developing and the devil loved it. It was a cosmology that centered on earth instead of the eternal. Every old truth and every sign, every manifestation of the supernatural, was questioned. There were doubts about the Bible. There was questioning of original sin. The rise of science gave men a nearly drunken belief in their power over nature, and their scoffing at anything supernatural allowed demons to begin operating unseen.

Mathematicians could now calculate probability instead of relying on Lady Luck and astronomers could calculate eclipses, stripping them of their aura, so who needed anything supernatural?

By way of Galileo and Newton, men reached to the stars, discovering sunspots and Jupiter's moons and no longer needing religion to glimpse "heaven" (which now seemed like nothing more than a bunch of desolate planets).

The universe became meaningless and mechanical. It was ruled not by a living force but by mathematical law. And with those new laws men could predict results with a precision that religion and magic could not.

The Renaissance had given birth to the Enlightenment. And whatever "enlightened" men could not explain they simply denied or ignored, especially spirits. Science could explain far less than it pretended, but it had control over much of the media including mass-distribution books, magazines, and newspapers which would purvey their view of a universe devoid of the supernatural. The first advertising was under way in Paris, and soon fashion would go beyond the daring styles of the high Middle Ages and into the stratosphere. Science and not the Church would soon reign as arbiter of cultural affairs and "scientism" would become a human-centric religion. In England and France the idea was already prominent that human reason could create a new earth or "golden age."

What *couldn't* man do? What *couldn't* he explain? Hadn't he already shown the force of gravity and that stars or comets could be explained in mathematical terms?

Yet there were always mysterious little events that slipped past the edge of knowledge. Although the materialists didn't see it, the veil was parting. There was the sound of tempests. Mournful groans. A strange time. A very strange time. Evil spirits and more eruptions of bubonic plague. The fever killed 68,596 in London and a year later, in 1666, a fire burned for a week in that same beleaguered city, consuming markets, wharves, the Guildhall, thirteen thousand homes, and eighty-four churches.

If that wasn't enough woe, the same year saw both the French and Dutch declare war on Great Britain, a nation which was the wellspring for much sophisticated occultism.

The subterranean smoke coming from the door swinging open was denser by the decade. There was a disquiet, an agitation of spirits, throughout Europe. In Germany where Luther had started his revolution, Protestants discarded icons, holy oil, and other tools of exorcism. This, along with the diminishing of the Mass, left many defenseless. Witchcraft was now in the big leagues, leading to the terrible and frenzied witch hunt that didn't end until 1666. The devil not only inspired residents to take up the occult, but then jumped over to the religious side and created a witch-hunting hysteria that would be repeated at Salem.

How the devil liked to confuse things by playing both extremes! Yet witches there were. They clustered in areas like the Black Forest, admitting to poisoning innocent victims in a practice known as *pharmakos*, which was similar to *pharmakeia*, the old Roman term for an abortifacient. They were also linked to the shockingly common practice of infanticide. A song published in 1666 told of forty people who had died in the witch hunt at Reutlingen and exhorted readers to turn to Christ "Who wants to save us from the devil and all evil."

Salvation was in the sacraments and if it looked like good and evil were fighting to a standstill in Europe, there were more encouraging signs in the West, especially in South America in 1651 or 1652 when Mary came to bring Coromoto Indians to baptism. In Guanare, Venezuela, a chief was on his way to a place he was cultivating in the mountains when, near a shallow ravine with a smooth-flowing stream, he and his wife suddenly saw a beautiful woman gliding over the water. The mysterious female spoke to the chief in his own language and told him to go see the missionaries and have them pour water over his head so that he could go to heaven.

Mary wanted the Indians baptized, and naturally the chief listened. Soon his small tribe underwent baptism, but oddly the chief had a change of heart and returned home without receiving the sacrament. On September 8, 1652, he was resting in his hut when the lovely woman appeared again, rebuked him for missing baptism, and asked him to follow the example of his own people. When the chief became angry and reached for his bow, a flash of light temporarily blinded him. Mary disappeared but word of the event led to yet more conversions.

In Auriesville, New York, where three French Jesuits had been slain by hostile natives, a Mohawk woman named Kateri Tekakwitha became Catholic and began an extraordinary life that would lead to her beatification. Kateri developed such a devotion to the Blessed Mother that in 1676 she visited a fabled statue of Mary in Tionnontoguen.

I mention her pilgrimage because it was on the Feast of the Immaculate Conception and it was under that title that the new nation, the United States, would one day be consecrated.

# 33

## Secrets in America and Europe

That Mary was so quietly involved with the development of America would come as a shock to many Catholics and non-Catholics. Yet not only would America one day be consecrated to her, but its oldest city, St. Augustine, Florida, was founded by Franciscans on the feast of her nativity, and as I said, the continent's greatest river, the Mississippi, was originally named by explorers Père Marquette and Louis Joliet the "River of the Immaculate Conception."

Montreal was "Ville-Marie" and Mary's name was also given to the Chesapeake Bay, which originally was known as the "Bay of St. Mary." The first Mass celebrated in Maryland was on the Feast of the Annunciation and the oldest prayer book in the United States, *Garden of the Soul*, contained five holy days of obligation dedicated to Our Lady. Up north, Canada was also consecrated to her.

While secularization would later erase her role, the early French and Spanish explorers had felt they were on a mission for the Blessed Mother. She was on the move and we'll see why in a short time but first, quickly back to Europe, where Mary's apparitions were truly awesome throughout the century—before, during, and after the wars and witch hunts and settling of America. She was credited with halting plague in dozens of places—Amberg, Passau, Lauffen—and after she rescued Vienna, Emperor Leopold I raised a baroque monument showing a woman holding the Cross over a defeated hag.

In Naples Mary warned the world that without penance there would be more scourges and in Spain she asked for the lighting of a "plague candle." In Paris miracles were flowing from a shrine dedicated to Our Lady of Victories and throughout the Church she was now known as "mediatrix," a title that like "co-redemptress" went back many centuries. The designation was now in wide use, opening the route to more grace and joining the declaration in Ireland of a holy day for the Immaculate Conception.

Cures abounded at the Belgian shrine of LaSarte and Pope Urban VIII, usually skeptical about miracles, sought Mary's help at Genazzano after reviewing the impressive documentation. Rumors floated of an apparition in Holland, while at Lyons Our Lady of Fourvière was invoked during a bubonic outbreak in 1643. "Instantly," said a chronicler, "all trace of pestilence vanished."

I could never recount or even synopsize all the miracles. On Saturdays or feast days of Our Lady there were inexplicable lights on a knoll along the Danube. In Elend, Germany, an apparition thought to be Mary came from the woods and freed a wagon stuck in snow. She was described as "a female form like the silver moon when she appears above the peaks of the mountains ... slender as the fir tree ... rosy as the early dawn."

Angels were heard for several hours at a shrine in Dieburg on the eve of All Saints' Day, and three years later Mary appeared to a girl named Eva in Mühlberg, interceding for Germany in a special way. A miraculous spring was discovered at a shrine in Albendorf and the voice of Mary predicted that a great prince would become ill but would find a cure when he built a monastery she wanted. This happened to Prince Ferdinand von Fürstenberg of Neuhaus Castle, who was healed after granting her wish.

In Wemding a Protestant was cured after praying before a wood-carved bust of the Virgin that later took on the appearance of a live person, and in München the eyes of a Sorrowful Mother image were seen to move, indicating her nearly desperate concern for the nation which, due to famine, war, and plague (and in keeping with Revelation 6:8), had seen its population shrink from seventeen million in 1618 to eight million by the middle part of the 1600s.

In the Black Forest at Rottweil in 1643 both Catholics and Protestants saw the colors on a statue change and the face reflect grief and sadness during a siege by French and Swedish forces. In Ireland during the persecution by Oliver Cromwell, a priest named John Turner saw a most beautiful woman ascending to the sky five miles from Wexford, where, unknown to him, Catholics were being slaughtered. Mary was also seen during the siege of Limerick and on March 17, 1697, thousands praying before an image that had been sent from Ireland to Győr, Hungary, watched for three hours as the image shed tears and blood.

The Győr case was noteworthy because witnesses included not just rabbis and Protestant ministers but the bishop, the city's mayor, and all the councilmen. Hungarians were sure this image had saved them from the Turks and other disasters. As before, Mary's apparitions were joined by reports of the Archangel Michael. He was seen at Old Bayly in England, while on a mountain in the French Alps not far from Grenoble, a seventeen-year-old shepherdess reported the apparition of St. Maurice. The saint pointed to a spring she had never before seen and told her to take her sheep the next day to graze closer to the area known as St. Etienne, where the girl, Benoîte Rencurel, saw a light coming from a grotto in a hollow of rock called Roche-aux-Fours and beheld a beautiful woman smiling at her.

The woman held Jesus and appeared for two months before Benoîte, prodded by a local magistrate, asked the apparition who she was. *"I am Mary, the mother of Jesus, and it is the will of my Son that I should be honored in this parish,"* she said, directing Benoîte to an old, ruined chapel in nearby Le Laus. *"I have requested Le Laus from my divine Son and He has given it to me. This church will be built in His honor and mine. Many sinners will be converted here."*

The doubts of Church officials were erased when a local woman regained use of her long-crippled limbs while worshiping there.

At Vinay, France, an event documented by a bishop's inquiry included the incredible story of a Calvinist named Pierre Port-Combet. Aggravated that Catholics had suspended work to commemorate the Feast of the Annunciation, Combet taunted them by engaging in manual labor, pruning a willow at the most conspicuous spot along the processional route.

He stopped in his tracks and was horrified when blood began to ooze from the bark. The tree was bleeding! For a moment Combet thought he'd injured himself until he jabbed the tree several more times and watched blood come from the wood. His wife and others witnessed the prodigy, which culminated on March 25, 1656, with Combet's sighting of a lady clothed in white and wearing a blue mantle and a black crepe veil that partly hid her face. She warned that he would die soon and risked hell, but he converted before his death.

Another case of blood occurred in Attersee, Austria, where a Protestant woman hit an image of Mary with a hatchet and a streak appeared on both the head of the Infant and Mary's neck.

In Siluva, Lithuania, where Protestants had confiscated Church property, the Virgin had been seen with Child on a rock. During the 1600s, when a liberalized law allowed Catholics to repossess the property, they couldn't find their records, which had been stored in a chest. Such documents were necessary to reclaim the land and that's when Mary was seen by young shepherds at the place of the church. One of them ran to tell Mikola Fiera, a local Calvinist teacher, who immediately denounced the apparition as a deception of the devil.

The next day Fiera went to the site and ridiculed a crowd gathered there, castigating them for believing the fantasies of children. In the middle of his harangue Mary appeared again on the rock. All saw her, including Fiera. "Why are you weeping?" asked the stunned teacher.

*"Formerly in this place my Son was adored and honored, but now all that the people do is seed and cultivate the land,"* she responded, holding Jesus.

The Blessed Woman disappeared, but when a local blind man heard about the apparition, he recalled the chest and when he went to the rock his sight returned. He was able to indicate where the chest had been buried—allowing the Catholics to regain the land—and in the chest was an image of Mary holding Christ just as she held the Infant in the apparition.

Many were the cases in Austria and Germany of hidden or forgotten shrines found on hills or in meadows or in forests. I could fill a book the size of this one with just these cases. Her statues were found in oak stumps and tree hollows. Legend related that during the Thirty Years' War a statue was tossed several times by Swedes into a village pond, but each time it was found back at its place in the church. There was also an image tossed into the Main River during the plundering of a chapel in Miltenberg but recovered when a local fisherman named George Ebert observed a mysterious brightness on the water. Reaching with his net, he found the light coming from a submerged statue of Mary. The accounts continued. Accounts of miraculous cures were reported, a myraid of stories converning Turks or Protestants whose attempts to ruin images were strangely thwarted. At a chapel in Luxembourg, there was a list of thirty-three authenticated healings.

The intervention in Austria was phenomenal. It was the hot spot of the 1600s. There was the complete range of Mary's miracles. None were more interesting than in Graz where an image of Mary supernaturally appeared on canvas stored by an artist named Pietro Giovanni de Pomis. As in Spain, there were also strange ghostly processions of white-clad figures and many cases of curative springs.

In 1667 a picture of Mary suddenly loosed itself from a wall, fell nearly to the floor, but before it hit raised itself back up to its former position as a Catholic priest and a Lutheran named Elias Seltenschlag ("Oh, you make entirely too much of your Mary!") were debating about her in Schwadorf. The phenomenon was said to have repeated itself a second time to forestall the excuse of hallucination.

Also confirmed was the story near Innsbruck of a farmer's wife who on

December 25, 1685, heard a weeping in her room. After searching she found behind a chest a long-forgotten picture of Mary with Jesus. It was dusty but streaked with tears that continued to flow even after it was wiped with a cloth. Church authorities investigated and deemed the case miraculous, as they did a number of similar events of this time period.

While it wasn't the usual custom to form ecclesiastical commissions except in special cases, the placement of miraculous images in churches or the construction of chapels, which occurred in the large majority of cases I've mentioned, was *ipso facto* Church approval. In Hungary the name of a village called "Pocz" was changed to "Mariapocz" after the bishop investigated the claim of more tears in 1696. The phenomena there and elsewhere were clearly associated with last-ditch efforts by the diminished Turks to menace parts of Europe. The following year, a spring with alleged healing qualities burst forth under the altar of a church in Bildstein, which had been built sixty-eight years before to commemorate a place where there had been both a venerated image and an associated apparition.

Chapels were illuminated by inexplicable lights or ghostly torches. Such was the history deep inside Ukraine at the monastery of Pochaiv, where the pillar of fire had been witnessed by shepherds in the twelfth century. There Mary was seen again in 1675 when the monastery was attacked by Turks. The sky parted to reveal her and a host of angels. The same thing happened at Czestochowa when Swedes had attacked in 1655. Mary intervened to help the sanctuary guards defeat them. So significant was the victory that Our Lady of Czestochowa was renamed "Queen of Poland."

When a vicious storm with high winds, ominous black clouds and vivid lightning attacked Ardesio, Italy, Mary seated on a golden chair with the Child appeared in a living tableau to a couple of young girls who were praying in their house. At that instant the storm stopped. The happening was witnessed by others in the village and repeated itself a few days later, when this time Christ appeared on the Cross with a circle of stars around His head. After an ecclesiastical investigation, the feast day of this happening was declared to be June 24 and Church officials approved construction of a new church.

When I visited Saragossa, I noted that it was during the amazing seventeenth century that an inconceivable and yet Church-documented miracle was said to have happened to a twenty-three-year-old man named M.J. Pellicer Blasco. Blasco's right leg had been amputated after a wagon ran over it. As a result he was reduced to begging in front of the church, which was soon built into a grand basilica.

On March 29, 1640, Blasco dreamt that he was in the chapel dedicated to Our Lady of the Pillar and that the Blessed Mother had restored his leg. When Blasco woke—and this was of course the incredible part—his missing leg had regenerated.

It seemed incredible to the point of the outlandish except that the case had been closely documented by authorities. Many testified they'd seen the one-legged man begging in front of the church on innumerable occasions and that the leg had been amputated in 1637 at Grace Hospital in Saragossa by surgeons named J. Estanga and D. Millaruelo and buried by an assistant named J.L. Garcia.

At a hearing initiated by the city government, twenty-five witnesses presented formal testimony and on April 27, 1641, Archbishop P. Apolaza formally declared in favor of the miracle.

Philip IV received Blasco in Madrid and Pope Urban VIII was notified.

From 1641 onward, reports of the Blasco miracle circulated in Spanish, Latin, and other languages throughout Europe. These were prodigies that would have been at home in the Bible. At Verviers, Belgium, on September 18, 1692, a sandstone statue of Mary and Jesus seemed to change during an earthquake, not as it would if shaken by the tremors, but rather in the way Jesus as a youngster turned to His mother and clung to her.

So tangible was Mary's involvement that the state of New York was consecrated to her even before it was known as "New York."

In a short time one of the first parishes in the colonies would be dedicated to her in Philadelphia.

Stunning was the claim in the Mexican village of San Juan Bautista Mezquititlan that a "dead" child had suddenly stirred in her burial shroud and come to life when she was placed before a statue depicting the Immaculate Conception.

Stunning too was a case in Antipolo, Philippines, where an image of Mary disappeared from the church on two occasions. Each time it was relocated in the branches of a tipulo tree, which was then cut and its trunk made into a pedestal for the statue. Mary obviously wanted that spot for unknown reasons.

Elsewhere images wept or were miraculously restored.

There were also conversions, none more exceptional than that of a Moroccan sultan who in 1660 had heard an apparition of Mary tell him to leave the faith of Mohammed and become a Catholic, which he did, making a pilgrimage to Rome instead of Mecca.

# 34

## Born in Hell

The love and humility of Mary are what won converts, along with faith. They were secrets that wove in and out of each other like needlepoint. Humility was an aspect of love because love led to selflessness and in its turn selflessness led to sharing the sufferings, glory, and faith—the beauty—of Christ.

Deep secrets. The key to happiness. The message of Mary. No grand prophecies were as powerful. Mary came on a cloud. She did not usually stand on the earth. That meant we were not to root ourselves in the world. It meant detachment from self. A new secret here: Mary was indicating that in addition to humility a key to inner tranquillity—peace—was detachment from self. Abandonment. It was the highest phase of humility. She demonstrated it every time. She showed it at every legitimate apparition. She was selfless and as a result majestic and tranquil. That little secret was so powerful it spoke louder than any literature, louder than the rising European philosophers, louder than Locke and Rousseau and Voltaire: When a person detached from ego, when all thought and action were dedicated to Christ, serenity was the surprising result. A person could go through life seeking every possible means of peace and never find it unless he or she lost *self*.

Sometimes that meant suffering. Christ gave each of His followers a cross. Suffering was a ticket to heaven, the test of life, which was itself one *constant* test!

But the Blessed Mother was always there and, as Margaret Mary Alacoque of the Sacred Heart revelations said, Mary never refused her encouragement. She never refused her help. The tougher the times and the more meaningful the times, the more conspicuous Mother Mary was. For eighteen centuries there had been a buildup. Now chapter 12 of Revelation was manifesting, prefaced by the signs of thunder, quakes, and hail. My, had there been thunder! And quakes: the seventeenth century had seen more than its share, with three hundred thousand dying in Calcutta, another major one in Hokkaido, Japan, as well as quakes in Quito, Catania, and Lisbon.

It was the thick of spiritual conflict. The devil had always been around, but the abyss, the earth, continued to open. Locusts were everywhere. In 1679 there had been a report from Lemster, England, of several people who claimed to have seen "a most strange and prodigious opening of the earth" and a form of "black mournful colors" rising from the ground. Was it real or metaphor? Seers expected a great quake as in Revelation 11:13 and some correctly saw that "quake" as a coming revolution.

There would be revolution. There would be many forms of disturbance. Mary would counter with silence and the force of faith. She spoke through her actions. She spoke through the shedding of tears. That was *her* prophecy and that was how she punctuated events. Her very coming was a warning. On August 5, 1715, pilgrims pressed into Pötsch, Hungary, to see a weeping picture of the Virgin, while around the very same time crying or bleeding pictures were also seen in Szent-Antal, Sajopálfalva, and other Hungarian cities as that region faced a final battle with the Turks, who had destroyed sanctuaries like Our Lady of the Golden Fountain.

If hers was a mantle of protection—which indeed it was, for in the end the Turks were repelled—it operated best when a person simply acknowledged her. She wanted an invitation. She honored free will. Most often her signs were low-key, not just lacrimation, but those precious little instances when she quietly offered herself by leaving an image in a dry lake bed or in a bush. If there was enough faith, the folks would see the image move or smile or exude fragrance. They would see images survive flood and fire and, in one case, a volcano. They would witness cases where statues mysteriously moved themselves. In Maria-Steinbach, Germany, in 1733, a statue emanated light to the chapel ceiling and changed shape and color before at least five hundred sworn witnesses.

There were also mysterious strangers who sounded like angels. In 1720 two young men coming from Acapulco, Mexico, had stopped for lodging at a small hostelry in Tlaltenango. The men were described as so unusually genteel and attractive they created a stir in the pueblo. They brought a richly decorated box or casket and on leaving asked a woman named Doña Agustina Andrade to take care of it until they returned.

They never did. Days, weeks, and then two months passed with no sign of the travelers. One night Doña Agustina heard music from the room where she kept the box. Entering she saw rays of light and smelled what seemed like an exotic perfume. When representatives of both the Church and crown arrived to investigate, they too smelled the fragrance and saw soft rays of light coming from the box despite shutting all sources of natural illumination. When they opened the chest, the astonished onlookers saw a statue of Mary in a blue cloak and rose tunic.

Mary also appeared to a future bishop named Alphonsus de Liguori who was soon to write a classic called *The Glories of Mary*, and there was a case in Turin where a seer known as Blessed Mary of the Angels had daily ecstasies, although she also had fierce struggles with demons. For eight months she had apparitions of spirits that beat her and sent temptations against faith, hope, and chastity. Faith was a target because it was the secret weapon. With faith, devils of any sort could be cast off. Faith elevated the person above attack.

And attacks there were. During the summer of 1780, a miner searching for passage through the mountains east of Copiapó, Chile, sought refuge in a cave with his muleteers when a tremendous storm hit the area. They began to pray in the midst of the lightning, the roar of thunder, and the howling wind. A particularly vivid bolt shattered the sky and the miner, Mariano Caro Inca, saw what seemed like the pale face of a small woman outlined momentarily among the rocky crags across from the cave. The next morning when Caro and his men investigated, on a flat stone they found the statue of a beautiful lady with a child in her arms. It was about eight inches high and its miraculous cures were soon to make it famous.

Another venerated statue was at the shrine of Lujan near Buenos Aires, Argentina. "On August 28, 1780, the inhabitants of Lujan were put into panic by the news of what they had long dreaded, that a huge army of ferocious Indians was sweeping the plains, massacring all in their path and advancing rapidly on the town," wrote Marian historian H.M. Gillett. "Utterly defenseless, the people fled to the shrine and in a body put their whole trust in their special Protectress. Suddenly, even as they prayed, a dense and unexpected fog rolled up and enveloped the town so that the savage hordes lost their way and passed by in another direction."

In North America there were rumors of a vision to none other than George Washington. Whether authentic and if so whether the figure he saw was the Virgin are two chief matters that will probably never be answered, but it's difficult to ignore the report in volume 4, number 12 of an old nineteenth-century veterans publication known as the *National Tribune,* now *Stars and Stripes.* A very old man named Anthony Sherman was quoted as relating a happening in 1777 during the retreat to Valley Forge. It was said that as the chilly wind murmured through leafless trees, Washington, who was known to wander alone praying, spent nearly the entire afternoon in his quarters, allowing no interruptions. "When he came out, I noticed that his face was a shade paler than usual, and there seemed to be something on his mind of more than ordinary importance," claimed Sherman, who reputedly fought alongside Washington.

Returning just after dusk, he dispatched an orderly to the quarters of the officer I mention who was presently in attendance. After a preliminary conversation of about half an hour, Washington, gazing upon his companion with that strange look of dignity which he alone could command, said to the latter: "I do not know whether it is owing to the anxiety of my mind, or what, but this afternoon as I was sitting at this table engaged in preparing a dispatch, something seemed to disturb me. Looking up, I beheld standing opposite me a singularly beautiful female. So astonished was I, for I had given strict order not to be disturbed, that it was some moments before I found language to inquire into the cause of her presence. A second, third, and even a fourth time did I repeat my question, but received no answer from my mysterious visitor except a slight raising of her eyes. By this time I felt strange sensations spreading through me. I would have risen but the riveted gaze of the being before me rendered volition impossible. I assayed once more to address her, but my tongue had become useless. Even thought itself had become paralyzed. A new influence, mysterious, potent, irresistible, took possession of me. All I could do was to gaze steadily, vacantly at my unknown visitant."

While there was plenty of room for skepticism (it was claimed Sherman remembered all this at the age of ninety-nine), and while the Washington account did not have the same documentation as many similar encounters by bishops, popes, or secular leaders in Europe, there was no doubt that such a legend was in print by 1880 if not before.

"Gradually the surrounding atmosphere seemed as though becoming filled with sensations, and luminous," Washington was quoted as saying. "Everything about me seemed to rarify, the mysterious visitor herself becoming more airy and yet more distinct to my sight than before. I now began to feel as one dying, or rather to experience the sensations which I have sometimes imagined accompany dissolution. I did not think, I did not reason, I did not move; all were alike impossible."

It was then that Washington was said to have heard a voice. *"Son of the*

*Republic, look and learn,"* said the apparitional woman, extending an arm eastward.

It was claimed Washington then beheld a white vapor that gradually dissipated, revealing "all the countries of the world," and saw a cloud rise from Europe and America, a cloud that moved westward.

Storm clouds. More thunder. If the legend was fiction, it was brilliant in capturing the obscure characteristics of legitimate apparitions. Others too saw thick rising vapors as the Revolution in America was followed by the French Revolution.

This was a huge moment in both French and world history. It was the culmination of rationalism. It was the crest of the Enlightenment. And it struck with hurricane force. In 1789 twelve hundred deputies arrived in Versailles from every part of France to solve a financial crisis. Once gathered, they decided the country needed radical change, which meant doing away with all privileges due to birth and giving power to the middle class. The deputies also stood for complete economic freedom. And while many of the goals were admirable and certainly drew popular support, the uprising soon turned bloody. In the way that Satan twists many things that start out noble, soon the liberals focused their wrath on the Church and began a horrifying persecution under the guise of rationalistic progress. Unlike the American Revolution, the French one was not against a foreign oppressor; it was against God. It was the extreme opposite of humility, the paragon of arrogance.

Rationalism had reached such an extreme that Catholicism was outlawed and thirty thousand to forty thousand French priests were driven from their native cities, hounded into hiding or slaughtered for not agreeing to declare the state instead of Rome the ultimate authority.

It was the Reign of Terror. The first slaughter of clerics occurred in Paris, where 220 priests and several bishops lost their lives. Many followed elsewhere. At Orange nuns imprisoned for "fanaticism and superstition" were brought to the guillotine and in the course of a few short years virtually every church in France was boarded up, destroyed, or turned into a "temple of reason."

"The Revolution began to take on the character of a religion in itself," wrote Bokenkotter. "Some of the patriotic ceremonies featured sacred oaths and sacred trees, and some of the localities substituted patriotic names for the religious names of the streets. Compiègne replaced the names of the saints with revolutionary heroes, as did many others. Infants were given 'un-Christian' baptismal names. Church bells and chalices were seized and melted."

All religious holidays were canceled, and all references to the birth of Christ were dropped by establishing a new era that started with the revolutionary republic in 1792. The Christian Sunday was suppressed by a new calendar that epitomized the cult of reason and reverence for an idealized nature that spread the seeds of atheism and globalism.

Many of the French shrines, many of the miraculous sites, many of the places where Mary had appeared in apparition, caused statue miracles, or healed the sick, where she had shown miraculous springs or rescued the destitute, where she had touched earth with the power of heaven, were desecrated, sullied, and destroyed. On August 30, 1792, the last Catholic Mass was celebrated at Fourvière, and the following year revolutionists invaded Chartres and snipped a large piece from an ancient and famous relic thought to be part of Mary's actual veil. They took it for "scientific" review, and to their disappointment, the analysis indicated that the veil might be authentic, perhaps two thousand years old. While the veil was eventually placed back in its case, the rest of Chartres was plundered, while in Cherbourg the sanctuary known as Our Lady of the Vow, where an empress caught in a tempest had been saved by Mary, was similarly demolished.

A chapel housing a miraculous statue in Luxembourg was devastated, and the seventh-century image that had arrived at Boulogne after the mysterious ship carried it to port was seized by revolutionary thieves and reduced to ashes.

Clairefountaine was also burned.

If there were legitimate points to the revolution, as there are often legitimate beginnings to things that turn evil, in the final analysis the revolution was born in hell. At the Cathedral of Notre Dame an actress was enthroned as the Goddess of Reason, and the same day a decree closed all churches in Lyons, where a donkey decorated in priestly insignia was made to trample on a Crucifix and drink from a chalice. "Even yet more horrible profanities were in preparation when they were put a stop to by what the miscreants themselves seem to have felt a preternatural sign of the divine displeasure," wrote James Northcote. "The sky suddenly darkened and such a terrific storm burst over the heads of the infamous assembly that with one accord they dispersed and fled from the spot in terror."

# 35

## Catherine's Secret

The signs continued to rumble and grow in fury. It was starting to be a repeat of medieval warnings. In 1807 lightning made a direct hit on a wood statue inside a convent in Guadalajara. While the Christ Child survived in His mother's arms, it was clearly an omen.

So were other occurrences. In Italy the rise of Napoleon and his preparation to seize the Papal States was presaged not only by tear-filled images but also oddly moving ones. In Rome a picture of the Mother of Mercy over an arch near the Piazza Santi Apostoli seemed to open and close its eyes. The old image, almost unrecognizable with age, suddenly showed distinct features and returned to its ancient beauty. "In the course of the same day the same supernatural appearance was observed in six other pictures, either in the streets or in churches, in different parts of the city," noted James Northcote.

It was a spiritual gyration and in America the rumblings, the stirrings, were literal. In 1811 and 1812 at New Madrid, Missouri, there were a series of quakes so powerful that the River of the Immaculate Conception, now known as the Mississippi, briefly flowed *backward*. Downstream in New Orleans a statue kept by Ursuline nuns was the focus. The statue was credited with a decisive victory during the battle over New Orleans, when a force of six thousand Americans under General Andrew Jackson defeated a British force of at least fifteen thousand.

"From the windows of their convent the Ursulines could see the smoke rising from the battlefield, and could hear the report of guns and the thunder of cannon," wrote historian William J. Walsh. "Jackson had sworn that, should he be vanquished, the enemy would find New Orleans a heap of ruin. In order to help in averting this imminent danger, the Ursuline chapel was continually thronged with pious ladies, all weeping and praying at the foot of the holy statue, which was placed on the high altar.... Just at Holy Communion a courier entered the chapel to announce glad tidings of the enemy's defeat.... Nobody could reasonably doubt of heaven's intervention on this occasion through the intercession of Our Lady of Prompt Succor. Jackson himself, the hero of the day, did not hesitate to admit of divine interposition in his favor; and in his first proclamation to the army, he said, 'By the blessing of heaven, directing the valor of the troops under my command, one of the most brilliant victories in the annals of war was obtained.'"

And with it was yet another sign that the spiritual conflict, the grinding of heavenly tectonic plates, was real and growing. While the revolution had simmered down and Napoleon was soon out of power, the seeds of godless humanism were sprouting. France was the spiritual battlefield. There were apparitions in Bordeaux, Grandchamps, and Brittany, then Bordeaux again, and in 1830 a statue at the Cathedral of Notre Dame wept so profusely a caretaker had to wrap it with a towel.

Something big was in the wind. It was getting to be crunch time again. In 1830, the same year as the crying statue, Mary appeared in the famous Miraculous Medal apparitions to Catherine Labouré in a Paris chapel at 140 Rue du Bac, saying, *"The times are evil. Misfortunes will fall upon France. The throne will be overthrown. The entire world will be overcome by evils of all kinds.* (At this point Mary looked very distressed.) *But come to the foot of the altar. There graces will be shed upon all, great and small, who ask for them.*

*"My child, the Cross will be treated with contempt,"* Mary went on. *"They will hurl it to the ground. Blood will flow. They will open up again the side of Our Lord. The streets will run with blood. Monsignor the Archbishop will be stripped of his garments.* (Now her face was in such anguish that she could hardly speak.) *My child, the whole world will be in sadness."*

It was true. An archbishop would be killed. The world would grow dark. The Medieval Chastisement threatened to repeat itself. But Mary didn't come to scare. She gave her messages with elegance. She was described as of average height and clothed with white array in a style called *"à la Vierge."* She wore a high neck and plain sleeves, with a veil that flowed over her head and fell to the floor. Under the veil her hair was in coils and bound with a fillet ornamented with lace. Her feet rested on a large white globe and she was stepping on a green serpent with yellow spots. "Her eyes were now raised to heaven, now lowered," recalled Catherine of an apparition on November 27, 1830.

Her face was of such beauty that I could not describe it. All at once I saw rings on her fingers, three rings to each finger, the largest one near the base of the finger, one of medium size in the middle, the smallest one at the tip. Each ring was set with gems, some more beautiful than others. The larger gems emitted great rays and the smaller gems, smaller rays. The rays bursting from all sides flooded the base, so that I could no longer see the feet of the Blessed Virgin. At this moment, while I was contemplating her, the Blessed Virgin lowered her eyes and looked at me. I heard a voice speaking these words: *"This globe that you see represents the whole world, especially France, and each person in particular."*

Mary showed Catherine an image of the Sacred Heart wrapped in piercing thorns and her own heart punctured by a sword. Then the Blessed Mother extended her radiant hands, saying, *"Behold the symbol of graces I shed upon those who ask me for them.*" An oval-shaped frame formed around her and on it were the words, *"O Mary, conceived without sin, pray for us who have recourse to you!"* She was also seen with twelve stars around her head as in Revelation 12:1. She instructed Catherine to strike a medal of her pose. She had also held a smaller globe with a cross on top and her lips moved in prayer while offering it to Jesus. "I did not hear but understood that she was praying for the whole world," said Catherine, adding that Mary held the globe "close to her merciful heart contemplating it with ineffable tenderness." At the moment that Mary pressed the globe to her chest, "light from diamonds, carbuncles, and other precious stones radiated from her maternal hands."

This information Catherine secretly gave to her confessor and then hid herself in a convent, withdrawing totally from the world and working as a lowly laundress for the infirm and aged even while countless medals circulated, twenty million pressed in a ten-year period by one Paris firm alone. For forty-six years Catherine kept it secret that she was the Miraculous Medal seer, until she had to reveal herself just before dying in order to have another request by the Virgin, this one for a particular statue, fulfilled.

The medal went on to become one of only three sacramentals to be liturgically honored, sharing that station with the brown scapular and the rosary. As an English bishop noted, "Except for the Holy Cross, no other Christian symbol was ever so widely multiplied, or was ever the instrument of so many marvelous results." Among the miracles was that of an obstinate Jewish atheist, a wealthy lawyer and banker named Alphonse Ratisbonne, who detested Christianity. He wore one of the medals to humor a friend or as sort of a dare but then himself experienced an apparition of Mary as he was waiting for his friend at the Church of Sant'Andrea in Rome. "I was in the church only a minute or two when a great feeling of distress gripped me," the French atheist later recounted. "I glanced round and the whole building seemed to have disappeared except for one chapel and there, in the midst of a blaze of light above the altar, stood the

Blessed Virgin as she is seen on the Miraculous Medal. I advanced towards her. She made a sign to me to kneel down and then seemed to say, *'That is right.'''*

Ratisbonne found it hard to verbalize much else, but did comment that as he tried to raise his eyes to the Virgin's face he couldn't look higher than her hands. "I cannot tell in words of the mercy and generosity I felt expressed in those hands," he said, adding that in those moments he understood and accepted the truth of traditional Christianity. Soon after he was not only baptized but gave up his life as a wealthy businessman to become a Jesuit priest. His conversion was so impressive it was investigated by an ecclesiastical tribunal that declared the perfect and instantaneous conversion "a true and signal miracle."

Such good fruit confirmed the authenticity of Catherine's apparitions, but mysteries about them remain. We don't know if the Blessed Mother confided secrets to Catherine. She almost certainly did. The motif of her apparitions in the nineteenth and twentieth centuries would often include confidential messages about the personal life of the seer, the Church's condition, or the world. Sometimes the secrets involved all three. At the very least, Catherine was told a personal secret concerning her own death, for she knew when it was impending.

While Mary's most important secrets, the secrets to life on earth, involved the practice of faith, humility, and love, there were always hidden meanings to Mary's visitations and often the message was in their moment. The secret was in the timing and location. Catherine's apparitions took place as Charles Darwin was collecting research for his theory of evolution and as the works of Hegel were setting the stage for Karl Marx. Only those who didn't know the ways of heaven would consider such events to be coincidence.

There was a great acceleration in apparitions around the world, including America, as mankind (intoxicated with new inventions like the steamboat and railroads) burrowed yet deeper into materialism. There was the amazing appearance by Mary in a tepee in Montana to a young Flathead Indian boy who saw her in a way that also resembled the Miraculous Medal (she appeared with a star over her head and a serpent under her feet and arrayed with incredible light), while in France two youngsters named Maximin Giraud and Mélanie Mathieu saw her sitting and weeping on a huge mountain in the French Alps just above LaSalette, where on September 19, 1846, she confided a secret to each visionary and also warned that a "great famine" was coming.

That very year was marked not only by crop shortages in France but by the great Irish potato famine, which took a million lives during the 1840s.

Mary warned that children under seven years of age would be seized with trembling and die in their parents' arm, and sure enough, the famine was accompanied by recurring epidemics of typhus, dysentery, and small-pox which caused children to die as she predicted. Such disease repeated with what one historian called "almost apocalyptic violence."

Those were the *known* predictions. There were also ones that were *not* known, secrets on a level not previously reported and first indicated within a week of the apparition, when Maximin was interviewed by the curé of Corps. Asked if there was anything else related by Mary, Maximin said, "Yes, there is something, but the Holy Virgin has forbidden me to tell it." It was learned that after Mary had enumerated various community sins, including using the Name of Jesus in vain and working on Sundays, and after she forecast the famine (as well as lesser crop problems), she had spoken to each seer individually. Although Mélanie could see her lips move, she could hear nothing of what she was saying to Maximin and Maximin could hear nothing as Mary confided the secret to Mélanie.

According to Sandra L. Zimdars-Swartz, a professor who has closely studied the situation, when asked by Marquise de Monteyard, sister of the bishop of Moulins, if he could say whether his secret was fortunate or unfortunate, Maximin's face took on an "ineffable" expression and in a lowered tone he said, "Ah, it is good fortune." When further prodded whether the secret would someday be known by everyone, the boy cryptically replied, "Yes, when all men will be judged." Indications that the two secrets pertained not just to the seers personally but to the public at large were first reported by a local lawyer named Armand Dumanoir who knew the seers and commented that each child had been given a secret "which appears to consist in the announcement of a great event, fortunate for some, unfortunate for others." Further attempts at gleaning information failed as the seers showed an extraordinary skill at deflecting inquiries with reserved, precise, and firm answers. In other words, these unsophisticated children were able to outmaneuver the most clever of interrogators.

But in 1851, five years after their apparition, the situation changed. Maximin and Mélanie were asked by a representative of Bishop Philibert de Bruillard of Grenoble if they would agree to write down their secrets and send them in a sealed envelope to Pope Pius IX. Both agreed despite those years of steadfast refusal, indicating they had since received supernatural signs—in the case of Mélanie, possibly an apparition—that gave them the green light. Maximin was taken to a school in Rondeau and seated at a desk with pen and paper, writing his secret as two men, one named Canon de Taxis, the other a local engineer, looked on. Maximin's secret consisted of seven numbered paragraphs. At one point he was ordered to copy it more neatly. While doing so, he requested the spelling of the word "pontiff." The secret was then sealed in an envelope as promised.

Mélanie's turn came the next day. She was more hesitant, even weeping, but finally sat down and penned a secret that was longer than Maximin's. Under equally watchful eyes she wrote calmly and seriously for an hour without pause, covering three pages of narrow-lined notepaper. Without looking it over, she sealed her secret in an envelope and addressed it to "His Holiness Pius IX in Rome." A few hours later she realized she had made a mistake in writing that two events would take place on a certain date when actually they were to occur on separate dates. So she requested and was allowed to rewrite the secret. Again she did so steadily, pausing only to ask for the meaning of the word "infallibly" and the spelling of "Antichrist" and "corrupt." At her request the secret was previewed by Bishop Bruillard, who emerged from reading it moved to tears. It was then sealed, and both secrets were taken to Pius IX. A believer in Mary's intercession, (he believed she had once healed him of epilepsy), Pius reflected great emotion as he read the prophecies. His lips tightened and his face reportedly flushed. When he finished he said in a grave voice, "I must read these letters again at my leisure. There are scourges that menace France, but Germany, Italy, all Europe is culpable and merits chastisements." When asked for further information by the Superior of the Missionaries of Our Lady of LaSalette, Pius replied, "So you want to know the secrets of LaSalette? Well, here they are: unless you repent you will perish."

The nuncio to Paris, Cardinal Nicolò Fornari, was more direct. "I am terrified," he said, "of these prodigies; we have everything that is needed in our religion for the conversion of sinners; and when heaven employs such means, the evil must be very great."

The question now was whether the Church and society were going to *use* the means God had granted them or whether humanity would slide toward some sort of oblivion, into a series of chastisements like those in the Roman Empire, which had seen quakes and fire and centuries of attacks until finally the entire old order had been destroyed. Many rumors circulated about the contents of the secrets, and rumors, false rumors, spread that Catherine Labouré had come to LaSalette on pilgrimage and received a revelation about the Second Coming. It was also said a second nun from Soissons had an apparition and likewise a tantalizing secret as confidential messages became a mainstay of Marian apparitions.

Away from LaSalette the action was also hot and heavy. In Paris a nun named Sister Justine Bisqueyburu who soon promoted the Green Scapular claimed revelations during an experience at Rue du Bac while a priest at Our Lady of the Victories in that same city had heard a voice say, *"Consecrate your parish to the Most Holy and Immaculate Heart of Mary."*

As if in further warning, in Germany lights were seen flashing in and around a chapel and on May 12, 1848, Johann Stichlmayer saw Mary in a Bavarian pasture sitting and weeping as she had at LaSalette. Eventually she was said to have appeared to at least fifty-six people in Obermauerbach, where she prophesied plague and warfare. *"I can no longer hold back the punishments of God,"* was the virtually constant refrain.

Two years later there was a noteworthy apparition involving the wife of a Protestant officer from France who claimed she saw the Virgin at the Vatican!

That same year Mary also appeared in Lichen, Poland, with dramatic messages. She begged the people to pray the Rosary and predicted a bloody and worldwide conflict if they didn't. She said millions would die in epidemics and bloodshed.

The Lichen messages were interesting because they met with official Church acknowledgment. They were also interesting because very shortly, in 1854 and 1855, 152,000 starved in France and cholera was killing thousands. Between 1849 and 1854 up to 750,000 died throughout Europe, including now Russia.

This was at the same time that Karl Marx was meeting Friedrich Engels in Paris. Marx captured the spirit of the times when he penned a poem called *Oulanem* which vowed in chilling and demonic fashion that "soon I shall embrace eternity to my breast, and soon I shall howl gigantic curses on mankind."

# 36

---

## *Borrowed Time*

In a grotto at the other end of the country, along the River Gave, the reply from heaven was a lady who emerged from a gold-colored cloud after the sound of a storm.

*"I am the Immaculate Conception,"* she said, not as an airy or ghostly image, not as a dream-vision, but as a delicate and dainty young woman of flesh and blood. She was short and calm, and her snow-white raiment was unlike the hoopskirt fashions of the day. Wavy ringlets of light brown hair escaped from under a veil. An incredible blue ribbon, lightly knotted at the chest, flowed around her, and two golden roses were placed above the slender toes on each foot.

It was the famous apparition to Bernadette Soubirous of Lourdes. The grotto had been a place where townsfolk feared demons and ghosts. Now it was taken over by a more potent force. In what would become one of the most powerful apparitions in all history, the message was that as the devil raged, as he threatened, as he cursed, God would not leave mankind alone. At Rue du Bac, Mary had showed herself in direct contention with the forces of dark. Now at Lourdes in 1858 she was showing that she was fighting the war not with the devil's weapons of pride and anger, but with humble beauty. She was confirming the dogma of the Immaculate Conception. She would win the war calmly and with goodness. She would win gently. That's what was shown in a series of eighteen apparitions that occurred in the mound of granite that was streaked with calcification and adorned with vines next to a river that was quietly swift, whispering loudly.

It was the most picturesque of all apparitions and while the Blessed Mother was not exactly pretty, she had an unearthly beauty, her skin clear and rosy, a frequent sparkle in her dark eyes, a pleasant smile as she appeared to young Bernadette and spoke with a soft and sparing but rich voice.

Actions spoke louder than words. She held a rosary. *"Pray for sinners,"* she said when she did speak. *"Penitence!"* And she prayed with the seer. As Bernadette recounted,

> Without thinking of what I was doing, I took my rosary in my hands and went on my knees. The Lady made a sign of approval with her head and herself took into her hands a rosary which hung on her right arm. When I attempted to begin the Rosary and tried to lift my hand to my forehead, my arm remained paralyzed, and it was only after the lady had signed herself that I could do the same. The lady left me to pray all alone; she passed the beads of her rosary between her fingers but she said nothing; only at the end of each decade did she say the *"Gloria"* with me. When the recitation of the Rosary was finished, the lady returned to the interior of the rock and the golden cloud disappeared with her.

Cholera raged, war threatened, and a local church had become a "temple of reason," but Mary had never abandoned any of her flock. As times hardened and got colder, as mankind slipped into a structure of philosophy that was perhaps worse than that of the ancient pagans, as great violence and war were prepared for Christians, Mary was coming with greater clarity. She came more clearly from behind the veil. During the apparitions at Lourdes, a healing spring was found and officials would count more than twenty-five hundred "extraordinary" or "inexplicable" cures. Those who came were delivered from epilepsy, ulcers, and tuberculosis. No site would equal its elegance and in that beauty was strength. Lourdes was the bastion for Europe as Satan raged against the woman, as he sought to sweep her away with a torrent of water (Revelation 12:15), as he sought to befuddle mankind with his pretension and even to directly attack the apparition, sending a horde of false visionaries.

One day rumor spread that Bernadette was coming for an apparition. As the crowd gathered they saw a woman kneeling with a *capulet* covering her face.

It wasn't Bernadette. It was something sinister. "With her back to the crowd, she washed in the spring, drank of its water, ate of its herbs, slid on her knees, uttered long quivering sighs, and whispered, 'Penitence! Penitence!'" wrote Franz Werfel in *The Song of Bernadette*. "The imitation was so perfect that almost none of the witnesses of the great fortnight was taken aback. Only the whole performance remained curiously ineffective, like a thing that had been and had been worn thin. At the end of ten minutes the figure leaped up and threw back the hood of the cape and revealed a merrily grinning, brown, pockmarked girl's face. She picked up her skirt and began to dance. Before she could be captured she escaped across the rock like a beast of these mountains."

There were more than fifty false or demonic seers at Lourdes, along with reports of a strange fiery "balloon" similar to one seen above Paris during the plague. But nothing, not even the most blatant attempts at obfuscation, could squelch the work of God.

Would Satan still try?

Of course he would still try. Of course he *did* try. It was the endgame. He knew that he was the one on borrowed time. He had his eye on that hourglass. The heat was up. The sand was dwindling. These were special times. With each decade, right into the twentieth century—which was approaching like a train—the times would become all the more special as Satan, operating in the new realm of science but with the same old viciousness, made unprecedented attempts at deceiving and destroying all who lived on the planet.

Bernadette too was given at least three secrets, but they were private. She made it clear they should not be seen even by the pope. The opposite had happened, of course, with the LaSalette secrets, which were now the subject of an intense rumor mill. Soon different texts or tracts claiming to reveal portions of those secrets circulated in France. Some had already proven to be inaccurate, predicting great events that were to take place in 1856, which would signal the end of the world. That year passed but the fervor had not. Eventually there would be brochures claiming to present Mélanie's secret, but the main one was eventually condemned by the Church (despite one bishop's imprimatur) and there were those who worried that the prediction had been influenced by outsiders since it was now twenty-five years since the apparition.

Some feared that the prediction may have been drawn from strident and sometimes morbid prophecies from non-Marian seers earlier in the century. These consisted of mystics who had spoken of huge natural disasters, dreadful persecution, and ravaging wars mirroring the spiritual turbulence, which would show itself with scandal, apostasy, and an exiled or otherwise incapacitated pope.

It was all a bit overheated but it got the point across that horrible events were in the future and the remedy was the Rosary. The remedy was Jesus and Mary. The apparitions were a crucial counter to the French Revolution, the spirit of which was radically altering the course of history and continued to menace Christians everywhere.

All we need to know about the LaSalette secrets is that the pope had used the term "chastisements."

Was that where Europe was heading? Was that where the world was heading? Was a time of testing and purification around the corner again?

If the resurrection of paganism was an indication, the answer was in the affirmative. Mankind had started to set a pious path during the Middle Ages, but had badly diverted. The godlessness of rationality was joined by the godlessness of the occult, which was now in the form of trance mediums and "spiritualism." Seances were taking over Victorian England and spreading to Boston, New York, and Washington. Thousands were claiming to communicate with spirits through mediums or rapping sounds. Their followers included the likes of Queen Victoria and Mary Todd Lincoln. In Paris an infamous medium named Madame Blavatsky was integrating spiritualism with Masonic and Eastern beliefs, so that soon there would be a hodgepodge of occultism known to the "illuminated" as part of the Age of Aquarius or "new age." It was said that in 1862 Lincoln himself witnessed a spiritualist gathering in the White House's "Red Parlor."

But the president was much more interested in biblical phenomena. He was especially interested in dreams. He experienced one himself in which he saw a grieving group at the White House and was told that the president had been killed by an assassin. "I kept turning the leaves of the old book, and everywhere my eye fell upon passages recording matters strangely in keeping with my own thoughts—supernatural visitations, dreams, visions," said the president. Lincoln was also interested in the concept of chastisement because he thought the Civil War was a punishment for slavery. "The Almighty has His own purposes," he said in a speech just weeks before the South surrendered on Palm Sunday of 1865.

If we shall suppose that American slavery is one of the offenses which, in the providence of God, must needs come, but which, having continued through His appointed time, He now wills to remove, and that He gives to both North and South this terrible war, as the woe due to those by whom the offense came, shall we discern therein any departure from those divine attributes which the believers in a living God always ascribe to Him? Fondly do we hope—fervently do we pray—that this mighty scourge of war may speedily pass away. Yet, if God wills that it

continue until all the wealth piled by the bondman's 250 years of unre-
quited toil shall be sunk, and until every drop of blood drawn with the
lash shall be paid by another drawn with the sword, as was said three
thousand years ago, so still it must be said, "The judgments of the Lord
are true and righteous altogether."

Lincoln knew that history was full of chastisements, and indeed purifications greater than the Civil War were lurking. The Lord hated false gods
and that was what scientism was creating: a god of technology. The tele-
graph was taking the place of prayer and electricity the place of the Holy
Spirit. Through chemistry men were transmuting reality and thus scientism—the obsessive overuse of science—was even denying God His role as
Creator. While expertly documenting evolution, which simply meant an
"unfolding," Darwin made the grave error of attributing that unfolding
not to God but to "natural selection." Such a theory purveyed the
mechanical and rationalistic notion that mere freaks of nature, mutation,
guided the way organisms developed.

Life was a grand mistake! The universe was mechanical and spiritless!
The fish in the deep with luminosity like lamps and the camel with its
cooling humps and the lizards that could change color to camouflage
themselves—not to mention fins, feathers, arms, eyes, and brain, the
tremendous process of digestion and a nervous system, of creativity—
these Darwin considered accidents of nature, along with a thousand other
examples, from amoebae to human beings, with incredible complexity and
countless interactions any one of which the human could not live without.

All an *accident*? All random mutations that nature "selected"?

It was absurd and arrogant, an affront to logic, but it's what the devil
wanted: denunciation of the supernatural element. If there was no supernatural, there was no God. If there was no supernatural, there was darkness, which is where Satan best operated. And it all undermined faith.
Faith was believing in precisely that spiritual element. Faith was the test of

trust. Faith was abandonment to God, which then empowered men to rise above the snares of Satan.

Thus Satan was trying to undermine faith. Thus was he trying to quash spiritual sight. But his problem was the Virgin Mary, who by her mere presence blasted a hole in atheism.

It was at Baños, Ecuador, in the region of Darwin's greatest research, that a woman visiting a hot spring found a conical limestone rock that bore Mary's image.

# 37

## "I Will Be Your Mother"

Coincidence?

According to one list, Mary manifested in a significant fashion at least ninety-eight times between 1800 and 1899.

There were hundreds of lesser or unreported manifestations.

In Robinsonville, Wisconsin, Mary allegedly appeared between two trees to Adele Brisse, a Belgian immigrant who had wanted to be a nun. "In God's name who are you and what do you desire of me?" Adele asked.

*"I am the Queen of Heaven, who prays for the conversion of sinners, and I wish you to do the same,"* was the answer. *"You were at Holy Communion this morning."*

"Yes, dear lady."

*"You have done well, but I wish you to do more. Pray for nine days. Go and make a general Confession and offer your Communion for the conversion of sinners. If they do not convert and do penance my Son will be obliged t o punish them."*

One of Adele's companions anxiously asked her who she was talking to. It looked like thin air. "Kneel," Adele quickly replied. "The lady says she is the Queen of Heaven." When the friend expressed distress over not seeing Mary, the Virgin looked tenderly in her direction and said, *"Blessed are they who believe and do not see."* Then turning back to Adele she asked, *"What are you doing here in idleness, while your companions are working in the vineyard of my Son?"*

Adele, who had aspired to mission work, began to weep. "What more can I do, dear lady?"

*"Teach the children,"* replied Mary.

"How shall I teach them, when I know so little myself?"

*"I do not mean the science of the world,"* she said. *"Teach them their catechism, that they may know and love my Son."*

Three years after, in 1862, the Virgin also appeared in St. Louis. The apparition was to a woman named Mary Wilson, whose family had rejected her when she announced a Catholic conversion. *"Weep not,"* Mary consoled her. *"I will be your mother."*

There would be other apparitions in the middle part of America and they would spread west as far as San Francisco. Mainly the Virgin came in a personal way, but she was also a sage and her messages were earnest. In Israel during 1858 she had told a woman named Mirjam Banardy that the devil was full of more guile than ever, an obvious reference to increased demonic activity. She confirmed it eight years later in 1866 when at Anglet, France, she showed a nun the vision of demons set loose and wreaking devastation. There were warnings in Austria of buildings engulfed by flames, and predictions of a time of "sad darkness" and "great affliction." The hellish door was no longer just swinging but kicked open. In France a bitter cold winter had sent wolves precariously close to the village of Pontmain, which had been hit hard with smallpox and now was also threatened with an attack by Prussians.

Between 5:30 and 6 P.M. on January 17, 1871, a boy helping his father in a barn at Pontmain went to look out the door and check the weather. Snow covered the roofs of the hamlet and the sky was very clear, dark blue and studded with stars. That's when Eugène Barbadette noticed something unusual. Above a house across the road, a patch of sky seemed *devoid* of stars. As Eugène stared, suddenly there was a beautiful woman, motionless but smiling at him from the odd void. She was wearing a deep blue gown with wide sleeves and decorated with golden stars. Her head was covered with a black veil and she wore a gold crown with a red band around its middle.

Eugène gazed for fifteen minutes and then pointed it out to his father, brother, and neighbors. Not all could see the Virgin but there were at least five others who became visionaries during an apparition that lasted more than three hours.

As onlookers recited the Rosary, Mary's image grew. When the Rosary was finished, the form of an incredible white scroll began to unroll across the sky, spelling words as if an invisible hand was forming each letter.

It was under the Virgin's feet and the children shouted out each letter as it appeared.

*"But pray, my children ..."*

The words were in gold.

*"God will hear you in a short time,"* it spelled out next, followed by, *"My Son permits Himself to be moved."*

Those words were underlined and it was later learned that at this time, on this very night, German troops poised to strike the nearby town of Laval were suddenly called off by Germany's Supreme Command. Within ten days the war with France was over.

In Germany itself the apparitions were so profuse that they were clearly warning of something. They were reported on both the eastern and western borders, especially in the region known as Alsace, where claims came from Krüth and Wittelsheim. There were also claims from the village of Guisingen, followed a month later by several children in Medelsheim who, though the war with France had ended, warned of a coming "bloodbath."

Most noteworthy was Marpingen, Germany, where three eight-year-olds reported apparitions and secret messages for fourteen months beginning in 1876. So prominent was the alleged appearance that the children were taken into custody, gendarmes occupied the village, and the apparitions were derided by the likes of Otto von Bismarck.

There were those who said they saw hell opening and hordes of demons. In Scotland there were at least four reports during the late 1800s of the Loch Ness "monster" and in the United States there was a rash of UFOs. In Rome legend had it that on October 13, 1884, Pope Leo XIII experienced a vision of the devil and the granting to him of enhanced power for the next century. We can't confirm that vision but the same year Pope Leo penned a strong denunciation of the Masonic threat in an encyclical.

At Pellvoisin, France, seer Estelle Faguelle saw Mary shoo away a demon during the first of fifteen putative apparitions. I can't vouch for every such case, but they were certainly vivid and they came amidst a great upsurge of occult force. In France, the country's best scientists and politicians were openly preaching humanism and joining Masonic lodges, while in Germany neopagan cults that had different rituals but the same naturalistic philosophy were quickly rising. These organizations would soon resurrect ancient mystical symbols and inspire ideas of Germanic or "Aryan" superiority.

Highly influential in the spiritual underground and immensely popular in Austria was an enigmatic, white-bearded occultist who wore long flowing robes. It was said that one morning the magician had gone to a hill overlooking Vienna, chanted his special incantations, and buried nine wine bottles in the shape of the ancient symbol called the swastika.

Was that why Mary was so often being seen in Austria? Was that why she was seen in Dolina by three shepherd children?

At Cap-De-La-Madeleine in Quebec on the north bank of the St. Lawrence River, a priest trying to build a church at the site of an historic chapel planned to have stone cut from a quarry across the river and hauled on the frozen river, but when the winter was unseasonably mild and no ice formed, the priest, Father Luc Desilets, prayed and the next day gale force winds began to pile up floes of ice until the next morning there was a span strong enough to sustain the loads. Although he had planned to replace the old chapel, Father Desilets left it standing as a gift to the Blessed Mother. And in 1888 he and another priest praying in the chapel saw the eyes of a statue rise from their usually downcast position and stare straight ahead. It appeared to Desilets "as if looking outwards, far into the distance. Her face was at times severe and sometimes sad."

These were not cute little vignettes. They were serious business. Mary was a mother but she could storm and trample on enemy turf like an Old Testament prophet. In India she converted a pagan teacher and in Pompeii she came to the aid of Bartolo Longo, a former satanist who was trying to convert but found himself deeply discouraged about his past life. He heard her voice say, *"One who propagates the Rosary shall be saved."* Longo went to work promoting the Rosary. In Lyons Mary wanted devotion to a medal of the "Forsaken Mother" and in Vallensanges, France, appeared to a thirteen-year-old girl named Jean Bernhard in a clover field, weeping over mankind's sins and the coming judgment. In Poland she made 160 visits to four seers at Dietrichswalde while on a rainy night in 1879 she appeared to fourteen Irish witnesses in the forsaken town of Knock, which had been ravaged by food shortages. There she was seen in a living picture with St. Joseph and a man they took to be John the Evangelist holding the Book of Revelation.

The vision at the wall of the local stone church lasted for two hours, lighting the wall bright as snow. The light at times mounted above the gable, a scene from heaven and totally silent. At times the apparitional figures moved. But mainly they stood looking toward the witnesses, with angels hovering.

The tableau would enter Mariology as a vision of historic import but Mary also manifested in lesser-known instances to people like Thérèse of Lisieux, who was cured of a malady on May 13, 1883, as she looked upon a statue in France on the other side of the English Channel. "All of a sudden the Blessed Virgin appeared *beautiful* to me, so *beautiful* that never had I seen anything so attractive," recounted the Little Flower. "Her face was suffused with an ineffable benevolence and tenderness, but what penetrated to the very depths of my soul was the ravishing smile of the Blessed Virgin."

It was the precise date, May 13, that an image was crowned in Italy and it was in Italy that Mary was seen in the diocese of Bojano near Castelpetroso as the Sorrowful Mother. The vision was beheld on a rocky mountain and it was very unusual. A light issued from the rock fissures and it was in that light that various images of Mary, sometimes like a statuette, perhaps also like a tableau, were seen, accompanied by Michael and troops of angels on occasion, or of course with the Child in her arms. She was seen under different aspects, including Our Lady of Grace, Our Lady of the Rosary, Our Lady of Carmel, and Our Lady of Seven Sorrows, the last phenomena attracting four thousand visitors within a few days. While it was first denounced as a delusion from the pulpit by the local archpriest, soon it was witnessed by another disbelieving priest who looked into one of the fissures and saw the Virgin with the Infant and then Christ bearing the crown of thorns and covered with blood.

In what would become a trend in apparitions, a scientist versed in medicine and physics was drawn to the site to prove or disprove the alleged apparitions, but like so many subsequent investigators at so many other places, he was not able to use physical science to capture something that was nonphysical. Although most of the local clergy were initially hostile, their skepticism turned to belief when they saw with their own eyes or were brought evidence by others, and in 1890 a beautiful Gothic church was built there. "I myself can bear witness that I visited the sacred spot, and, after some time spent in prayer, saw the apparition of the Blessed Virgin," wrote Bishop Macarone-Palmieri of Bojano. "At first the image of Our Lady appeared faint and indistinct, but at length she appeared in the attitude and proportions of the representation of the Mother of Sorrows published in [a religious journal]. Besides myself and the very large number of persons whose names are recorded in the official report, there are the vicar-general of the diocese, the archpriest of the cathedral, and many other ecclesiastics who also beheld the apparitions."

In Spain the Virgin was crowned again on October 13, 1889, and while that was a happy event, in 1892 the Church acknowledged a statue that wept at the Italian town of Campocavallo.

In the northern French village of Tilly sur Seulles, the Virgin was seen from March 3 to July 26, 1896, by dozens of nuns and schoolchildren. It was extraordinary how they could look out the school window to a meadow and see her there for long periods at a time. "Across the fields, at a distance of some twelve hundred yards, they saw, as distinctly as was possible such a long way off, a figure of Our Lady such as is represented on the Miraculous Medal, with her hands extended, and surrounded by an oval of dazzling light," wrote William Walsh.

There was no clear message but near Frankfurt Mary *again* stressed a time of "trembling."

*"You poor sinners,"* she allegedly said at Corsica in 1899.

And on September 8, 1900, a hurricane and tidal surge killed more than six thousand in Galveston, Texas. Seawater flooded the entire island, leaving only the sight of floating debris and surreal flashes of lightning. Afterward the island, once a famous party town ("Beelzebub and the Devils" was the recent theme of a Mardi Gras there), was covered with an inch-layer of foul-smelling slime. An article in *National Geographic* described it as "a scene of suffering and devastation hardly paralleled in the history of the world" and it was an especially sad day because September 8 was Mary's official birthday.

# 38

## The Great Sign

A nd sad because it was the opening for the twentieth century, the stormiest of centuries, the most exciting of centuries, a century full of the greatest good and the greatest bad, a century that saw the strongest outpouring of supernatural forces yet as man headed into a new and unknown millennium.

In a short one hundred years it would be the year 2000. Was the world finally ready to end? Odds were that it was not ready to end, but odds were that Mary's apparitions were building to some sort of final denouement.

Something was in the wind just as something had been in the air before the schism and Black Death, something that would involve not one event or crisis, but a long series of crises spanning the next century or two. It was indicated precisely by the spiritual outpouring. As the very face of reality changed, as men introduced cars and phones, as the world was soon linked by television and satellite, as men left the earth in rockets for other worlds and transformed the nature of this one, the apparitions of Mary, far from fading as a superstition, would reach biblical proportion.

Had it all been a deception? Was it possible that the nontraditional Christians, the antagonists who came after Luther, were correct? Was she just a random peasant woman whose womb had been used by the Holy Spirit?

Nothing could have been more removed from fact and to Christ few notions could have been as disturbing. She was not just a woman and she was not just a saint. She was His mother. He loved her as His mother. He remained in her arms. He was the Savior and Son of God, part of the Trinity, but He was also her Son and as portrayed in those countless statues she was there to hold the Infant and show Him to the world.

*Hail Mary, full of grace, the Lord is with thee.* Anyone who knelt at an altar dedicated to her knelt not in worship of Mary but to enter the heart of Jesus, Who was everywhere she was and Who is the greatest of all forces. There was no quicker way into the heart of a son than through his mother and in Lisbon Cardinal Dom Manuel Goncalves Cerejeira would one day describe her appearance as confirmation and witness to the reality of God. "It is a renewed appeal for the extraordinary circumstances of miracles, because of the tragic anguish of the time in which we live, and because of the hopes which are offered it has the significance of a supreme attempt at salvation, or as a certain French writer said, 'the final sign,' the 'last attempt at salvation.'"

She had guided mankind for all those centuries and now she was determined as a mother hen to get her children through the exquisitely dangerous twentieth century which, with its billions of people, would see as many souls as all the previous centuries combined. Perhaps half the people who'd ever lived would be part of this century, making it the greatest of all spiritual battlefields.

She had appeared this year—1900—even in Africa. There were manifestations in Peking, Tong-Lu, and Manchuria. She was sad and in a warning mode—her strongest and most explicit warnings ever—because mankind was tempting and would continue to tempt chastisements. Just weeks after the great 1906 San Francisco quake, an astonishing picture of Mary as Sorrowful Mother was seen to open and close its eyes at a Jesuit boarding school in Quito, the site of so many of her miracles. It was perhaps the most authentic-looking of her many pictures and the phenomena were witnessed by both professors and students, who in fact had been discussing the quake when the picture began to move. "On one occasion the whole student body was in the school chapel in the evening saying the Rosary when the lady of the picture, which had been moved to the chapel, again repeatedly closed and opened her eyes," wrote Broschart of the painting (which is on the cover of this book). "At the same time the chapel bells began to ring with no hand touching them."

It was known as Our Lady of Seven Sorrows, and not only did it come on the heels of San Francisco but also just months before a worse quake killed twenty thousand in Valparaiso. They were the first of many quakes that would shake up the twentieth century as no century had been shaken before. They included a 1908 tremor at Messina, Italy, that killed eighty-three thousand and caused a famous relic alleged to be a letter from the Virgin to disappear in the wreckage.

If they were not random natural events, they were harbingers. Such was indicated by the accompaniment of apparitions, especially the kind of secret messages that had been initiated at LaSalette and now became a common component of Mary's appearances. I had no way of discerning each apparition and the Church didn't formally rule on most, so all I can do is report on the more pronounced claims like that of Gray, France, which started on September 9, 1909 (a day *after* her birthday), and occurred to a priest who said he had received secrets that could be told only to a few pious souls. Of the secrets revealed later was one that predicted world wars unless people did penance and placed holiness in family life. The priest said millions would die and all of Europe would be set afire.

Such was likewise prophesied on May 12, 1914, during an apparition witnessed by twenty-two Ukrainian peasants laboring in the fields of Hrushiw. It was the site of a miraculous well that had flowed from an old tree which had long borne a miraculous image. During the apparition, Mary predicted eight decades of hardship for believers. She warned that Ukrainians would witness a series of wars.

A coming tribulation, the beginning of a series of events, was also implied when she appeared to about five hundred in Alzonne, France, leaving another warning of war. She continued her presence in the often turbulent and once barbarian nation of Germany, which with Austria had *exploded* with visions in the past century and soon exploded with combat as World War I was initiated by the assassination of Archduke Francis Ferdinand in Sarajevo.

Turks were again involved, but the main action was now between Germany, Austria, and those many other nations that had hosted her apparitions. The war pitted Germany, Austria, and Turkey against France, Britain, and Russia, then the United States. In the very heat of battle, Mary appeared at LaMarne, France, to German troops who reportedly saw a woman dressed in white. Because of her they stopped an advance from September 5 to 12, 1914. Afterward they were forbidden under penalty of death to talk about it. The activity stepped up in 1917 with reports of Mary appearing in Paris, Moscow, and the famous site of Fatima, Portugal, where the Blessed Mother had once come to help a hungry peasant child and where she had also healed a deaf shepherd girl. It was also where the Archangel Michael had been seen by the knight known as D. Nuno just as an angel bearing the Eucharist came to announce the Virgin of Fatima, who in a magnificently momentous apparition from May 13 to October 13—dates that had always figured into prodigies—to three young shepherds named Jacinta, Francisco, and Lucia. These three had all the earmarks of classical seers, and the apparitions in 1917 involved events of such magnitude that, like Lourdes, Guadalupe, and the Miraculous Medal, they would have been at home amid biblical occurrences.

A white cloud seemed to descend on a holm-oak during the apparitions, just as a light had issued from a holm-oak to a Spanish shepherd in 1213 and Mary left to the sound of thunder in a luminous globe. Most famous was her last apparition in October when more than fifty thousand onlookers witnessed incredible movements of the sun above Fatima. It gyrated and spun and caused authorities to pay much more attention to the youngsters, who claimed that the previous July they had been given three secrets concerning the future, prophecies that said World War I would soon end—which it did—but that if mankind did not cease offending God a worse one would erupt during the pontificate of Pius XI. *"When you see a night illuminated by an unknown light, know that this is the great sign given you by God that He is about to punish the world for its crimes, by means of war, famine, and persecution of the Church and of the Holy Father,"* the Virgin said in the secret.

It was a prophecy strikingly similar to that of the 1914 Hrushiw apparition, but the Virgin of Fatima went on to request the consecration of Russia to her Immaculate Heart and the devotion of first Saturdays. *"If my requests are heeded, Russia will be converted, and there will be peace. If not, she will spread her errors throughout the world, causing wars and persecutions of the Church. The good will be martyred, the Holy Father will have much to suffer; various nations will be annihilated. In the end, my Immaculate Heart will triumph. The Holy Father will consecrate Russia to me, and she will be converted and a period of peace will be granted to the world."*

These were the first two parts of a great secret. There was the sound of thunder and Lucia shouted, "There she goes!" With a last fond look, the Blessed Lady had glided slowly toward the east and as Lucia said, "disappeared in the immense distance of the firmament." There was the third part of the message that has never been revealed. As the seers listened, Lucia had taken a deep breath, turned pale, and let out a shriek. "Why do you look so sad?" people asked when the July apparition was over.

"It's a secret," insisted Lucia. "It's a secret."

"Good or bad?"

Repeating nearly exactly what had been said at LaSalette, she responded, "Good for some, for others, bad."

The third secret would not be written down until late 1943 or January of 1944, when Sister Lucia, possibly inspired by another visit from Mary (for her apparitions continued), was to sit down in the chapel at Tuy and after great impediment, after a block that lasted for more than two months and seemed supernatural, finally wrote it out. And while it would be kept a strict secret at the Vatican, where it was placed in the archives of the Sacred Congregation for the Doctrine of the Faith, we know the 1917 message began with the words, *"In Portugal, the dogma of the Faith will always be preserved ..."* This indicated that elsewhere the faith would not be preserved, that the secret which Lucia said could be publicly revealed if the pope chose to do so after 1960 (when it would make more sense) had to do with a horrible trial of doubt and the erosion of belief by way of materialism that would become all the more profligate and engrained as a spiritual chastisement, a spiritual suffering, began to strip the Church of its spirit and install a cold secularism in a society that would one day abandon the pews and veer even more radically toward lust and money just as happened during the Medieval Chastisement.

That was the indication—a loss of faith and deepening division among Christians, with serious misunderstandings and confusion, in Lucia's own later words, a "diabolical disorientation." It was not the end of the world, not necessarily any earth-stopping calamity, although calamity may have played a part in the secret, but more than anything it was an indication that mankind was entering a decisive period of the world's history without knowing how long that period would last.

To identify the secret only with catastrophic events was to obscure what seemed to be its main warning: that mankind was facing eternal perdition, that the afterlife was far more important than anything on earth, and that sin would lead to a dismal eternity, which is why the seers were shown a vision of hell.

One day there would be a period of peace, a time of mercy, but before that there would be great upheaval—the annihilation of nations—and indeed just three weeks after the October sun miracle Lenin rose to power in Russia and there was a revolution that marked the onset of Communism.

Russia was ready to spread her errors and annihilate the identities of neighboring nations that were soon swallowed by the godless Soviets. Those were the first two parts of the secret as recorded by Lucia. There was also the third that she said could be revealed after 1960 if the pope so chose and that seemed to predict future distress. Although it would never be released, there were indications it had to do with a falling away of the faithful and crises in the Church. There were also things said in private to Francisco and Jacinta, who died within a few years of the apparition when they took ill in an incredible epidemic of influenza that killed twenty *million* throughout the world.

The epidemic wasn't up to the proportion of bubonic fever because so many more people were alive, lessening the proportion, but it was unquestionably part of a chastisement, a hint at what else may come in the next couple of centuries, and it came with more rumblings and then major quakes that soon were to claim 570,000 lives in the Orient. It was a breathless century in the way of both disasters and prognostication. Prophecies were given in Brussels, Belgium, to an alleged seer who said England would have succumbed in World War I had the cardinal not consecrated that nation to Mary's Sorrowful and Immaculate Heart, and in 1918, acknowledging her help, the title "Queen of Peace" had been added to the Litany of the Blessed Virgin. More consecration was needed. It was essential. The seer saw trouble that would spread to all countries as humankind rushed to what the Brussels revelation called a "dreadful storm." She claimed to see Jesus Himself, Who said He wanted recourse to His mother under her title of Immaculate Heart as the *"last help I shall give before the end of time."*

In France a nun received the message that love and suffering could obtain anything and that if there was one thing humankind needed to do it was *"love, love, love."* The future would be dim if mankind did not devote itself to Our Lady and with humility abandon itself to God. The nun said Christ warned it was the devil who tried to otherwise sway us and the devil who tried to persuade men that confidence in Mary subtracted from tenderness and regard for Christ. The devil inspired the thought that Mary was a deception when the real deception, the real lie, was that Mary usurped her own Son. *This* had deceived even the elect, the many good faithful, Protestants and Catholics alike, and it was a brilliant ploy by Satan to make sure there was always a breech between Catholics and Protestants. Such division could be healed only by humility, which was also emphasized to the nun with two simple words: *"Humble yourselves."*

Humility and love were both a giving of self and when self was gone there was unity.

There was also a secret given to the French sister who took it to her Mother General in Rome on August 20, 1923.

Was the secret apocalyptical?

No one knew. The times certainly warranted it. They may not have been the end of the world, but they were apocalyptical on a spiritual level. Seer after alleged seer emphasized the unusual darkness. Pius IX had foreseen terrific Church suffering followed by a "great prodigy." But before the sign, which reminds us of the sign in the sky given to Constantine or the cross over Golgotha in the fourth century, there was to be trouble. Most worrisome to Pius was modernism. The pope had hurled eighty paragraphs of condemnation at it, concluding that it was wrong to believe "the Roman Pontiff can and should reconcile himself to and agree with progress, liberalism, and modern civilization" that made men deities and ignored God. The Church wasn't opposed to progress that helped human beings but it *was* opposed to progress that saw everything in mere human terms. It was his successor Leo XIII who seemed to indicate a special trial of evil. Pius X also viewed doctrines of modernism as "the synthesis of all heresies."

Ignoring God was not only the synthesis of all heresies, but the mother of them. It aimed to demystify all of His creation and declaim anything supernatural. This was done by muddling the public with a kind of science that was little more than minutiae and jargon. The devil was indeed in the details, especially when those details were meant to confuse and complicate. Confusion was never of the Holy Spirit. Simplicity was. Simplicity and clarity were wisdom. They were diluted or obscured by technicality, yet men didn't see that; when it came time to choose, humans were going to choose complexity because they figured it was complexity and not simple inspiration that had created the great new conveniences of the day, the cars and fashions and movies that made life so titillating as they headed through the Roaring Twenties.

There was even the undercurrent of certain "intellectual" priests who, bowing to rationalist pressure, were starting to look skeptically at the Church's rich mystical history, including the miracles in Scripture. No self-respecting and modern mind accepted such hokum, such fairy tales! Where for nineteen centuries bishops had welcomed miracles and personally led processions to miraculous sites, ordering hundreds of shrines, basilicas, and chapels to mark the Virgin's marvels, suddenly in the 1900s they began to feel superstitious and self-conscious. Now when they heard of a miracle they proceeded in the other direction.

It was the intimidation of science, which could be a great force and which made remarkable and hugely beneficial discoveries, but which was being twisted as the devil twisted many things that were initially good. He did this through pride. He did this through rationalism. So great became the pretension of science that it began to attack spirituality. As a physical system, science could not document, understand, or control something that by its very definition was nonphysical, and as I have stressed, what science could not control, it denied, which was not just arrogance but dishonesty. *No* scholar worth his bifocals could deny the almost *endless* accounts of miracles. No scholar who bothered to objectively review a fraction of the mountainous mystical literature could come away thinking it was all hallucination.

True, it wasn't documented like a doctoral thesis. It wasn't something that could be replicated in a lab. But that was because miracles were beyond experimentation. It was because heaven didn't play by human rules. There always had to be an element of faith. As we've seen, Mary most often chose the uneducated and humble, the faithful, not the intellectual, as her witnesses. Her mystics didn't seek acclaim. They didn't want a Nobel Prize. They were men like Padre Pio and their strength, their sinew, was selflessness.

Selflessness was more important than any prophetic secret. Selflessness was both mercy and love. Selflessness led to abandonment to God and that created a sense of direction so essential when sin multiplied as it was now multiplying—as it was now skyrocketing—in sensuous, loveless times promoted by the new glamour of Hollywood. Mary said as much in an apparition near Luxembourg. Love and mercy. Love, not sensuality. Love came from the spirit. Love could include sensuality in a marital setting, but it was *not* its definition. Love wasn't meant as the kind of plaything it became during the Roaring Twenties. When love was a plaything it meant trouble, and at Aichstetten, Germany, the Virgin reappeared as Our Lady of LaSalette saying the miseries would soon be everywhere. World War I was only the start. Penance, penance, penance, she repeated in yet another apparition near Grenoble in 1927. Sin reopened the wounds of her Son, which were symbolized in the stigmata suffered by mystics like one woman in the 1930s who said simply, "The furies of hell are now set loose. Divine punishment is inevitable."

Oh, yes! There was going to be persecution and there were going to be martyrs. There were going to be more martyrs in the twentieth century than in all the rest of history. There were already martyrs in the Soviet

Union as Communists began ruthlessly killing millions of Catholics in what became, in sheer number, the greatest persecution of all time. The chapel at Hrushiw was boarded shut and other churches were ripped down, turned into warehouses, or renovated into museums of atheism. It made its progenitor, the French Revolution, look like kids' play. The horrors were especially severe in the Ukraine. During 1932 and 1933 Stalin, seeking to quash Ukrainian nationalism and terrorize private farmers, hauled all the republic's wheat to Russia and created a severe, almost incomprehensible famine. In 1933 alone at least 4.6 million and perhaps as many as 10 million Ukrainians perished. "Practically every village has a mass grave from the artificial famine of 1933," Dr. James Mace, director of the Commission on the Ukraine Famine, told me. "There was tremendous demographic damage, epic figures." According to another scholar, Lubomyr Hajda of Harvard, it qualified as a case of actual genocide. The number of dead from this period alone may have equaled or exceeded the number of people killed a few years later during the Nazi Holocaust. Said Hajda: "In terms of absolute data the Ukrainian numbers are probably higher than any other mass atrocity we're familiar with. It's not proportionately as high as what happened to the Jews—whose entire European population was nearly exterminated—and we don't have a good reckoning from China, but the Ukrainian experience has certainly been one of the most horrific of this century."

Their crops stolen by the Muscovites and their herds slaughtered for Russian consumption, Ukrainians were forced to eat nettles, tree bark, leaves, milkweed, worms, rodents, and crows. Entire villages were devoid of life. The cats and dogs were devoured when the crows and rats were gone. Numerous incidents of cannibalism were reported, and in cities where children were abandoned by parents who couldn't provide so much as a morsel of black bread, trucks came each night and picked up corpses that littered every major thoroughfare. Thousands of priests and nuns were sent to Siberia.

The United States escaped with only the Great Depression as the chastisement bore on, but overall the world was in terrific distress. It was so in need of a mother that between 1928 and 1971 there would be at least 210 major claims of apparitions along with the many others that were considered minor or had not even been reported. How many were true? One guess was as good as another. The Church ignored or rejected the majority. Some of that was because of rationalists and the new skepticism, but some of it was also prudence. The Church sensed the rising evil and knew the devil loved twisting or counterfeiting miracles. Could the devil come as Mary? Of course he could. Of course he *did*. And it could be excruciatingly difficult to discern him. The true test was permanent fruits (Matthew 7:16). Mary healed the soul, and when she appeared there was perfect joy and peace; when there was confusion, on the other hand, it indicated a serious problem. No matter how nice and bright a vision initially seemed, no matter how much phenomena, any form of disturbance, according to ancient Church doctrine, any unrest in the soul, indicated Lucifer.

He was the angel of light and there were concerns he had stepped into or even initiated a mind-boggling series of events in northern Spain. They were centered in the village of Ezkioga. There in Basque country apparitions had begun in 1931 and spread to the point where by 1936 approximately 250 people would formally claim to see Mary.

There were many others who were casual or one-time visionaries. They came from dozens of villages that stretched from Pamplona to the vicinity of Santander. No one really knows how many seers there were. In the first month alone there were a hundred. Whether some of the initial experiences in which visionaries again saw Mary as the sad Mother were authentic, there were serious concerns about the strange nature of ecstasies in which the visionaries' eyes were raised in a strained fashion or the seers virtually convulsed on the ground. There were apparitions. There were materializations of the Eucharist. There were equally dramatic predictions, resurrecting an old prophecy of a great and imminent "miracle." As early as 1910 the theologian Augustin Francois Poulain had questioned prophecies that said the world was about to be suddenly changed by a miracle, with everyone becoming holy in an instant, and while such predictions had not come from the Virgin, now at places like Ezkioga they were being attributed to her. Some of the seers believed the miracle would consist of Mary appearing with three angels and a half-moon under her feet and an extraordinary light that would illuminate everything around— an entire mountain. Also, the Archangel Michael would descend on a white horse and explain the reason for the appearances. It would begin at quarter to five in the afternoon and end at 11 P.M. There would also be chastisements. Many of the Ezkioga seers warned of great calamities like earthquakes and three days of darkness. There would be a major war and ravaging hurricanes. Afterward there would be a new era, a world in peace. The earth would be renovated after a third of the people died. One seer had permission from the apparition to tell people the dates of the miracle and chastisement eight days before they were to happen. This seer said the chastisement would come before the miracle. There was also talk of the Antichrist, who as in past centuries was said to be alive. He would come to power in 1949 and die in 1956 at the age of thirty-three.

It was all very exciting and the part about war, storms, and chastisement had the ring of truth. But specific dates were given for prodigies that never came and at least two seers later admitted fabricating their stories. In September of 1933 the bishop wisely condemned the apparitions, denying that they had supernatural content and prohibiting Catholics from retaining pictures, photographs, and books relating to them. One prohibition was backed by Pope Pius XI. The bishop went so far as to request priests to deny Communion to seers who persisted in visiting Ezkioga. Some observers were concerned about sorcery. The ecstasies were often weird and this was the region of Spain where there had been an explosion of witchcraft during the seventeenth century. Had that left a residue, a curse? There were those who spoke of seeing a witch in the sky or a monkey that turned into an ugly woman near a stream. Others saw the devil in human form.

These were not pleasant topics, but they showed how vexed the times were. They indicated confusion and demonism as Spain was ready to suffer a civil war as well as an intense persecution of clergy. As elsewhere, the nation was also in the throes of modern immorality. Sexually explicit literature was surging and couples were staying out late and wearing more and more revealing clothes. Sensuality was sweeping both Europe and America. Pius X had said that "all the strength of Satan's reign is due to the easygoing weakness of the Catholics" and with all the immorality, all the Communism and warfare, all the martyrdom, Pius XI added that "this is the darkest [time] in history since the Deluge."

As if to ward off a vampire, villagers at a remote place in Bosnia-Herzegovina hauled cement up a mountain and erected a cross that could be seen for miles around. It wasn't far from Sarajevo where World War I had been born. In other places the palladium, the vehicle of exorcism, appeared to be Mary. People were starting to see reports from places like Verdun, Quebec, and Woonsocket, Rhode Island. Mary was most prevalent in Germany and Belgium, especially two Church-approved sites called Beauraing and Banneux. How beautiful she was, and how tender were these reports compared with those that contained prophetic harshness. At Beauraing she was an eighteen-year-old with beautiful deep blue eyes and at Banneux she resembled Our Lady of Lourdes and called herself the "Virgin of the Poor." Seers saw a brilliant heart of gold surrounded by glittering rays or a spotless white gown chastely closed at the collar and a golden rose on her right foot. On January 3, 1933, the Virgin disappeared and then reappeared at Beauraing after a crack of thunder and a ball of fire that landed on a hawthorn and was visible to everyone present. That day she gave secrets to three of the five Beauraing visionaries and on February 5, 1933, confided secrets to Mariette Beco, the sole seer at Banneux.

As in most cases, no one ever learned their contents but the medium was the message. *Blessed art thou among women, and blessed is the fruit of thy womb, Jesus.* That's where the blessings, the grace, originated. The spread of apparitions in little Belgium was astonishing. Between 1933 and 1937 there were at least fourteen public cases. This was interesting not only because Belgium bordered Germany, but because 1933 was the year Adolph Hitler was appointed as German chancellor and given dictatorial powers.

It was also the year of the first concentration camps and warnings of a coming judgment, another part of the chastisement, resounded in Switzerland, Italy, and most especially Heede, Germany. At Heede four girls were given secrets that were to be sent through a parish priest to the Holy Father during putative apparitions that lasted from 1937 to 1940. These took place under great duress as the gestapo tried to stop them by arresting the seers and tossing them in an insane asylum. The girls were released after many weeks, but now the apparition had to appear surreptitiously in a meadow.

There were other portents. In January of 1938 an unprecedented display of what scientists explained as the "northern lights" was seen in the skies of Europe. In London awestruck residents watched two magnificent arcs of light rising in the east and west, "from which radiated pulsating beams like searchlights in dark red, greenish blue, and purple," according to the *New York Times* on January 26. It was the most brilliant display of the northern lights in memory and "one of the novel features of tonight's show," said the *Times*, "was the vivid red glow."

Astronomers claimed it was caused by sunspot activity. Red balls of light. From an airplane it looked like a "shimmering curtain of fire." In London they thought Windsor Castle was ablaze. The phenomenon was seen as far east as Vienna. In southern Germany it struck special fear into the hearts of Catholics who knew that this day was the feast of St. Paul—who was blinded by a light from heaven (Acts 9:3)—and in Portugal peasants ran through villages fearing the end of the world.

Shortwave radio transmissions were disrupted, and in Grenoble near LaSalette *huge* blood-red beams of light further convinced scientists that it was an aurora borealis of "exceptional magnitude."

From her lonely window at a convent in Tuy, Spain, Lucia dos Santos, the lone surviving Fatima seer, now a religious, marveled at the meteorological spectacle and remembered the words spoken to her in secret twenty-one years before. *"When you see a night illumined by an unknown light, know that this is the great sign given you by God that He is about to punish the world for its crimes, by means of war, famine, and persecutions of the Church...."* In a letter to the bishop, Lucia pegged the northern lights as the long-awaited oracle. "God manifested that sign, which astronomers chose to call an aurora borealis," she wrote. "I don't know for certain, but I think if they investigated the matter, they would discover that, in the form in which it appeared, it could not possibly have been an aurora borealis. Be that as it may, God made use of this to make me understand His justice was about to strike the guilty nations."

A similar display of the northern lights had preceded the apparition at Pontmain, but this was far more spectacular and far more foreboding. A week after the aurora borealis, on February 4, 1938, Hitler, who had been influenced by the Templars and had an acute interest in the occult (especially Woden, the old pagan god of destruction), promoted himself to military chief and a month after marched his Nazis into Austria and annexed that nation, declaring victory in Vienna.

In certain ways it was the beginning of World War II. There were pogroms in Germany followed by a war unlike any in history, a war that saw Germany invade Poland and attack France while smoke billowed around St. Paul's Cathedral in London. Hitler aimed his forces in all directions, including Russia. Pius XII now weighed in with his own evaluation, agreeing with his predecessors that it was "perhaps the gravest hour since the beginning of Christianity."

Within several years, virtually all of Europe was engaged or severely affected. In Portugal, which was spared participation in the war, ceremonies for the twenty-fifth anniversary of Fatima were capped in 1942 with a radio address by Pius, who in a solemn tone reminded his listeners that in such a "sinister spreading of conflict" Mary had to be invoked. He acknowledged her prophecy by mentioning the Virgin's "foreknowledge of this great disaster with which the justice of God mortifies the world." In a nearly desperate prayer Pius pleaded, "Queen of the most holy Rosary, help of Christians, refuge of the human race, winner of all the great battles of God, at your throne we prostrate ourselves, confident in obtaining mercy and in finding grace and the necessary help in the present calamities, not through our merits, which we do not presume, but solely through the great goodness of your maternal heart."

The war raged from Norway to Egypt, then east to Russia and out to the Philippines. By 1945 concentration camps would imprison eight to ten million people, half of whom would be executed. The chastisement that began with World War I, thirty years before, had a long way to go but already the horrid persecution of Jews resurrected the old witchy way of poisoning victims or sacrificing them with fire, which was known in sorcery as *holokaustein* or "burnt offering."

It was an atrocity that rivaled the Ukrainian genocide. About 5.9 million Jews, or two-thirds of the European Jewish population, died. The war itself took an even ghastlier toll. Before it was over forty-four million would die and churches, including many of Mary's precious shrines, were destroyed with demonic fervor as the ancient occult symbol of the swastika was unfurled from flagpoles. At Auschwitz Maximilian Kolbe, who as a boy had seen Mary and been offered the crown of martyrdom, placed that crown on his head by giving his life in 1941 so that a condemned man with a family could be spared.

Finally on the Fatima anniversary date of October 13, 1945, the horror came to an end as Allied bombers pounded the Nazi headquarters. In the rubble were little miracles. At St. Kolumba Church in Cologne, air raids had almost completely destroyed a chapel enshrining an image of Mary, but one pedestal was left standing. It was the one supporting her image. In Hiroshima four Jesuits praying the Rosary in the church of Our Lady's Assumption just eight blocks from ground zero somehow survived the incredible blast of the atomic bomb on August 6. The church was left standing in the historic rubble and by August 15, Feast of the Assumption, Japan had surrendered. Fascinating was the fact that atomic blasts created atmospheric effects—refractions and balls of light, red shock waves—that were nearly identical to some of the effects reported with the northern lights. This was later seen in tests over Johnston Island, where there were similar reflections and striations. There were similar colors.

Thus the sign which had announced the beginning of the war had also shown how it would end.

# 39

## Queen of Eternity

After the debacle of Hiroshima, Mary entered the phase of apparitions that led to what we see today. Far from fading, the apparitions of this amazing woman, this astonishing and underestimated woman, grew to remarkable proportion. It was the hour of battle with Satan and there came other apparitions with other secrets, the appearances especially intense at the beginning of the cold war. Similar miracles were soon reported around Italy and the rest of the continent—including the old site of Saragossa. At place after place the sun whirled and pulsed and spun. It moved. It turned colors. Mary's time had arrived. The episode had begun with the Miraculous Medal and, according to Father Johann G. Roten, director of the International Marian Research Institute, "between 1830 and 1981 there were close to a thousand major, minor, and related apparitions."

Others gave estimates far higher. If every daily or weekly apparition is counted in cases where a seer had more than one, the number would not be calculable. I don't know how they derived their figure, but the French periodical *Le Monde* once estimated twenty-one thousand apparitions between 1976 and 1986! Mary's era, her most intense intervention, was at full throttle. Now apparitions that were once centered in Italy and France fanned across the nations. There were reports in Ephesus. There were reports at Bethlehem. In Poland Sister Faustina had visions. In Dublin the Blessed Mother appeared during World War II in front of a green clover-shaped cloud with the dragon at her feet. *"Have faith,"* she said. *"The war will not reach Ireland."*

Up through 1946 she had also been reported as a luminous figure over a mighty cliff in Kerrytown.

She was in Hungary. She was in Michigan. She was reported by four French girls in a major case at L'ile Bouchard. She came with a sun miracle at Casanova, Italy. In one of the most dramatic cases, she appeared in Rome on April 12, 1947, to a virulent anti-Catholic named Bruno Cornacchiola who had made a vocation of speaking against Catholicism and who had planned to assassinate the pope. While writing a speech against the Virgin as his children played in a field, Cornacchiola was drawn to a small cave where, to his shock, he saw his children in ecstasy and witnessed a small light that grew brighter and stronger until it lit the whole grotto. In the light was a heavenly woman surrounded by gold. She asked Cornacchiola why he was persecuting her and described herself as *"the Virgin of Revelation."* She wore a cascading green mantle and a brilliant white dress and it certainly convinced Cornacchiola. He was given a secret to bring to the pope and immediately converted to Catholicism, changing his name to Brother Maria Paolo.

These weren't ancient myths. These were visions recorded in our own era. My frustration has been in being able to relate but a fraction. I have a study from Austria alone that with a miracle per page is a couple inches thick. Apparitions were claimed from eastern Canada to Bellmullet, Australia. In a visit to a nun in Fostoria, Ohio, the Virgin asked America to dedicate itself to the Immaculate Conception and pray the family Rosary. She needed help. She needed prayers. The period of great trial was only beginning. She wanted Americans to form special pilgrimages to the National Shrine of the Immaculate Conception and dedicate itself to her purity. While World War II had ended, she was here to prevent another atomic tragedy. She was here to prevent World War III. From April 25 to June 25, 1946, she appeared at the German town of Marienfried, a name which means "the peace of Mary." There, another secret was given to a visionary and she again urged recitation of the Rosary to ward off Satan. She warned that if mankind didn't take advantage of Christ's mercy, there would be disaster. It wasn't meant to provoke fear but rather, like any good prophecy, to initiate action. The iniquities of the world had not all been purged and mankind had not learned from the wars. They tempted another holocaust. This time it would be a global holocaust. This time it would destroy much more of the world. This time it would involve something like radiation, which may have been what a seer at Seredne, Ukraine, was alluding to in the 1950s when she saw the danger, as did many subsequent seers, of "fire" falling.

In 1950 Mary's recognition and thus her ability to intercede were magnified when Pope Pius XII defined the dogma of her Assumption. On the day he announced this intention, the pope witnessed a solar phenomenon. It happened immediately behind the Vatican gardens above the land that had once belonged to Nero and Caligula. "The sun, which was fairly high, looked like a pale yellow opaque globe completely surrounded by a luminous halo, which nevertheless did not prevent me at all from staring attentively at the sun without the slightest discomfort," Pius wrote in a note to a cardinal. "The opaque globe began moving outward, slowly turning over upon itself, and going from left to right and vice versa. But within the globe very strong movements could be seen in all clarity and without interruption."

On November 1, the actual day for definition of the new dogma, the sun again moved so oddly that afterward Pius made inquiries to the Vatican Observatory.

The more Mary was invoked, the more she was officially recognized, the more she could intervene. She had kept the lid on the cup of justice but if matters kept going as they were, the world would have to drink that cup to its bitter dregs. A stern warning had been launched. A warning had been issued against the prevailing frivolity. A warning had been issued against atheism and the immoral. I take such words from a Vatican official.

While many might guess the period after World War II would have seen apparitions slack off, the opposite had happened. There was a surge. There was a great increase. Between 1947 and 1954 four times as many apparitions were reported as in preceding or subsequent years and what Mary seemed to be saying was that a danger lurked that would make World War II but a prologue.

Never in a reputable apparition did Mary proclaim the end of the world. Never did she say that the final chapters of Revelation would soon be realized. "To all the curious I would say I am certain that the Virgin does not engage in sensationalism," noted the Vatican official, Cardinal Joseph Ratzinger, who read the third Fatima secret. "She does not create fear. She does not present apocalyptic visions, but guides people to her Son."

In other words, she was moving through the verses of Revelation, but she was nowhere near the final ones. She was concerned with chapter 13. The rising beast. She was concerned with the evil that ruined men's souls and brought earthly destruction. There had to be much more good than evil prevailing in order for her to prevent what the Fostoria apparition called *"the holocaust that is so near approaching."* Time after time she halted local chastisements. Time after time she relieved man of plague and drought. She couldn't do that forever. One day there would be a reckoning. One day there would be too many holes in the dam. That was how chastisements worked. They were mainly localized events. But as sin grew so did they. As sin grew the local chastisements became regional chastisements. If sin were great enough, the chastisement crossed national borders.

Something on the level of bubonic fever was now hanging over the horizon. Already floodwaters had killed 4.9 million in pagan China during the past sixty years and while the mid-1900s saw the rise of many sensational and questionable seers, it was to be noted how consistently they warned of the same disasters. Churchmen like Ratzinger were correct to call the flock back from sensationalism, but one had to be careful not to go too far in the other direction and ignore legitimate warnings in the same way that God spoke in floods and tempests throughout the Old Testament.

In some way humankind faced an awesome condition that portended a series of warnings and chastisements. Otherwise it was difficult—nay, impossible!—to understand why so many of Mary's images began crying. Many of her tears were shed over immorality and Communism. In 1953 the Vatican approved a weeping plaque of the Immaculate Heart at a home in Syracuse, Sicily, a rare event because the tears lasted long enough for formal chemical analysis. They proved to possess the alkalinity and character of human secretion. Investigators sent by the bishop saw it for themselves, the tears collecting in a cavity formed by the hand over her heart. There could be no fraud. In a radio address on October 17, 1954, Pius XII acknowledged "the unanimous declaration of the Episcopal Conference held in Sicily on the reality of that event," and asked, "Will men understand the mysterious language of those tears?"

From 1953 to 1954 there were at least thirteen other weeping pictures representing the same image as that in Syracuse. Surely Mary was not crying because all was going so well and mankind had nothing to worry about! Surely she didn't shed tears just to draw spectators! "It is all too clear that God, angered and offended by the waywardness of men, who forget to render homage to their Creator, and who fight among themselves like savage wolves, wishes to punish humanity with individual and collective chastisements," noted Enrico Contardi, who wrote a pamphlet about Cornacchiola. "But then the sublime lady whom He chose for Immaculate Mother and Virgin, and whom He left at the foot of the Cross to be our mother, intervenes in our favor, interposes herself between the wayward sons on earth and the divine Son in heaven."

Precisely that kind of intervention seemed to have happened in Austria in 1955 when the Soviets were trying to plant troops in that country.

Faced with becoming a Communist satellite, Chancellor Julius Raab urgently requested a Rosary Crusade to begin praying twenty-four hours a day. Shortly afterward, Moscow invited a delegation from Austria to discuss the situation. In a stunning reversal on May 13, 1955, the Soviets agreed to withdraw from Austria and signed a peace treaty.

Such were the faith-building incidents. Faith was what the Blessed Virgin had come to build. Faith was needed for prayers to work. Faith was a shield against the flurry of fiery darts (Ephesians 6:16) just as it had turned back the arrows of Muslims and Turks in past centuries. Faith girded man and let loose the powers of God. Faith was the combination to the hidden safe and it tied into humility because the humble abandoned themselves. Faith was the great shield as demons ran across the globe in a period of temptation and mischief. There was still time, but the clock ticked. Sand continued to move in that cosmic hourglass. According to Sister Lucia, the devil was "in the mood for engaging in a decisive battle against the Virgin." The seer was told that the two last remedies for the world were the Rosary and devotion to the Immaculate Heart. Such was also the message of an apparition in Romania, where Mary had even appeared in Dracula's old haunt of Transylvania!

Nowhere was unconquerable. No place and no person could *not* be reclaimed. It was faith that brought fifty thousand praying spectators to witness supernatural images over the dome of St. Augustin Church in Communist Warsaw and it was faith with which an estimated one million pilgrims prayed at Fatima on the night of October 12–13, 1960, for protection against the threat of Russia. (That same night a new Soviet missile exploded during a test run, setting back the Russian military and taking the wind out of Khrushchev.)

Two years later, in Sao Paulo, Brazil, a huge and moving demonstration of hundred of thousands of women praying the Rosary sounded the death knell for Communism in that nation.

Faith was saving the earth. Faith was stilling the arm of justice. Millions were now visiting Lourdes and Guadalupe, where, in 1921, a terrorist bomb planted in the church had shattered the stained glass and twisted a metal crucifix directly below the image, but left the picture and its protective glass miraculously unharmed.

Mary could not have picked a more crucial time to expand her presence. She was the Mother of the Church, proclaimed as such in 1964, and her Church was in great trouble. According to Pope Paul VI himself, the smoke of Satan had entered. Something "preternatural" was afoot. Suddenly there was disenchantment throughout the mystical body. The fruits of Vatican II were distorted. Statues of Mary were soon hauled from churches, the Blessed Sacrament was downgraded, and for good measure the powerful prayer to St. Michael (which should immediately be reinstated) was abandoned.

Smoke. Confusion. A loss of faith. Once-pious religious orders began wandering into secularism. While it wasn't as bad as Avignon, that was the direction in which many nuns and priests were heading. The confessional? It was about to be turned into a mop closet. Altar boys? No one wanted to serve. Nuns? They were suddenly made to feel weird for wearing a habit. Perhaps that's why from 1963 to 1965 Mary appeared in Saigon at a convent. There she pleaded not only for loyalty and faith but also charity, coming once more with a message of peace and with a sun miracle.

She was also witnessed above a Coptic Orthodox church in Zeitoun, Egypt, where during the next several years more than a million people of all religions, including former president Abdul Nasser, would see her.

It was the Sixties. It was time for the sexual revolution. It was time for every sort of rebellion. From 1966 to 1969 it was time for rock, drug, and love fests in places like Monterey and Woodstock. It was time for wanton fornication and the frenzy of lust and selfishness which led to abortion.

The fruit of abortion, as Mother Teresa would say, was nuclear war.

Fire falling? In 1969 a profile of the Virgin was seen in a photo of a mushroom cloud over the atomic test site of Moruroa in the Pacific. It was formed by the smoke and was accompanied by the miraculous image of Jesus on the Cross.

Clearly, they were warnings. Sister Lucia had said the third secret did not have to be released, that it was totally up to the pope, but that if he did want to release the message, it would be clearer after 1960 because it had to do with the flood of evil and faithlessness into our world. Never did Mary's images weep like they did in the wake of abortion! Doctors, lawyers, and professors were witness to an image of Our Lady of Pompeii that bled from January to May 1971 at Maropati, Italy. Two years later—the very year that abortion was legalized in the United States—a statue at a convent in Akita, Japan, shed tears that were also analyzed and found to be human. There was a warning at Akita of schism and a fiery holocaust, and Mary also came to Betania, Venezuela, seeking reconciliation of all peoples. She warned of nuclear war during a Church-approved apparition in Cuapa, Nicaragua. She was in China. She returned to Vietnam.

And there were secrets. There were many apparitions that claimed secrets. There were seers claiming secrets in at least twenty-one countries. I can't ignore that. I can't soft-pedal that. We should never underplay the seriousness of the world situation. I don't know how many prophecies are real and it's a shame how Satan has mocked legitimate prophecy with his false seers and far-out predictions, but I know that nothing quite like this episode has happened in the past. I know that secret messages about the future have become as much a motif as illuminating images or apparitions that pointed to buried statues had been in earlier ages.

Why secrets? Because they galvanized. Because they sought the prayers and sufferings of the seer. Because they brought gravity to the apparition and indicated that while the main message of Mary has always been hope, there is also seriousness.

I know many and perhaps most are bogus, just as many predictions were bogus in the past. They are the result of a demon or the subconscious, especially those that are sensational. But I also know that there is a strong and legitimate movement of the Spirit and I'm not going to underplay that. I'm not going to ignore that. I'm not worried about those who so hastily dismiss any warning as "apocalyptical" or "doom and gloom" as they bury their heads in the sand.

On June 24, 1981, the Virgin made her first appearance on a hillside just outside Medjugorje in what was then the Communist country of Yugoslavia. She came to the parish of St. James, holding the Child just as she came with the Child to the apostle James at Saragossa. It was the start of thousands of apparitions to six credible young people who *daily* saw her as the Queen of Peace, just as she had been known during World War I. Evil was still rising, and so she pleaded for peace. As in Constantine's time there was a great wonder in the sky during 1981 when the word *MIR*, meaning "peace," was seen by a number of witnesses above the incredible village. There were many other signs, sun miracles and visions of Christ and stars that seemed to move, unfixed as in the days of the plague. I visited there myself and saw the phenomena a number of times. No question there was something coming. The feeling was there each of the five times I visited. The feeling was there when I spoke privately on May 13, 1997, with one of the key seers, Vicka Ivankovic, who said the apparitions at Medjugorje "are the last apparitions on earth."

If Saragossa was her first, Medjugorje would be her last. Once the apparitions at Medjugorje halted, so would her other appearances.

After that she would be at her place in heaven.

I have no idea what that means for earth, but if true it means Mary's role will be very different. I don't know if it will need a definition of a dogma and I leave all such discernment to the pope, but I do believe something is coming. I think she will return to the side of the King in heaven, which she has related to visionaries as a place of incredible peace, joy, and love, a place where light radiates instead of reflects, where there are beautiful colors that saints have always described as like gold or emerald or sapphire.

In apparitions that may one day rank with Lourdes, Guadalupe, and Fatima if the seers remain credible and if the Vatican keeps it from a hostile local bishop, Mary stood on a cloud as a full-bodied, corporeal person, twelve stars circulating around her head, granting each seer up to ten secrets. With the Fatima secrets finding their fulfillment, the Medjugorje secrets seem to take up where Fatima left off and seem yet more dramatic. There was the sense that while Fatima dealt with the first part of the general chastisement, Medjugorje dealt with its conclusion. The first three Medjugorje secrets contain warnings. In the case of at least one visionary, her first has to do with a regional event, an event in a city, country, or part of the world, that will be reported through the media and recognized as a special warning by those waiting for such an omen.

The second secret is also a warning that seems like regional calamity or events that will be followed, according to all the seers, by a third warning and "great sign," which was precisely the language used to predict the aurora borealis at Fatima.

The remaining secrets appear to concern the parish of Medjugorje, the personal lives of the seers, the overall Church, and chastisements that threaten the world.

It was Vicka's impression that before any of the secrets transpire, she will be given the signal by Mary to print a book on the life of Mary that was dictated to her by the Virgin. But she's not sure when the book will be released and she doesn't know what's in the other visionaries' secrets. They've never spoken about them. She told me that while the Blessed Mother comes more joyfully than before, there is still a great struggle with Satan and the spiritual darkness has not yet been broken. When I asked if she'd ever heard anything about a single great "warning" coming, she said she has never been told about any single global event (as prophesied at an alleged site in Spain) but that "the Blessed Mother's presence is a warning."

Indications from Medjugorje have always been that we face several warnings that will occur at a regional level, followed by certain chastisements and events in the Church that will affect the entire world. Vicka said the punishment in her seventh secret was reduced by half through fasting and prayer. What might be in the remaining secrets is totally unknown but the hint is that after the events, men will worship as in ancient times when miracles were accepted as a matter of daily life and God was glorified through Mary and the ringing of the *Angelus.*

When I asked Vicka if her secrets have anything to do with the end of the world, the Antichrist, or the Second Coming, Vicka said that her particular secrets have "nothing to do with that."

Will Vicka, a seer who may well rank someday with Sister Lucia, live to see all her secrets unfold?

She said she doesn't know.

Can the last three secrets still be lessened?

Yes, she said; it depends on us. Instead of awaiting calamity we must fast and pray.

Was the war in Bosnia, the horrible war right there in the vicinity of Medjugorje, the one that seemed prophesied by the Blessed Mother's very coming, part of her secrets?

No. They pertain to other things. It's a time of reckoning. It's a time for action. There will be strangeness. There is already much strangeness when one turns on the television to nearly any channel, or sees the coldness that has spread from places like Los Angeles and New York to the rest of America.

Partial-birth abortion! Cloning! Euthanasia!

Time and again Mary has prevented tragedy, time and again she has convinced her Son to postpone His judgment, but the divine cup is close to overflowing and there is no denying her stridency. While two world wars have ended, mankind faces other crises. Like the Medieval Chastisement, the wars are but an accompaniment or prelude. There could yet be decades or even centuries of unusual suffering. There could be plague, schism, and scares from the frontiers of space or the depths of the ocean. The trial is not over. There are lulls, but it could pick up at a moment's notice. No one knows what will happen after the heroic John Paul II is gone, but a good bet is that there will be anxiety. A sure bet is either that men will get better and stand up for their Christianity or face the consequences.

*"God is giving me this time as a gift to you, that I may teach and lead you on the way of salvation,"* the Virgin said on August 25, 1997. *"Dear children, now you do not comprehend this grace, but soon the time will come when you will lament for these messages."*

How far man had strayed! How pretentious he had become! Even those who called themselves theologians questioned the supernatural and that was true blindness because the supernatural was operating at the highest levels. This was evident when the bullet that had pierced Pope John Paul's abdomen on May 13, 1981, miraculously missed his aorta and vital organs. *He* knew. He credited Our Lady of Fatima with saving him. And he had the bullet placed in her crown at the shrine.

While recovering he also witnessed a sun miracle.

Such phenomena were soon seen at apparitions claimed in at least forty nations. The interventions were often invisible and without phenomena but still earth-shaking. On May 13, 1984, as one of the largest crowds in the history of Fatima gathered to celebrate the anniversary, a massive explosion at Severomorsk in the U.S.S.R. destroyed a *third* of the Northern Fleet's stock of surface-to-air missiles, greatly lessening their ability to strike at a time when there had been great tension.

The Blessed Woman had long concerned herself with Russia and on

March 25, 1984, her pope, John Paul II, knelt before her and consecrated the world and Russia to the Immaculate Heart of Mary, who had said at Fatima that if her requests were heeded, Russia would be converted and there would be a *"period of peace"* given to the world. According to Sister Lucia, we currently live in that "period of peace."

According to Sister Lucia, the Triumph of the Immaculate Heart began with the remarkable—the miraculous—collapse of Communism. On the very day Lech Walesa of Poland was celebrating new freedom, he was pictured on the *International Herald Tribune* with a statue of the Fatima Virgin behind him. Clearly the apparition at Fatima was chiefly concerned with Russia, Eastern Europe, and Communism. And for the moment, Communism has fallen in Europe. It's a gift. It's a result of the consecration. According to Sister Lucia, *it averted fire from falling—a nuclear exchange.*

"The consecration of 1984 prevented an atomic war that would have occurred in 1985," said Lucia during a startling meeting on October 11, 1993, with Cardinal Ricardo Vidal of the Philippines and a journalist named Carlos Evaristo, startling by the very thought of such a thing but also startling because this was precisely when the Soviets had their most dangerous leaders and when Mary was begging prayers for peace at Medjugorje, a peace that did in fact come to most of the world though ironically not there in Bosnia. "The era of peace does not refer to a civil peace, but rather to a peace that we are now living with the end of the spread of the errors of Communist Russia," Lucia explained, indicating that our time has been a time for mercy, a window of opportunity, a lull before the potential storm. Indeed, despite regional flare-ups like Bosnia and Rwanda (which was also foreseen by apparitions in Kibeho), most of the remaining years in the second millennium, militarily speaking, had been as peaceful a time as there had been in two thousand years.

While even one lost life is a tragedy, the numbers lost in recent wars are but a tiny proportion of the world's populace and nothing like the centuries of warfare that rocked all of Europe during its formation. It has been one of the most peaceful times in history but there are still great dangers and time continues to run. The window of opportunity will not be open forever. If there is not an adequate response to the mercy of God, a calamity or series of calamities similar to the plagues, quakes, fires, storms, and endless war that bedeviled the Middle Ages and Roman Empire will almost certainly recur. We'll revisit a calamity like that of the bubonic plague or relive on a larger scale destruction of the Temple or severe change in climate. No doubt about it: the first century of the third millennium is going to be most interesting!

I believe mankind faces a new and barely perceptible evil the likes of which we have never before encountered. This evil is not currently known to men. It has arrived almost imperceptibly, with few people noticing its depth, for it will appear to have beneficial and convenient aspects. This evil is being allowed as a test because of the prayers inspired by Mary to put off chastisements. How mankind responds to this new evil will determine the extent, length, and severity of the chastisements. These chastisements will differ according to regions, and like the great evil, will not always or usually be immediately noticeable for what they are. In this period there also will be a warning that involves not fire from the sky so much as the *fear* of fire from the sky, and strange loud rumblings. This, according to mankind's response, will then be followed by another chastisement, or the inevitable onset of the change of era.

Our era is ending. One day soon the world will not be the world we know. I'm not speaking of a barren world, or one depopulated, but of the end of modernism and the technological obsession. Many inventions of mankind will be broken down and there will be more of a peasant attitude and way of life as in past eras. After the breakdown of artificial reality I would not be surprised to see major spiritual manifestations and the dangers of a new world order.

I am well aware that there have been many false alarms about the Antichrist and while warning about not *repeating* those false alarms, let me also urge vigilance as always Christ said we must be vigilant. The Lord will manifest and break the evil one day in a series of supernatural events similar to Mary's apparitions but much more powerful. When that occurs it will be spectacular to many but also unknown initially to many, or disbelieved. Yet the pretensions of the world will have been broken. Some day, no one knows when, He will come in towering light. His mother held Him as an Infant in her arms from Saragossa until Medjugorje and He will come as she has come, in light and as the Lord Who strikes down human arrogance.

Things are interesting already. We have already seen warnings. The greatest hurricane in history hits Florida and is followed from the East Coast to Hawaii by "storms of the century." Floods cover large parts of North Dakota and California and the farms along the River of the Immaculate Conception. Quakes rock St. Mary Queen of the Angels of the Portiuncola or "Los Angeles" and also strike Assisi. Floods in Florence. Drought in England. In 1980, the year before Medjugorje, America saw twenty-three federal disaster declarations. That figure rose to thirty-one in 1989 and seventy-five during 1996 with at least *seven* of America's ten all-time greatest disasters occurring since 1989.

As the graphline of apparitions rises, so do the disasters. But so does the hope, the magnificent incredible hope, the main message of happiness that comes from Mary, because her very presence, more than a warning, more than an admonishment, is proof of eternity.

Let's not forget this. The bottom line is that God exists. He is there. He watches. He listens. He loves us all equally and He sends us Mary. She is proof of heaven and with her we fear no death. With her, there *is* no death. That's her last and greatest secret: if we live as we should, with purity, humility, and faith, if we are truly close to Christ, death will be a fearless transition. We'll hardly feel it.

Death is the happiest event in life for those who have prepared for it.

And in all the centuries Mary has brought no greater message.

She will be standing next to Christ when we are ready for judgment. What a secret!

*"I call on each of you to consciously decide for God and against Satan,"* she said at Medjugorje. *"I am your mother and, therefore, I want to lead you all to complete holiness. I want each one of you to be happy here on earth and to be with me in heaven. That, dear children, is the purpose of my coming here and it's my desire. If you would abandon yourselves to me you will not even feel the passage from this life to the next life. You will begin to live the life of heaven from this earth."*

It was her last and greatest secret because with a life of prayer death not only loses its sting but ceases to exist. There is no blackness. There's no panic. We leave this earth fully conscious, aware of the separation of spirit from body, and at that moment all those *Hail Mary's* will come back with interest. All the invocations for Mary to pray for us at the final hour are there waiting at death's glorious door.

What a secret! What a secret when the door opens to a place beyond what any writer of any caliber could write, beyond what any seer could see, beyond what any mind still trapped in the body could hope to conceive. Heaven is not only real but more real than earth and there's no time there, no beginning or end, and it makes any suffering on earth but a minor price of entrance. The door will open to a light that is at the same time brilliant and soft and that's when we will finally see her. That's when we will finally embrace! That's when we'll see the Virgin in her true glory arrayed as no jewels, no gold, no sapphire could be arrayed, and that's when she'll show us not the Infant in her arms this time, not the Child, but Christ as God and King.

# NOTES

### ONE
### *A Huge Mystery*

Unless otherwise indicated the Bible I use is *The New American Bible* (Camden, N.J.: Thomas Nelson, 1971). At times I employ the King James Version (also published by Thomas Nelson or as related in a computer Bible manufactured by Franklin Electronic Publishers in Mount Holly, New Jersey). From time to time I use *Roget's Thesaurus of the Bible* by A. Colic Day (New York: HarperCollins, 1992) and the *Reader's Digest Bible* (Pleasantville, N.Y.: Reader's Digest Association, 1982). John Paul II's view on Mary comes from page 6 of *Madonna* by Frederick M. Jelly, O.P. (Huntington, Ind.: Our Sunday Visitor, 1986) and page 213 of the Pope's book, *Crossing the Threshold of Hope* (New York: Knopf, 1994). The figure from the International Marian Research Institute comes from personal communication. *The Catechism of the Catholic Church*, which I use as background, was published through Liberia Editrice Vaticana and St. Paul Books and Media in 1994. As a general background text I also use the Penguin *History of the World* by J.M. Roberts (New York: Penguin, 1992). Throughout I also use *A Concise History of the Catholic Church* by Thomas Bokenkotter (New York: Image, 1979) and *History's Timeline* edited by Fay Franklin (New York: Crescent, 1981). One of the main lists of apparitions I used was *Lexicon, der Marienerscheinungen* by Robert Ernst (Druck und Verlag: Anton Ruhland, Rudolf-Diesel-Strabe). Another source consisted of a series of mostly unpublished manuscripts by Charles B. Broschart, who did yeoman's research for a series of research books and papers under the title *All Generations Shall Call Me Blessed*, or often shortened to *Call Her Blessed*, which is the title I will use. They are available to my knowledge only through the University of Dayton's Marian Library. The manuscripts are categorized according to nation.

### TWO
### *Strong and Demure*

There are those who not only dispute the apparition at Saragossa, but who dispute that James even visited Spain. It's like anything else so long ago: there are even disputes about who wrote certain books of the New Testament. For more on the debate about James and Spain, and for background on James and other saints, see *Butler's Lives of the Saints*, edited and supplemented by Herbert J. Thurston, S.J., and Donald Attwater (Allen, Tex.: Christian Classic, paperback edition, 1956). When I use *Butler's* there is no need for page numbers, as the entries are indexed. Note that some say James was accompanied to Spain by Mary of Cleopha. I state that there were eight followers with him because that's the number of men in the artwork inside the basilica. Others say it was seven disiciples. The description of Spain comes in part from a personal visit to Saragossa in November of 1996.

The history of Neanderthals can be found in *Humankind Emerging* by Bernard G. Campbell (Boston: Scott, Foresman, 5th ed., 1988). For the account of the apparition at Saragossa I used many sources, primarily "Saragossa's Our Lady of the Pillar" by John E. Keller in *The Irish Catholic*, November 7, 1968; *Historic Shrines of Spain* by Isabel Allardyce (New York: Franciscan Missionary Press, 1912); *Shrines to Our Lady Around the World* by Zsolt Aradi (New York: Farrar, Strauss, and Young, 1954); and *Apparitions and Shrines of Heaven's Bright Queen* by William J. Walsh (London: Burns & Oates, 1904). See also *Historia de la Virgen del Pilar* by Francisco Gutierrez (published in Saragossa and available at the Marian Library at the University of Dayton); *La Santisima Virgen del Pilar* by Dr. Julian Cantera Orive (Bilbao, 1958); *Historia Critica Y Apologetica de la Virgen Nuestra Senora del Pilar de Saragossa* by D. Mariano Nougues Y Secall (Madrid: D. Alejandro Gomez Fuentenbro, 1862); *La Venida de la Virgen* by Roman de Arnels (Saragossa: Talleres Editoriales, El Noticiero, 1963); *La Virgen del Pilar* by Archbishop D. Rigoberto Domenech Y Valls (Saragossa, 1955); and *Novisima Apologia Hispanica* by Francisco Gutierrez Lasanta (Saragossa, 1960). For background on the Virgin's life and looks I used *Ephesus, Legends and Facts* by Dr. Ahmet E. Uysal (Ankara: Ayyildiz, 1962); and *Butler's Lives of the Saints*. See also *Favourite Italian Shrines of Our Blessed Lady* by M.D. Stenson (Dublin: Catholic Truth Society of Ireland, 1992). For the A.D. 47 chapel in France see *Lexicon, der Marienerscheinungen* (cited in chapter 1), which lists apparitions chronologically. There are some who claim the Virgin arrived in Ephesus between A.D. 42 and 48 and died there (see *Ephesus, Legends and Facts*, cited above). Mystics have disagreed on Mary's death, some saying she died thirteen years after Jesus, while others have reckoned she lived on for another fifteen or even, according to Mary of Agreda, twenty-one years after the Crucifixion, which means what James saw indeed may have been a bilocation, whereby a living mystic is seen in two places at once.


## THREE
### Days of Darkness


For Le Puy see page 212 of *Celebrated Sanctuaries of the Madonna* by Reverend James Spencer Northcote (Philadelphia: Peter F. Cunningham and Son, 1875). For how Mary may have lived, see *The Book of Mary* by Henri Daniel-Rops (New York: Hawthorn, 1960). For the pagan gods, see *A History of Pagan Europe* by Prudence Jones and Nigel Pennick (New York: Routledge, 1995); *Mystic Italy* by Michael I. Rostovtzeff (New York: Henry Holt); *Man, Myth, and Magic* edited by Richard Cavendish (New York: Time Books), under "Gnosticism," "Mystery Religions," "Rome," "India," "Germanic Mythology," "Incas," and "Simon Magus"; *Religions of India* by Louis Renou (New York: Schocken, 1968); *The Worship of the Romans* by Frank Granger (London: Methuen, 1895); and the article "Of Gnosticism and the Spark Within," *New York Times*, September 27, 1996 (book review). For paganism in Rome see *The Long Year A.D. 69* by Kenneth Wellesley (London: Paul Elek, 1975). For Pompeii see *Pompeii, The Day a City Died* by Robert Etienne (New York: Harry N. Abrams, 1992). For the swastika see *The Twisted Cross* by Joseph J. Carr (Shreveport, La.: Huntington House, 1985); and also the entry for

"Swastika" in *Man, Myth, and Magic* (cited above). For Caligula and Nero see *Caligula, Emperor of Rome* by Arthur Ferrill (London: Thames and Hudson, 1991); *Caligula, The Corruption of Power* by Anthony A. Barrett (London: B.T. Batsford, 1989); and *Nero, Emperor in Revolt* by Michael Grant (New York: American Heritage Press, 1970). See also *Antichrist, Two Thousand Years of the Human Fascination with Evil* by Bernard McGinn (San Francisco: HarperSanFrancisco, 1994). For Peter's crucifixion and also the fire of Rome, see *Butler's Lives of the Saints* (cited in chapter 2), henceforth known simply as *Butler's*. For the church in Malta, see page 281 of *Miraculous Images of Our Lady* by Joan Carroll Cruz (Rockford: TAN Books, 1993). For the Madrid statue, see *Call Her Blessed* (cited in chapter 1), page 36. For the well at Ein Karim see a volume of Broschart's that was published, page 273 of *Call Her Blessed* (New York: Society of St. Paul, 1961). For the statue of Barcelona, see *Historic Shrines of Spain* (cited for chapter 2), page 47. For the account of Glastonbury, see *Butler's*, volume 1, page 618. For sexual and abortion practices in ancient times, see *Sexual Life in Ancient Egypt* by Lise Manniche (London: KPI, 1987); *Sexual Life in Ancient Rome* by Otto Kiefer (London: George Routledge & Sons, 1934); and *Abortion: The Development of the Roman Catholic Perspective* by John Connery, S.J. (Chicago: Loyola Univ. Press, 1977). For A.D. 69 see *The Year of the Four Emperors* by P.A.L. Greenhalgh (London: Weidenfeld and Nicolson, 1975), and *The Long Year A.D. 69* by Kenneth Wellesley (cited previously). The account of the comet comes from an old English pamphlet entitled, "Prodigies and Apparitions," privately published in England during the seventeenth century. For the fall of Jerusalem see *The Walls of Jerusalem* by Chaim Raphael (New York: Knopf, 1968) and *The Fall of Jerusalem and the Christian Church* by S.G.F. Brandon (London: S.P.C.K., 2d ed., 1957). For Pompeii see *Pompeii, The Day a City Died* (cited previously); *Pompeii, Its Destruction and Re-Discovery* by Sir William Gell and J.P. Gandy (New York: A.W. Lovering, n.d.); *Pompeii and Herculaneum* by Marcel Brion and Edwin Smith (New York: Crown, 1960); and *Pompeii, Its Life and Art* by August Mau (London: MacMillan, 1904). Due to the nature of narratives, certain facts and chronologies to do with Pompeii and surrounding towns are sometimes confusing and blurred.

## FOUR
### *"Mother of the Lord"*

For the ghosts at Nero's tomb, see *Call Her Blessed* (cited for chapter 1), page 200. For the account of Placidas, see *Call Her Blessed* (cited for chapter 1), Book 2, page 119; and also *Butler's* under St. Eustace, martyr. For the image in the Catacomb of St. Priscilla, one source, *Famous Shrines of Our Lady* by H.M. Gillett (Westmister, Md.: Newman Press, 1952) says it was the second century while the Catholic *Catechism* (cited in chapter 1), page 13, says it's the third century. For Gregory the Thaumaturge see his entry in *The Catholic Encyclopedia* (New York: Robert Appleton, 1910); the book *Apparitions and Shrines of Heaven's Bright Queen*, cited for chapter 2, page 103; *The Fear of Freedom, Studies of Miracles in the Roman Catholic Church* by Rowan A. Greer (Pennsylvania State Univ. Press, 1989), pages 109-11; *The Madonna*, page 406 (cited for chapter 3); *Mary, A*

*History of Doctrine and Devotion* by Hilda Graef (New York: Sheed and Ward, 1963); the entry in *Butler's*; and perhaps most engagingly of all, Raphael Brown's *Saints Who Saw Mary* (Rockford, Ill.: TAN Books, 1994). We note here that the sources for Gregory the Thaumaturge, while as usual open to criticism, are surprisingly good. There is Gregory's own recounting and a strong oral tradition reflected in the panegyric penned by an author thought to be Gregory of Nyssa, who lived in the fourth century; *Historia Miraculorum* by a historian named Rufinus, who lived around 400; and a sixth-century manuscript of Syriac origin. St. Basil also wrote of Gregory.

FIVE
*Above the Sun*

For the number of emperors who died violently see *Germany the Aggressor* by F.J.C. Hearnshaw (New York: Dutton, 1842). For St. Nicholas (who, by the way, appeared to Constantine in a dream) see his entry in *Butler's*. For Catherine see *Apparitions and Shrines of Heaven's Bright Queen* (cited for chapter 2), page 141, and also *Butler's*. For Julian and Basilissa see *Butler's* as well as *Celebrated Sanctuaries of the Madonna* (cited for chapter 3), page 406; and *Apparitions and Shrines of Heaven's Bright Queen*, page 149. For Philomena and Monica I draw from *Visions of Mary* by Peter Eicher (New York: Avon, 1996). See also *Saint Philomena, Powerful with God* by Sister Marie Helene Mohr (Rockford, Ill.: TAN Books, 1988). For Constantine see *Constantine the Great, The Man and His Times* by Michael Grant (New York: Charles Scribner's Sons, 1993); and *Constantine* by Ramsay MacMullen (New York: Dial, 1969); *Constantine the Great, The Reorganization of the Empire and the Triumph of the Church* by John B. Firth (New York: G.P. Putnam's Sons, 1905), from which is the quote on Constantine asking God to declare Himself; and *Constantine the Great* by Lloyd B. Holsapple (New York: Sheed & Ward, 1942). The historian I quote for Constantine's effect was J.M. Roberts, cited too for chapter 1.

SIX
*Gog and Magog?*

For the attribute of Pallas, see *A History of Pagan Europe* (cited for chapter 3), page 68. For establishment of the Eucharist and other sacraments, along with the issue of morality and celibacy, see *A Concise History of the Catholic Church*, cited for chapter 1. For Mary and the shrines in Italy, see again *Call Her Blessed* (cited in chapter 1), page 173. For excavations at Nazareth see *Dictionary of Mary*, no specific editor (New York: Catholic Book Publishing, 1985). For Mary as mediatrix see *The Blessed Virgin's Co-Redemption Vindicated* by Rev. J.B. Carol (Florence: Quaracchi, Tipografia Del Collegio Di S. Bonaventura, 1937). For the doctrine of her perpetual virginity and divine motherhood see *The Book of Mary*, cited for chapter 3. For St. Helena see her entry in *Butler's* as well as *Miraculous Images of Our Lady* (cited for chapter 3), page 380 as well as *Dictionary of*

*Mary*, page 63. For Our Lady of the Snow see *Apparitions and Shrines of Heaven's Bright Queen* (cited for chapter 2), page 151. See also *Famous Shrines of Our Lady* (cited for chapter 4). For images of Luke see *The Madonna of Luke* by Henrietta Irving Bolton (New York: G.P. Putnam's Sons, 1895). For the Goths and Huns and barbarians in general I rely upon the following: *Germany, 2000 Years* by Kurt F. Reinhardt (Milwaukee: Bruce, 1950); *Germany the Aggressor* by F.J.C. Hearnshaw (New York: Dutton, 1942); *The World of the Huns* by Otto J. Maenchen-Helfen (Berkeley: Univ. of California Press, 1973), from which I draw the quote about Huns; and *A History of Attila and the Huns* by E.A. Thompson (Oxford: Clarendon, 1948). For paganism I often refer to *A History of Pagan Europe*, cited in the notes for chapter 3. For sexual practices in the Roman Empire see again *Sexual Life in Ancient Rome* by Otto Kiefer (London: George Routledge & Sons, 1934). For Oropa see *Miraculous Images of Our Lady*, from which I draw the quote on stupendous miracles. For the account of Simeon the blind man I used *Call Her Blessed*, one of the Broschart manuscripts that was published (as cited for chapter 3); and also *Miracles of Mary* by Michael S. Durham (New York: Blackberry, 1995). It was a man named Bishop Chorene who called Mary co-redemptrix according to *The Blessed Virgin's Co-Redemption Vindicated* as previously cited.

SEVEN

*Through the Streets of the City*

For Our Lady of Good Counsel see *The Virgin Mother of Good Counsel* by E.A. Selley (Boston: Cashman, Keating & Co., 1889). For Ephesus, especially the little prayer quoted, see among other sources *Legends of the Blessed Virgin* by J. Collin De Plancy (New York: P. O'Shea, 1864). For Ireland I used: *Mary: A History of Devotion in Ireland* by Peter O'Dwyer (Four Courts); *Our Lady's Island* by the Very Reverend Patrick Canon Murphy (Wexford: People Newspapers, n.d.); and *How the Irish Saved Civilization* by Thomas Cahill (New York: Anchor, 1995). See also Patrick's entry in *Butler's*. And for the wells see *Man, Myth, and Magic* (cited for chapter 3). For the epidemic see *The Black Death* by Robert S. Gottfried (New York: Free Press, 1983). I take the account of Gregory the Great mainly from *Butler's* and encyclopedias; it is well documented. For Gregory and theories of Antichrist, see *Antichrist, Two Thousand Years of the Human Fascination with Evil* (cited for chapter 3) and also *Visions of the End* by Bernard McGinn (New York: Columbia Univ. Press, 1979), from which I draw the Gregory quotes. For references on early devotion to Mary see *The Middle English Miracles of the Virgin* by Beverly Boyd (San Marino, Calif.: Huntington Library, 1964). For Narses see pages 393-94 of *Celebrated Sanctuaries of the Madonna* (cited for chapter 3). For the singing of angels during the procession, see *Famous Shrines of Our Lady*, page 34. For the history of the Assumption, see *Mary, A History of Doctrine and Devotion* (cited for chapter 4), pages 133-34. This section also discussed the origin of her association with the woman in Revelation. For Gallus see *Call Her Blessed*, the Broschart manuscripts cited in chapter 1 (page 161 of volume under that nation). For Mary's exemption from original sin, see *Mary, A History of Devotion in Ireland*, page 13. For Ildephonsus see his entry in *Butler's* and also *Apparitions and Shrines of Heaven's Bright Queen* (cited for chapter 2). See also *A Dictionary of Miracles* by Rev. E. Cobham Brewer (Philadelphia: J.B. Lippincott, 1966), page 485. For Guadalupe see *Historic Shrines of Spain* (cited for chapter 2), page 74; and Jody Brant Smith's wonderful *The Image of Guadalupe* (originally published by Image Books in 1983). The location of Guadalupe and further details can be found in *Shrines to Our Lady Around the World* (cited for chapter 2), page 46; and Broschart's *Call Her Blessed* (the published version from the Society of St. Paul, Alba House, cited for chapter 3).

## EIGHT
### From Highest Mountains

For the statue on the boat see *Miraculous Images of Our Lady* (cited for chapter 3). For Bonitus see *Apparitions and Shrines of Heaven's Bright Queen* (cited for chapter 2), page 203. For the angel and the alleviation of conditions for women, see *Mary: A History of Devotion in Ireland* (cited for chapter 7), page 46. For Bishop Egwin see *Apparitions and Shrines of Heaven's Bright Queen*, page 211, and *Miracles of Mary* (cited for chapter 6). Some say the actual date was 709. See also *Our Lady's Shrine Evesham* by Rev. A.J. Proudman (Birmingham, England: Catholic Truth Society, n.d.). For Mary of Egypt see *Butler's* and for the mother of St. Stephen as well as the patriarch in Constantinople, see *Lexicon, der Marienerscheinungen* (cited for chapter 1). For Montserrat, see *The Monterrat* by José María de Sagarra (Barcelona: Editorial Noguer, 1956); *All Montserrat*, a tourist publication issued by Editorial Escudo de Oro and as far as I know available only in Spain; and *Historic Shrines of Spain* (cited for chapter 2), page 47. I also use *Miraculous Images of Our Lady*, page 413. For Our Lady of Antocha and also the account of Pelayo and Covadonga, see *Historic Shrines of Spain*.

## NINE
### Little Secrets

For Muslims and image smashing, see the *Penguin History of the World* (cited for chapter 1), page 317. For the Vikings I used *A History of the Vikings* by Gwyn Jones (Oxford Univ. Press, 1984); *Everyday Life in the Viking Age* by Jacqueline Simpson (New York: Dorest, 1967); *Man, Myth and Magic*, cited for chapter 3; and *A History of Pagan Europe* (see notes for chapter 3). For iconoclasm see also the *Penguin History of the World*, page 343; *The Birth of the Middle Ages* by H. St. L.B. Moss (New York: Oxford Univ. Press, 1964); and the *Dictionary of Mary* (cited for chapter 6), pages 131-32. For Germanus see the entry in *Butler's*. The account of John Damascene comes from his entry in *Apparitions and Shrines of Heaven's Bright Queen* (cited for chapter 2). For Charlemagne and Ostro, see Broschart's *Call Her Blessed* (unpublished, Book 5, available through the Marian Library as cited in chapter 1). For Rocamadour and Aachen see *Shrines to Our Lady Around the World* (cited for chapter 2), pages 42 and 49. For the shepherd near Itra, see Broschart's *Call Her Blessed*. For Einsiedeln see *Celebrated Sanctuaries of the Madonna* (cited for chapter 3) and also

*Saints Who Saw Mary* (cited for chapter 4). For Archbishop Gondisalve see *Lexicon, der Marienerscheinungen* (cited for chapter 1). For the German chapel see *Call Her Blessed*. For the bishop of Argos see *Mary, A History of Doctrine and Devotion* (notes for chapter 4), pages 175-99. For Coimbra see *Call Her Blessed*, as with all these volumes available only at the Marian Library in Dayton. For the bishop in Utrecht see *Lexicon, der Marienerscheinungen*, which is also the source for Herford, Sion, and Canterbury. I also use *Apparitions and Shrines of Heaven's Bright Queen* (chapter 7), page 243, for Canterbury. For Athos see *Mother of Nations* by Joan Ashton (Great Britain: Lamp, 1988).

## TEN
### *The Stroke of Twelve*

For John XII and the description of St. Peter's Basilica at the turn of the millennium, see *AD 1000, Living on the Brink of Apocalypse* by Richard Erdoes (New York: Harper & Row, 1988), which is also the source for the Glaber and Hervee quotes (pages 5-6). For Antichrist see *Antichrist, Two Thousand Years of the Human Fascination with Evil*, cited for chapter 3. The quote on immorality in the papacy comes from *A Concise History of the Catholic Church* by Thomas Bokenkotter (see notes for chapter 1), page 101. For apocalyptic fervency at approach of 1000, see *Visions of the End* by Bernard McGinn (cited for chapter 7). For the flurry of apparitions in France, Spain, the North Sea, England, Belgium, and Italy, see *Lexicon, der Marienerscheinungen* (cited for chapter 1). I also use for St. Albert and for Arras a list of apparitions provided by the 101 Foundation, a Marian group in New Jersey. For the intercession in London, see *Celebrated Sanctuaries of the Madonna* (first cited for chapter 3), pages 316-17. For the sites in Austria see *Call Her Blessed*, Book VI (cited for chapter 1).

## ELEVEN
### *Lights, Sounds, Graves*

For Turin see *Favourite Italian Shrines of Our Blessed Lady* (as cited for chapter 2), pages 48-50; and *Miraculous Images of Our Lady* (cited for chapter 3). For Emperor Henry see *Apparitions and Shrines of Heaven's Bright Queen* (as cited for chapter 2), page 249. The quote on Chartres is from page 225 of *Celebrated Sanctuaries of the Madonna* (see notes for chapter 3). The quote on Montserrat is from pages 9-10 of *The Monterrat* by José María de Sagarra (cited for chapter 8); for the other quotes see pages 48-49 of *Historic Shrines of Spain* (cited for chapter 2). See also the entry in *Miraculous Images of Our Lady*. Bokenkotter's quote is from his book *A Concise History of the Catholic Church* (see notes for chapter 1), page 113. Cahill's quote is from page 4 of *How the Irish Saved Civilization* (see notes for chapter 7). For Alberic see his entry in *Butler's*. The quote from Bishop Fulbert comes from pages 205 and 206 of *Mary, A History of Doctrine and Devotion* (see notes for chapter 4). For the shrine in the Belgian marsh see *Famous Shrines of Our Lady* (cited for chapter 4). The quote is from pages 34-35. For Walsingham I used *Miracles of*

*Mary* (cited for chapter 6). For the "Crowned Madonna," see *Call Her Blessed*, cited for chapter 1. See also this reference for the case in Castellammare de Stabia and also for the visions in Sicily and the account of Nero's tomb. For the Spanish cases see Broschart's volume under that national category. As for the reliability of the site of the Holy Sepulchre, which Catholics hold as the site of Crucifixion and thus sent Crusades to defend, I consulted the director of the Rockefeller Museum when I was in Jerusalem.

## TWELVE
### *"The Bells Are Ringing"*

For the case of Borbiago, see "One Hundred Italian Madonnas," part of the *Call Her Blessed* series (cited in chapter 1). For the miraculous images in Spain, see Book 4 of Broschart's unpublished manuscript. For Bernard see *Saints Who Saw Mary* (cited in chapter 4); and *Life and Teaching of St. Bernard* by Ailbe J. Luddy (Dublin: M.H. Gill & Son, 1937). For Monte Vergine see *Miraculous Images of Our Lady* (cited in chapter 3). For Turin and Arras see *Lexicon, der Marienerscheinungen* (cited in chapter 1). For Norbert see his entry in *Butler's*. See also page 275 of *Apparitions and Shrines of Heaven's Bright Queen* (cited in chapter 2), which was also the source for Thetford, King William the Good, and Thomas Becket. For Innocent and Anacletus, I used *The Oxford Dictionary of Popes* by J.N.D. Kelly (Oxford: Oxford Univ. Press, 1986). The account of Abbot Kingston and Basse-Wavre comes from *Celebrated Sanctuaries of the Madonna* (cited in chapter 3).

## THIRTEEN
### *A Distant Thunder*

I draw much about medieval times from *The History of Western Civilization* by Harry Elmer Barnes (New York: Harcourt, Brace, 1935), an excellent history from which I paraphrased and drew the direct quotes (pages 589 and 629). I also used the *Penguin History of the World* (cited for chapter 1); *A Concise History of the Catholic Church* (also cited in chapter 1); and *Handbook of Medieval Sexuality* edited by Vern L. Bullough and James A. Brundage (New York: Garland, 1996).

## FOURTEEN
### *The Secret Presence*

The account of the count and black knight is from *Call Her Blessed* (cited in chapter 1), Book 6, page 95. The legends of Mary delivering people from the devil come from *Miracles of the Blessed Virgin* by Johannes Herold (London: George Routledge & Sons, 1928), pages 11-135. For monster myths, see *The Monsters of Loch Ness* by Roy P. Mackal (Chicago: Swallow, 1976) and *Mysterious Creatures*, edited by the editors of Time-Life

Books in New York (1988). For Hildegard and Joachim see *Antichrist, Two Thousand Years of the Human Fascination with Evil* (cited in chapter 3), pages 128-41.


FIFTEEN
*Pillar of Fire*

The legend of Mary speaking to Jesus about chastisement comes from *Miracles of the Blessed Virgin* (cited in chapter 14), page 27. The account of Theotonius is from his entry as a saint in *Butler's*. The information on Our Lady of Vladimir is from the Marian Library web site (http://www.udayton.edu/mary/.). For Zarvanystya, which I visited and found very special, see my book *The Final Hour* (Milford, Ohio: Faith Publishing, 1992). The case in Tortosa is from Book 4 of Broschart's *Call Her Blessed* (the abbreviated title for *All Generations Shall Call Me Blessed,* cited in chapter 1). For Conrad see his entry in *Butler's*. Other snippets are from *Lexicon, der Marienerscheinungen* (cited in chapter 1). For the account of Schillings see Book 5 of the Broschart volumes. For Warwickshire see *Apparitions and Shrines of Heaven's Bright Queen* (cited in chapter 2), page 325, and for Pochaiv see "The Miraculous Icon of Pochaiv," a pamphlet by John Bird (Dublin: Veritas, 1989). For the fisherman in Marseilles see *Miraculous Images of Our Lady* (cited in chapter 3), page 96.


SIXTEEN
*Secrets of the Rosary*

The Martin quote is from his book *The Rise of Chingis Khan and His Conquest of North China* (New York: Octagon, 1971), page 6. For Chinese occultism see *Ancient China* by John Hay (New York: Henry Z. Walck, 1973) and *Ancient China* by Edward H. Schafer and the editors of Time-Life Books in New York, 1967. See also *A History of Chinese Civilization* by Jacques Gernet (London: Cambridge Univ. Press, 1982). For the discussion of paganism see *A History of Pagan Europe* (as cited for chapter 3). For a history of the Rosary see *Dictionary of Mary,* as cited in chapter 6. For Dominic see his entry in *Butler's*. See also *Apparitions and Shrines of Heaven's Bright Queen* (cited in chapter 2), pages 353-365, and an article entitled "St. Dominic and the Rosary" by Robert Feeney in *Catholic Faith,* volume 2, number 5 (September/October 1996); and *Cause of Our Joy* by Sister Mary Francis (Boston: Daughters of St. Paul, 1976). I also visited Prouille.


SEVENTEEN
*The Omen*

For St. Francis I used *Saint Francis of Assisi* by Johannes Jörgensen (New York: Image Books, 1955) and *The Little Flowers of St. Francis* by Raphael Brown (New York: Image Books, 1958), as well as the entry in *Butler's*. For the city of Assisi I used a tourist booklet,

"Assisi," published by Pama Graphicolor and obtained during a visit there. For the struggles between Frederick II and the popes, see *A Concise History of the Catholic Church* (cited in chapter 1), pages 153-56. See also *Visions of the End* by Bernard McGinn (New York: Columbia Univ. Press, 1979). For the Communion accounts see *Eucharistic Miracles* by Joan Carroll Cruz (Rockford, Ill.: TAN Publishers, 1987). Reguengo do Fetal near Fatima is from *Call Her Blessed* (cited in chapter 1), Book 7, page 142. See also its entry in *Miraculous Images of Our Lady* (cited in chapter 3), pages 386-88.

## EIGHTEEN
### The Seven

For Clairefontaine see *Apparitions and Shrines of Heaven's Bright Queen* (cited in chapter 2), pages 9-11, as well as *Miracles of Mary* (cited in chapter 6) and *Visions of Mary* (cited in chapter 5) by Peter Eicher (New York: Avon, 1996). For Blessed Reginald see *Apparitions and Shrines of Heaven's Bright Queen*, pages 17 and 18. For the Alvarez case see *Call Her Blessed* (cited in chapter 1), page 117. For St. Anthony of Padua see *A Dictionary of Miracles* (cited for chapter 7). For Lutgardis see her *Butler's* entry and for Albert I use his entry in *Butler's* as well as *Visions of Mary* and *Apparitions and Shrines of Heaven's Bright Queen*, page 37. For Hyancinth see *Apparitions and Shrines of Heaven's Bright Queen*, pages 26-27. For the Seven Servites of Florence see Brown's *Saints Who Saw Mary* (cited for chapter 4); Durham's *Miracles of Mary* (cited for chapter 6); the entry in *Butler's*; and *Apparitions and Shrines of Heaven's Bright Queen*, pages 57-65. See also *Favourite Italian Shrines of Our Blessed Lady* (cited for chapter 2), page 31. For the Order of Mercy see Broschart's *Call Her Blessed*, the published manuscript (cited for chapter 3). For King James I, I used *Apparitions and Shrines of Heaven's Bright Queen*, pages 47-49.

## NINETEEN
### The Foreboding

For Mechtilde see *Saints Who Saw Mary* (cited in chapter 4), pages 48-53; *Apparitions and Shrines of Heaven's Bright Queen* (cited in chapter 2), pages 115-23; and the entry in *Butler's*. For Gertrude see *Saints Who Saw Mary*, pages 54-59; and her entry in *Butler's*. For Blessed Benvenuta see *Apparitions and Shrines of Heaven's Bright Queen*, pages 147-50. For conditions in the Middle Ages see *The End of the Middle Ages* by A. Mary F. Robinson (London: T. Fisher Unwin). For Chartres see *Apparitions and Shrines of Heaven's Bright Queen*, pages 67-75, as well as *Celebrated Sanctuaries of the Madonna* (cited in chapter 3), which also served as a source for Le Puy with *Famous Shrines of Our Lady* (cited in chapter 4), Volume 1. For *Las Cantigas* see *The Supernatural in Early Spanish Literature* by Frank Collcott (New York: Instituto de las Espanas, 1923), pages 15-129. For Zweibrucken see *Call Her Blessed* (or sometimes under the full title *All Generations Shall Call Me Blessed*, cited in chapter 1, also the source for the town of Lucca and the rose.

For Cambridge and Oxford see *Celebrated Sanctuaries of the Madonna*, page 378. For Depedale see *Apparitions and Shrines of Heaven's Bright Queen*, pages 341-43.

## TWENTY
### Signs and Curses

For the climate changes and also for the quote on the gallows, see Robert S. Gottfried's fine *The Black Death* (also cited for chapter 7). For lifestyles and many other facts in the Middle Ages used in this chapter see Barbara M. Tuchman's *A Distant Mirror* (New York: Knopf, 1978), which I paraphrase at some points. The Robinson paraphrase comes from pages 2 and 3 of *The End of the Middle Ages* (cited for chapter 19). The Knighton quote is from Tuchman's book. For Loreto see *Miracles of Mary* (cited in chapter 6). For the Church turmoil see *A Concise History of the Catholic Church* (cited in chapter 1), pages 158-61, which is also the source for the Bokenkotter quote (page 153). For Antichrist see again McGinn's *Antichrist, Two Thousand Years of the Human Fascination with Evil* (cited in chapter 3). For St. Bonaventure see page 345 of *The Graces of Interior Prayer* by Augustin Francois Poulain (Westminster, Vt.: Celtic Cross Books, 1910 and 1978). For the apparitions in Avignon see *Apparitions and Shrines of Heaven's Bright Queen* (cited in chapter 2), pages 175-77, and *Lexicon, der Marienerscheinungen* (cited in chapter 1). For the Templars see Tuchman and also *The Shroud of Turin* by Ian Wilson (New York: Image, 1979), pages 176-90.

## TWENTY-ONE
### Horrible Wonders

For Guadalupe see *Historic Shrines of Spain* (as cited in chapter 2), from which is drawn the quote on Our Blessed Mother's beauty, page 77. See also *Miracles of Mary* (cited in chapter 6), page 135. For the Guillaume de Nages quote and disasters in China see Gottfried's *The Black Death* (cited in chapter 7). For other facts on plague and especially disasters in China and India, see *The Black Death* by Philip Ziegler (New York: John Day, 1969), from which I draw his quote and further details, along with the quote of the Flemish cleric (page 14) and the phenomena of lights above Avignon and Paris. For spirituality in India see *The Religions of India* by Edward Washburn Hopkins (New Delhi: Munshiram Manoharlal, 1885). For medieval morality I used *Handbook of Medieval Sexuality* (cited for chapter 13), which is where the quote on omnipresent rape comes from. See also *A Distant Mirror* (cited for chapter 20), which is the source for Henry of Hereford. For St. Bridget see *Saints Who Saw Mary* (cited in chapter 4), pages 60-67, *Visions of Mary* (cited in chapter 5), pages 105-9; *Apparitions and Shrines of Heaven's Bright Queen* (cited in chapter 2), pages 181-87; the entry in *Butler's*, *Revelations of St. Bridget* (Rockford, Ill.: TAN, 1984); and *Visions of the End* (cited in chapter 7), pages 244 and 245. For St. Angela of Foligno see *Apparitions and Shrines of Heaven's Bright Queen*, pages 163-65, which was also the source for St. Nicholas Tolentine, pages 170-73. For Antony of the Desert see *The Fear of Freedom, Studies of Miracles in the Roman Catholic Church* (cited for chapter 4), page 105. For Christina Bruso see her entry in *Butler's*. For Blessed Angela see *Apparitions and Shrines of Heaven's Bright Queen*, page 163.


## TWENTY-TWO
### *The Chastisement*

For the plague I rely mainly upon *The Black Death* by Gottfried (cited in chapter 7) and *The Black Death* by Ziegler (cited in chapter 21), although certain facts, including the population in China, are drawn from *Plagues and Peoples* by Will H. McNeill (New York: Anchor, 1976). For Lamech see *The Black Death* by Francis Aidan Gasquet (London: George Bell and Sons, 1908), page 2. The quote on "pestiferous wind" comes from the Ziegler book, page 111. The quote on "engines of war" comes from Ziegler, page 17. For the Muslim aspect see *The Black Death, The Impact of the Fourteenth-Century Plague,* edited by Daniel Williman (Binghamton, N.Y.: Center for Medieval and Early Renaissance Studies, 1982), page 66. For the demonic dogs and the quote from Michael of Piazza, see page 41 of the Ziegler book. For the Clement VI quote see chapter 5 of *A Distant Mirror* (cited in chapter 20), which is also the source for the Clyn quote. For the Ziegler quote see page 85 of *The Black Death* cited above. See also *Peasants' Revolt* by Leonard W. Cowie (London: Wayland, 1972). For Willesden see the pamphlet "Our Lady of Willesden," Catholics Truth Society in London, 1980.


## TWENTY-THREE AND TWENTY-FOUR
### *Aftershock*
### *Where Devils Trembled*

For the aftereffects of plague and the slide in morals, see *The Black Death and Peasants' Revolt* (cited in chapter 22). See also Ziegler's *The Black Death* (cited in chapter 21), pages 270-73. For the Church's interpretation of God's final triumph and the Second Coming, see entries 676-77 in the *Catechism* (cited in chapter 1). For the Antichrist see *The Antichrist* by Vincent P. Miceli (Harrison, N.Y.: Roman Catholic Books, 1981), especially chapter 6. For Bonaria see page 28 of *Call HerBlessed* (cited in chapter 1), the one subtitled "One Hundred Italian Madonnas." See also *Famous Shrines of Our Lady* (cited in chapter 4), page 208. For Edward III see *Celebrated Sanctuaries of the Madonna* (cited in chapter 3), page 230. For St. Bridget see *Saints Who Saw Mary* (cited in chapter 4), pages 62-63 and her entry in *Butler's*. For the Versano woman see page 259 of "One Hundred Italian Madonnas." For Catherine of Siena I used these same two sources (pages 69-76 in *Saints Who Saw Mary*). For Aljubarrota and the apparition to Catarina see page 84 of *Call Her Blessed*, Book 7. For the angelic apparition at Fatima see the pamphlet "Saint Michael and the Fatima Connection" by Carlos Evaristo (Fatima: St. Anne's Oratory, 1992). For Prince Ferdinand see his entry in *Butler's*. For Vincent Ferrer see *Lexicon, der*

*Marienerscheinungen* (cited in chapter 1). For Salembier see his book *The Great Schism of the West* (London: Kegan Paul, Trench, Tübner & Co., 1907), page 124. For the Eucharistic miracles see again *Eucharistic Miracles* by Joan Carroll Cruz (cited in chapter 17). For St. Bridget's report of Christ's time frame see her entry in *Visions of the End* (as cited for chapter 7).

## TWENTY-FIVE AND TWENTY-SIX
### Secret Martyrs
### The Secret of Obedience

For Czestochowa see *Marian Library Studies*, Volume 8, "Theology of a Marian Shrine, Our Lady of Czestochowa," by Marian Zalecki (Dayton, Ohio: Univ. of Dayton, 1976). See also *Miracles of Mary* (cited in chapter 6), page 117. For the woman in Holland see *Miraculous Images of Our Lady* (cited in chapter 3), page 354, and for Rimini see *Apparitions and Shrines of Heaven's Bright Queen* (cited in chapter 2), page 161. For Garaballa see *Call Her Blessed* (cited in chapter 17), Book 4, page 228. For the fascinating account of Pedro and Juan I used William A. Christian's excellent *Apparitions in Late Medieval and Renaissance Spain* (Princeton, N.J.: Princeton Univ. Press, 1981), pages 26-35. For the papal disputes and the owl, see Bokenkotter's *A Concise History of the Catholic Church* (cited in chapter 1), page 169. For the prophecy on various feast days, see page 5 of *Prophecy For Today* by Edward Connor (Rockford, Ill.: TAN Books, 1956). The account of the ortiga bush and apparition near Fatima is from *Miraculous Images of Our Lady*, pages 393-94. For Bernardine see *Saints Who Saw Mary* (cited in chapter 4), pages 80-84. For Florence see *Lexicon, der Marienerscheinungen* (cited in chapter 1). For Jaén see *Miracles of Mary*. For Caravaggio see *Lexicon, der Marienerscheinungen* and also *La Madonna di Caravaggio, La Regina della Pace* (Caravaggio: Storia-Guida del Santuario). For Bologna see *Lexicon, der Marienerscheinungen*. For Czestochowa see again *Marian Library Studies*, Volume 8, "Theology of a Marian Shrine, Our Lady of Czestochowa," page 57. For Cordova see *Call Her Blessed*, published version, 236-37. For Saluzzo, Italy, see *Lexicon, der Marienerscheinungen*. For the apparitions in Cubas see *Apparitions in Late Medieval and Renaissance Spain*, pages 57-73. For Betharram see its entry in *Lexicon, der Marienerscheinungen*.

## TWENTY-SEVEN
### The Secret of Faith

For Dracula see *Dracula, A True History of Dracula and Vampire Legends* by Raymond T. McNally and Radu Florescu (Greenwich, Conn.: New York Graphic Society, 1972). See also the entry for vampires in *Man, Myth, and Magic* (cited in chapter 3). For the Hungarian picture that bled see *Lexicon, der Marienerscheinungen* (cited in chapter 1). For El Miracle see *Apparitions in Late Medieval and Renaissance Spain* (cited in notes for chapters 25 and 26), pages 113-26. For Good Counsel and the quote see Monsignor

George F. Dillon's *The Virgin Mother of Good Counsel* (New York: Benzinger Brothers, 1886) and also Cruz's *Miraculous Images of Our Lady* (cited in chapter 3), pages 179-82, and *Cause of Our Joy* as cited in chapter 16. For the Northcote quote see his *Celebrated Sanctuaries of the Madonna* (cited in chapter 3), pages 42-43. For Rhodos, Alsace-Loraine, Pope Pius II (whom from what I can tell was mixed in this source with Paul II), Locarno, and Alanus de Rupe see *Lexicon, der Marienerscheinungen*. For El Torn (actually Sant Andrés de Torn) and for his quote see Christian's *Apparitions in Late Medieval and Renaissance Spain*, pages 133-37. For Prato see *Mother of Nations* (cited for chapter 9), page 114. For the Rome plague see *Call Her Blessed* (cited in chapter 1), Volume 2, page 238. For the apparition near Morschwihr (really closest to Ammerschwihr) see *Apparitions and Shrines of Heaven's Bright Queen* (cited in chapter 2), page 309. My main sources for Columbus are *Columbus, The Great Adventure*, by Paolo Emilio Taviani (New York: Orion Books, 1991); *The Life of the Admiral Christopher Columbus* by his son Ferdinand (New Brunswick: Rutgers Univ. Press, 1959); and The *Diario* of Christopher Columbus's First Voyage to America (Norman, Okla.: Univ. of Okla.).

## TWENTY-EIGHT and TWENTY-NINE
### *"I Await You"*
### *The Spirit of Rebellion*

For the swastika see pages 41-42 of *The Migration of Symbols* by Count Eugene Goblet D'Alviella (New York: University Books, 1956). For Guadalupe I rely mainly upon Jody Brant Smith's wonderful *The Image of Guadalupe* (originally published by Image Books in 1983 but now in revised form from Mercer Univ. Press). I also use the classic book *A Woman Clothed With the Sun* edited by John J. Delaney (New York: Image, 1961) and *Quetzalcóatl and Guadalupe* by Jacques Lafaye (Chicago: Univ. of Chicago Press, 1987). For Luther see *Young Man Luther* by Erik H. Erikson (New York: W.W. Norton, 1958); Bokenkotter's *A Concise History of the Catholic Church* (cited in chapter 1); *Luther and the Reformation* by V.H.H. Green (New York: Capricorn Books, 1964); and "Was Luther a Marian Devotee?" by the Rev. William J. Cole in *Marian Studies*, Volume 21 (published by the Mariological Society of America, 1970).

## THIRTY
### *Mercy and Justice*

For Cortés see Joseph L. Cassidy's excellent *Mexico, Land of Mary's Wonders* (Paterson, N.J.: St. Anthony Guild, 1958), page 37. For the nativity fresco see *Call Her Blessed* (cited in chapter 1), Book 2, pages 81-82. For Frascati see Cruz's *Miraculous Images of Our Lady* (cited in chapter 3), pages 202-3, and *Miracles of Mary* (cited in chapter 6). For Savona see *Mary vs. Lucifer* by John Ireland Gallery (Milwaukee: Bruce, 1960), pages 42-43. The apparition on the stormy sea is from *Call Her Blessed* (cited in chapter 1), Book 2, pages 183-84, which is also the source for Vaciago, pages 25-26; the Turkish pirate, page 76; the

Casalbordino case, page 123; and Rho, page 134. For Chartres see *Celebrated Sanctuaries of the Madonna* (cited in chapter 3), page 230. For Lake Titicaca see *Miraculous Images of Our Lady*, page 51. For St. Alphonsus see *Apparitions and Shrines of Heaven's Bright Queen* (cited in chapter 2), page 63. For Fourviere see *Celebrated Sanctuaries of the Madonna*, pages 183-84. For Garsten see *Call Her Blessed*, Book 6, page 76. For La Paz see *Call Her Blessed*, Book 3. For Quito see *Call Her Blessed*, Book 3, page 441. For Matamargó see *Apparitions in Late Medieval and Renaissance Spain* (cited in notes for chapters 25 and 26), pages 138-39. For St. Cajetan see *Apparitions and Shrines of Heaven's Bright Queen*, page 335, which was also a source for some of Teresa of Avila, pages 32-33, although my main source is her own book *The Life of Teresa of Jesus* (New York: Image, 1960), a masterpiece of spirituality. For Nun X *The Graces of Interior Prayer* (cited for chapter 20), page 340. For John of the Cross see his entry in *Butler's*. The Thalbach case comes from *Call Her Blessed*, Book 6, page 183. For Flochberg see *Call Her Blessed*, Book 5, page 343. For Zapopan see *Miraculous Images of Our Lady*, page 286, and for Tlaxcala see *Mexico, Land of Mary's Wonders*.

## THIRTY-ONE
### The Prophecy

For the Lepanto account I rely upon encyclopedic sources as well as *The Galleys at Lepanto* by Jack Beeching (New York: Scribner's Sons, 1892); *Cause of Our Joy*, cited in chapter 16; and *Butler's* entry on Pius, along with *The Image of Guadalupe* by Jody Bryant Smith (cited in notes for chapter 28 and 29) for a paraphrase of the Doria account. For Quito see *Call Her Blessed* (cited in chapter 1), Book 3, page 424. For Cuba, see *Miraculous Images of Our Lady* (cited in chapter 3), page 63. For Orcotuna see *Call her Blessed*, Book 3, pages 483-84. For Father De La Fontaine see *Apparitions and Shrines of Heaven's Bright Queen* (cited in chapter 2), page 105, which was also the source for St. Rose, page 127, and the Aberdeen mention, page 339. For Ráquira and the Broschart quote see his tremendous *Call Her Blessed*, Book 3, page 265. For witchcraft in Germany see *Germany, 2000 Years* (as cited for chapter 6). For the Lima image see *Call Her Blessed*, Book 3, page 510, which is also the source for San Cristóbal, page 557; and Cormoto (pages 561-64). Esperanza is from *Mexico, Land of Mary's Wonders* (cited in chapter 30), page 34. For the Quito prophecy I used *Lexicon, der Marienerscheinungen* (cited in chapter 1), as well as *The Thunder of Justice* by Ted and Maureen Flynn (Sterling, Va.: MaxKol Communications, 1993).

## THIRTY-TWO
### Past the Edge of Knowledge

For the quote on wonders see the privately published pamphlet "Fearful and Strange News From the Bishopric of Durham," printed in 1641 for John Thomas. For the alehouse demon I use a pamphlet entitled "A Relation of a Strange Apparition In an Ale-house Next

Door to the White Horse," printed in London during 1641 for Richard Smethrust. The account of Woodstock comes from another pamphlet entitled "The Just Devil of Woodstock, a True Narrative of the Several Apparitions, the Frights, and Punishments upon the Rumpis Commissioners," privately published in England in the seventeenth century. Avignon comes from the John Thomas pamphlet "Strange News from France," February 4, 1641. Dublin comes from the pamphlet "Ireland's Amazement, or the Heaven's Armada," printed in London, 1641, for John Thomas. Northamptonshire comes from the John Thomas pamphlet "Strange News from France," signed February 4, 1641. For Constantinople see the pamphlet "Extraordinary News from Constantinople," printed in London during 1641 for Francis Constable and John Thomas. The Vatican vision comes from the pamphlet "Fearfull Prodigies in Italy, Seene Neere the Citie of Rome In the Aire," printed in London, February 6, 1643, for John Dobson. For witchcraft I used *Witch Hunting in Southwest Germany 1562-1684* by H.C. Erik Midelfort (Stanford, Calif.: Stanford Univ. Press, 1972). For the two Huron Indians see *Lexicon, der Marienerscheinungen* (cited in chapter 1). For Kateri see *Kateri Tekakwitha, Mystic of the Wilderness* by Margaret R. Bunson (Huntington, Ind.: Our Sunday Visitor, 1992); and *Adventures With a Saint* by Marlene McCauley (privately published, 1992).

## THIRTY-THREE
### Secrets in America and Europe

For Mary and America I used Volume 3 of *Marian Studies*, 1952, Proceedings of the Third National Convention of the Mariological Society of America, headquartered at Holy Name College and containing an article by Rev. Dr. Wilfrid Parsons entitled "Marian Devotion in the Early United States." For the quote about Lyons see page 119 of Gillett's *Famous Shrines of Our Lady* (cited in chapter 4). See *Call Her Blessed* (cited in chapter 1), Book 5, for a number of citations throughout the chapter, including the lights along the Danube, page 301; Amberg, page 308; Mühlberg, page 235; Albendorf, page 90; Prince von Fürstenberg, page 191; Wemding, page 107; Rottweil 348; München page 236; Swedish troops, page 215; Lauffen, Book 6, page 80. The plague in Vienna is mentioned in *Plague!* by Charles T. Greeg (New York: Charles Scribner's Sons), page 18. For Luxembourg see *Miraculous Images of Our Lady* (cited in chapter 3), page 277. Most of the German and Austrian anecdotes come from Broschart's *Call Her Blessed*. For Pochaiv see "The Miraculous Icon of Pochaiv," the previously cited pamphlet by John Bird (cited for chapter 15). For Czestochowa see *Miraculous Images of Our Lady* by Joan Carroll Cruz; and *Marian Library Studies*, Volume 8, "Theology of a Marian Shrine, Our Lady of Czestochowa," by Marian Zalecki, cited in notes for chapters 25 and 26. For Ardesio see Book 2 of *Call Her Blessed*, pages 78-79. For Wexford and Limerick see *Mary: A History of Doctrine and Devotion* (cited in chapter 4), page 221. For the Irish image in Hungary see *Shrines to Our Lady Around the World* (cited in chapter 2), pages 102-5. For Elend see *Apparitions and Shrines of Heaven's Bright Queen* (cited in chapter 2), page 152. For the apparition of Michael see the pamphlet "A Narrative of a Strange and Sudden Apparition of an Archangel at the Old Bayly," printed privately in 1681. For Le Laus see *Famous*

*Shrines of Our Lady*, Volume 1, pages 163-64, and *Miracles of Mary* (cited in chapter 6), pages 107-9, which was also the source for the New Mexico image. For the willow tree see *Famous Shrines of Our Lady*, Volume 2, pages 121-26; *Mary vs. Lucifer* (as cited for chapter 30), pages 22-23, and *Miraculous Images of Our Lady*, pages 104-8. For Attersee see *Call Her Blessed*, Book 6, page 72. For Lithuania see *Miraculous Images of Our Lady*, pages 270-71. For Antipolo see *Miraculous Images of Our Lady*, page 373. For Graz, Schwadorf, Innsbruck, Mariapocz, and Bildstein see *Call Her Blessed*, Volume 6, pages 120, 61, 148, 201, and 178, respectively. For Vienna see *Miraculous Images of Our Lady*, page 13. The Saragossa account of Blasco is on a plaque inside the basilica. For the statue in Belgium see *Lexicon, der Marienerscheinungen* (cited in chapter 1). For the child brought back to life in Mexico see *Miraculous Images of Our Lady*, page 323. For the sultan from Morroco see *Lexicon, der Marienerscheinungen.*

## THIRTY-FOUR
### Born in Hell

For the opening earth see the pamphlet "Strange News from Lemster in Herefordshire," printed in London for B. Harris, 1679. For Pötsch, Szent-Antal, and Sajopálfalva, see *Lexicon, der Marienerscheinungen* (cited in chapter 1). For Maria-Steinbach see *Call Her Blessed* (cited in chapter 1), Book 5, page 53. For Tlaltenango see *Mexico, Land of Mary's Wonders* (cited for chapter 30), pages 78-79. For Blessed Mary of the Angels see page 452 of *The Graces of Interior Prayer* (cited in chapter 20). The account of the images on the crags is from Broschart's splendid *Call Her Blessed*, Book 3, page 204, which I paraphrase here. The Gillett quote is from *Famous Shrines of Our Lady*, Volume 1, page 141 (cited in chapter 4). For Chartres see *Celebrated Sanctuaries of the Madonna* (cited in chapter 3), pages 228-29.

## THIRTY-FIVE
### Catherine's Secret

For Our Lady of the Lamp see *Call Her Blessed*, "One Hundred Italian Madonnas," (cited in chapter 1), page 108. For New Orleans see *Apparitions and Shrines of Heaven's Bright Queen* (cited in chapter 2), pages 266-67. For Guadalajara and Ancona see pages 346 and 233 of *Miraculous Images of Our Lady* (cited in chapter 3). The Northcote quote is from pages 54-55 of *Celebrated Sanctuaries of the Madonna* (cited in chapter 3). For Fourvière see page 120 of *Famous Shrines of Our Lady* (cited in chapter 4). The Walsh quote is from page 271 of *Apparitions and Shrines of Heaven's Bright Queen*. For the Miraculous Medal I visited the site and relied upon *A Woman Clothed With the Sun* (cited in notes for chapters 28 and 29); "The Saint of Silence and the Message of Our Lady," a pamphlet issued at the site; another pamphlet called "Our Lady of the Miraculous Medal" by the Daughters of St. Paul in Boston (1980); *Blessed Catherine Labouré* translated from the French, Edmond Crapez (Emmitsburg, Md.: St. Joseph's, 1933); and *The Sun Her Mantle* by John Beevers

(Westminster, Md.: Newman Press, 1953). For Montana and the Indian boy see page 291 of *Apparitions and Shrines of Heaven's Bright Queen*. For Ratisbonne see *Miracles of Mary* (cited in chapter 6). For LaSalette see *A Woman Clothed With the Sun*. I also visited there. For the secrets I chiefly rely upon the highly detailed and well-researched *Encountering Mary* by Sandra Zimdars-Swartz (Princeton, N.J.: Princeton Univ. Press, 1991). For famine see *The Irish Famine* edited by Cathal Póirtéir (Dublin: Mercier, 1995). For Our Lady of Victories see page 171 of *Famous Shrines of Our Lady*, Volume 1. For Marx see *Marx and Satan* by Richard Wurmbrand (Crossway Books).

## THIRTY-SIX and THIRTY-SEVEN
### Borrowed Time
### "I Will Be Your Mother"

My main sources for Lourdes in addition to my own visits were *The Song of Bernadette* by Franz Werfel (New York: Viking, 1942), from which I draw the Werfel quotes (pages 305 and 309); *A Woman Clothed With the Sun* (cited in notes for chapters 28 and 29); and *Encountering Mary* (cited for chapter 35). For Lincoln see *Lincoln, Addresses and Letters* edited by John M. Avent (New York: Allyn and Bacon, 1924); *Why the Civil War Came*, edited by Gabor S. Boritt (Oxford: Oxford Univ. Press, 1996); *Abraham Lincoln, The War Years*, Volume 4 (New York: Harcourt, Brace, 1939); and *Mary Todd Lincoln* by Jean H. Baker (New York: W.W. Norton, 1987). For Wisconsin see pages 158-60 of *Mary vs. Lucifer* (cited for chapter 30). The quote from Mary Wilson is from page 48 of *Apparitions and Shrines of Heaven's Bright Queen* (cited in chapter 2). For San Francisco and Israel see *Lexicon, der Marienerscheinungen* (cited in chapter 1), and for Anglet see *Marpingen* by David Blackbourn (New York: Knopf, 1994), pages 11 and 36, a book that is also the main source for the Marpingen account. For Austria see *Lexicon, der Marienerscheinungen*. For Pontmain see *The Sun Her Mantle* (cited in chapter 35) and the pamphlet "What Happened at Pontmain" by Abbe M. Richard (Washington, N.J.: Ave Maria Institute, n.d.). For the German apparitions see *Marpingen* and *Lexicon, der Marienerscheinungen*. For Dassapore see page 35 of *Apparitions and Shrines of Heaven's Bright Queen*. For Longo see *Miraculous Images of Our Lady* (cited in chapter 3), page 241. For Poland, Lyons, and Vallensages see *Lexicon, der Marienerscheinungen* and *Marpingen*. For Cap-De-La-Madeleine, see *Miracles of Mary* (cited in chapter 6), page 109-10. The Knock quote is from *A Woman Clothed With the Sun* (previously cited), page 155. I visited the site twice and relied upon original literature as well as *The Sun Her Mantle*. For Thérèse the Little Flower see pages 65-66 of *Story of a Soul*, her autobiography (Washington, D.C.: Institute of Carmelite Studies, 1976). For Castelpetroso and Tilly see *Apparitions and Shrines of Heaven's Bright Queen* from which I draw the Walsh quote. For both Vallensanges and the chapel in Poland see *Lexicon, der Marienerscheinungen*.

## THIRTY-EIGHT
### The Great Sign

Unless indicated otherwise apparitions mentioned briefly are from *Lexicon, der Marienerscheinungen* (cited in chapter 1), the excellent list compiled by Robert Ernst. For Cardinal Cerejeira see *Paulo VI* (Porto, Portugal: Publicacao Do, Centro de Caridade Nossa Senhora Do Perpétuo Socorro), which is also the source for Pius XII's radio address later in the chapter. For Quito see *Call Her Blessed* (cited in chapter 3), the published manuscript, pg. 41. For Gray see Chapter 1 of *A Guide to Apparitions of Our Blessed Virgin Mary* by Peter Heintz (Sacramento, Calif.: Gabriel Press, 1992). This is an excellent compendium. For Hrushiw see *Witness* by Josyp Terelya (Milford, Ohio: Faith Publishing, 1991). For Fatima see *Our Lady of Fatima* by William Thomas Walsh (New York: Image Books, 1954); *The Secret of Fatima* by Joaquin Maria Alonso (Cambridge, Mass.: Ravengate, 1976); and *The Final Hour* by Michael H. Brown (Milford, Ohio: Faith, 1992). For Brussels see *A Guide to Apparitions of Our Blessed Virgin Mary*, chapter 2. This is also the source for Portiers, chapter 4. For Pius IX and the prodigy see page 13 of *Catholic Prophecy* previously cited. For Leo XIII see the pamphlet called "'Neath St. Michael's Shield," published by the Daughters of St. Paul, and *Leo XIII* by Brother William J. Kiefer (Milwaukee: Bruce, 1961). For the quotes on the grave hour by Pius XI and Pius X and then Pius XII see page 33 of *The Message of Fatima* by Lawrence F. Harvey (Glasgow: John S. Burns & Sons, n.d.). The mystic in the 1930s was Teresa Neumann and her quote is on page 13 of *Catholic Prophecy*, previously cited. For the horrors in Ukraine see *The Final Hour* and *Witness* (previously cited). For Ezkioga see *Visionaries* by William A. Christian Jr. (Berkeley: Univ. of California Press, 1996). For the Belgian apparitions see pages 215-66 of *A Woman Clothed With the Sun* (cited in notes for chapters 28 and 29). For Heede see Chapter 9 of *A Guide to Apparitions of Our Blessed Virgin Mary*. For the Lucia quote on "immense firmament" see *Fatima in Lucia's Own Words*, edited by Louis Kondor (Fatima, Portugal: Postulation Centre, 1989) while her quotes on the devil and his time are in Frère Michel de la Sainte Trinite's volumes entitled *The Whole Truth About Fatima* (Buffalo, N.Y.: Immaculate Heart Publications, 1986). For Hitler and the occult see *The Twisted Cross* by Joseph J. Carr (Shreveport, La.: Huntington House, 1985). For Maximilian Kolbe I used a number of sources, key among them *A Guide to the Saints* by Kristin E. White (New York: Ballantine, 1992). For St. Kolumba Church see *Call Her Blessed* (cited in chapter 1), Book 5, page 186. For Hiroshima see *The Power of the Rosary* by Rev. Albert J.M. Shamon (Milford, Ohio: Riehle Foundation, 1990), page 29.

## THIRTY-NINE
### Queen of Eternity

For Pius and the sun miracle see *The Whole Truth About Fatima* (cited for chapter 38) and *Lexicon, der Marienerscheinungen* (cited in chapter 2), which was also the source for the Irish apparitions in Dublin and Kerrytown. For Cornacchiola see the pamphlet "The Virgin of Revelation" by Don Giuseppe Tomaselli, issued at the Grotta Tre Fontane in

Rome. For Fostoria see chapter 20 of *A Guide to Apparitions of Our Blessed Virgin Mary* (cited for chapter 38). For the Ratzinger quotes see *The Ratzinger Report* by Joseph Cardinal Ratzinger with Vittorio Messori (San Francisco: Ignatius Press, 1986), page 110, and page 3 of "The Marian Library Newsletter" issued by the Marian Library at Dayton University, spring 1997, number 34. For the number of apparitions between 1947 and 1954 see page 241 of *Religion, Power and Protest in Local Communities* edited by Eric R. Wolf (New York: Mouton, 1984). For Syracuse see page 249 of *Miraculous Images of Our Lady* (cited in chapter 3). For the Contardi quote see page 255 of *Religion, Power and Protest in Local Communities,* cited above. For Lucia's quote see page 107 of *The Final Hour.* For Guadalupe see page 293 of *Miraculous Images of Our Lady.* For Syracuse see the 1954 entry in *Lexicon, der Marienerscheinungen.* For the assassination attempt on John Paul II see page 31 of *Pope John Paul II* by Tad Szulc (New York: Scribner, 1995). For the Soviet explosion see *The Timetables of History* by Bernard Grun (New York: Simon & Schuster/Touchstone, 1975). See also page 34 of *The Power of the Rosary,* cited in chapter 38. For the consecration of the world see page 2? of *The Secret of Fatima* (as cited in chapter 38). For Lucia's quote on the atomic war and er. of peace see "Two Hours With Sister Lucia," a pamphlet by Carlos Evaristo, St. Anne's Oratory, Fatima, Portugal.

# OTHER BOOKS BY THE AUTHOR

*After Life*

*Secrets of the Eucharist*

*The Day Will Come*

*The Trumpet of Gabriel*

*The Bridge to Heaven*

*Prayer of the Warrior*

*The Final Hour*

*Witness*

*The Search for Eve*

*The Toxic Cloud*

*The Greenpeace Story*

*Marked to Die*

*Laying Waste: The Poisoning of America by Toxic Chemicals*

*PK: A Report on Psychokinesis*